ployee Relations in the
blic Services

The erosion of the British public sector over the past twenty years has b means diminished the political and economic significance of our public ices. Yet to date, few have looked at the huge changes across the secto g that period or examined their impact on employee relations in the ic services as a whole.

In t important new work, specialist authors consider key aspects of pub vice people management – pay, equal opportunities, flexibility, com e tendering and quality – in the context of dramatic financial, lega structural developments. At the same time the book highlights bot u nique features that make the sector such a fascinating and vital are o uly and the degree to which employee relations have increasingly mirror private sector practice.

Th unique, wide-ranging overview draws on contributions from a range of acknowledged experts in the field, representing a more rigorous and coherent critique than can be found in more descriptive, organisation-based texts.

Susan Corby is Senior Lecturer in Human Resource Management at the University of Greenwich Business School. **Geoff White** is Principal Lecturer in Human Resource Management at the University of Greenwich Business School. Both have written extensively in the area of public sector industrial relations.

WITHDRAWN

ROUTLEDGE STUDIES IN EMPLOYMENT RELATIONS
Series editors: Rick Delbridge and Edmund Heery *Cardiff Business School*

Aspects of the employment relationship are central to numerous courses at both undergraduate and postgraduate level.

Drawing on insights from industrial relations, human resource management and industrial sociology, this series provides an alternative source of research-based materials and texts reviewing key developments in employment research.

Rethinking Industrial Relations
Mobilisation, collectivism and long waves
John Kelly

Employee Relations in the Public Services
Themes and issues
Edited by Susan Corby and Geoff White

The Insecure Workforce
Edmund Heery and John Salmon

Employee Relations in the Public Services

Themes and issues

Edited by
Susan Corby and Geoff White

London and New York

First published 1999 by Routledge
11 New Fetter Lane, London EC4P 4EE

Simultaneously published in the USA and Canada
by Routledge
29 West 35th Street, New York, NY 10001

© 1999 Susan Corby and Geoff White

Typeset in Baskerville by The Florence Group, Stoodleigh, Devon
Printed and bound in Great Britain by Creative Print and Design
(Wales), Ebbw Vale

British Library Cataloguing in Publication Data
A catalogue record for this book is available from the British
Library.

Library of Congress Cataloguing in Publication Data
Employee relations in the public services: themes and issues /
    [compiled and edited by] Susan Corby and Geoff White.
        p. cm.
    Includes bibliographical references and index.
    1. Employee-management relations in government–Great
Britain.
I. Corby, Susan, 1941– . II. White, Geoff, 1949– .
HD8005.2.G7E48 1999
331'. 04135141–dc21   98–36487
                         CIP

ISBN 0–415–17444–9 (hbk)
ISBN 0–415–17445–7 (pbk)

Contents

List of figures and tables

Figures

Tables

The editors and the contributors

The editors

Susan Corby is senior lecturer in human resource management at the University of Greenwich. She has published widely on various aspects of public sector industrial relations in the civil service and the NHS (in both of which fields she was previously a full-time union official) and on equal opportunities in the public services. She has worked for ACAS and the industrial relations research organisation Industrial Relations Services. She is a member of both the Employment Appeal Tribunal and the Central Arbitration Committee.

Geoff White is a principal lecturer in human resource management at the University of Greenwich. He has written widely on remuneration matters and especially on pay in the public sector. Before becoming an academic, he was managing editor for research at the major pay research body Incomes Data Services, and ran its Public Sector Unit for many years. In 1998 he was seconded to the Low Pay Commission Secretariat as remuneration adviser. He is the joint author, with Janet Druker, of *Managing People in Construction* (IPD 1996).

The contributors

Stephen Bach is a lecturer in industrial relations at the University of Warwick. Formerly at the Centre for Health Planning and Management, University of Keele, he is co-author of *Case Studies in Health Policy and Management* (Nuffield Provincial Hospital Trust 1991). His current research interests focus on industrial relations developments in the public services and comparative public sector industrial relations.

Trevor Colling is senior research fellow at Leicester Business School, De Montfort University. He has published widely on various aspects of public sector industrial relations, particularly the implications of privatisation and contracting out in local government. Currently he is examining the dynamics of contracting more broadly and the management of labour within business service companies active in outsourcing markets.

Sandra Fredman is reader in law at the University of Oxford and Fellow of Exeter College. She is a specialist in employment law and has written widely on public sector law, co-authoring the book *The State as Employer* with Gillian Morris (Mansell 1989). Recently she has published *Women and the Law* (Oxford University Press 1997).

Ariane Hegewisch is a senior researcher and teaching fellow at the Centre for European HRM at Cranfield School of Management. Previously she worked as a policy adviser on employment and industrial policy in local government. She joined Cranfield in 1989 as a founding researcher on the Price Waterhouse/Cranfield survey of international strategic HRM and has written widely on employment and contract flexibility, equal opportunities policies, remuneration and human resource management trends in the public sector in Europe. She is joint editor, with Chris Brewster, of *Policy and Practice in European Human Resource Management* (Routledge 1994).

Miguel Martinez Lucio is a lecturer in the industrial and labour studies division of the University of Leeds. He has written many articles on the public sector and new management practices and has edited a book, *The Politics of Quality in the Public Sector* (Routledge 1992), with Ian Kirkpatrick. He is currently researching industrial relations at Royal Mail.

Robert MacKenzie is a doctoral student at the University of Leeds researching the impact on employee relations of commercialisation and deregulation in the privatised industries.

Hamish Mathieson is a senior lecturer in industrial relations at Manchester Metropolitan University. His research has focused on management and union strategies in the privatised power industry, on which he contributed a chapter in *Cases in Human Resource Management* (Pitman 1996), edited by Ann McGoldrick, and he is currently researching trade unions in Britain and Sweden.

Jean Shaoul is a lecturer in accounting and finance at the University of Manchester, where she concentrates on the public sector. Her research interests include the use of company accounts to evaluate public policy decisions and her papers include the impact of corporatisation and capital charging on NHS acute hospital trusts, accrual accounting in the public sector and comparisons of public and private sector provision of services.

Part I
Introduction

1 From the New Right to New Labour

Susan Corby and Geoff White

The public services are those public sector organisations providing public goods to citizens, excluding the public corporations. The main UK public services are central and local government, health care, education, the police, fire services and the armed forces and their employee relations have always differed from those in the private sector. This difference does not relate primarily to the absence of profit, a characteristic the public service sector shares with the private 'not for profit' sector, although clearly this limits the resources and strategies of both types of organisations. Nor does it relate to the greater strength of trade unions and collective bargaining in most of the public services compared with the private sector, because this has not always been the case and in some public services, i.e. the police and the armed forces, trade unions are outlawed. The difference is that, unlike the private sector, the fabric of public service employee relations is shot through with the all-important dimension of political power. As Storey has commented, the dilemmas for public sector managers 'derive . . . from the inherently political nature of the values and objectives which must inescapably govern the direction taken' (Storey 1992a: 55).

We start from Storey's proposition. Public service employee relations are different from those in the private sector because of the overarching importance of the political dimension and hence require separate detailed description and analysis. We begin by considering in depth the distinguishing characteristics of the employment relationship in the public services but, because today's public services do not exist in a vacuum, we then examine the context. Accordingly, we trace the historical development of employee relations in the public services and show how they have been affected from the 1980s by neo-classical economics and new public management. This has led to major changes in organisational structures and occupational composition. Next we discuss the issues posed in the book and the themes and trends common to many of the aspects of the employment relationship in the public services: the public/private sector boundary; decentralisation; flexibility; the erosion of collectivism and the decline of the public service ethos. Finally, we consider the implications of the election of a new Labour government in 1997.

A distinct approach

Public service employment relationships are unique in the degree of political control to which they are subject, as we have emphasised. Admittedly the private sector is also subject to the outcomes of political power through the employment policies and legislation of government and its economic and social programmes. In the final analysis, however, private sector employers remain free to regulate the employment relationship as they choose. In contrast, public service managers are governed by the political objectives of their elected masters, who – in a democracy – will normally change from time to time.

Five main features have been identified in the role of the state as an employer (Fredman and Morris 1989: 6). First, the state has the powers to initiate legislation and to govern. Second, it is not dependent on the output of its employees for its income, which it gathers through taxation. Third, it claims to represent the 'national' interest in order to justify its actions, which gives moral authority to its employment decisions. Fourth, constitutional constraints apply, at least in theory, to many public service employers which do not apply to others. For example, employment decisions in the public services may be subjected to judicial review (as in the case of the withdrawal of trade union recognition at GCHQ – the intelligence-gathering centre – without consultation), whereas similar decisions in the private sector would not be reviewable in the courts (Fredman and Morris 1989: 9). Fifth, public service employers operate through bureaucratic structures; a system of power relationships built on hierarchy rather than ownership of capital. This bureaucracy is designed to ensure that there are clear chains of command leading ultimately to ministerial accountability to Parliament and that there is consistency, equity and impartiality in the delivery of services to the public, even if on occasions bureaucracy may appear to impede such delivery. The public services have also been noteworthy for the power of professional interests over general management objectives. All these features have important implications for the employment relationship.

Nevertheless, the degree of political control varies. Civil servants are directly subject to the wishes of the government. There are no mediating forces and so employee relations changes in the civil service may be accomplished by ministerial decree, such as the introduction of contracting-out and the ending of national collective bargaining. In other public services there are mediating forces which may limit the authority of central government. They range from the relatively powerful, as in local government, where the controlling political party may differ from that of central government, to the relatively weak, such as the courts of governors of universities or the directors of NHS trusts. Whether there are mediating forces or not, however, the government controls the purse strings. Even local government, which has powers to raise revenue, derives half its funding from central government and other public services, such as the NHS or the police, are almost completely dependent on government funds.

Accordingly, central government can influence the way that employee relations are conducted through either the allocation of funds or legislation. An example of the first was when the government held back part of the funding for a pay increase for universities in 1992/93 until they could demonstrate that performance appraisal systems had been introduced, despite the supposed independence of higher educational institutions from central government. An example of the second was the passing of specific local government legislation aimed at introducing compulsory competitive tendering in 1980 and 1988.

At the same time, the public services are subject to other sources of power apart from central government: local democratic structures in the case of municipal government, Parliament and its committees in the case of central government, community health councils in the case of the NHS and local police authorities in the case of the police. So the political dimension encompasses a plurality of interests and the public services 'are enveloped in a much more complex web of relationships than simple customer-provider' (Storey 1992a: 56).

Historical background

Regularised employment in the public services can be traced back to the mid-nineteenth century and, in particular, to the social reforms which led to local government systems for towns and counties and to a growth in central government. The Northcote–Trevelyan report of 1853 introduced the concept of a meritocratic civil service with open recruitment conducted by independent boards and promotion based on performance, and led to the establishment of the Civil Service Commission in 1855, although open competition for jobs did not become obligatory on all departments until 1870.

Employee representation in the public services largely stems from the end of the nineteenth century, although there were unions organising in the public sector from as early as the 1870s. Not only did the craft unions organise their specific trades within the Royal Ordnance factories, Royal Dockyards and Stationery Office but there were also specifically public sector unions. The Post Office telegraphists held their first strike in 1870 and the National Union of Elementary Teachers was founded in 1870, partly in response to grievances over the 'payment by results' system for schoolteachers introduced in 1862 (Clegg *et al.* 1964: 31). Writing in 1920, the Webbs noted that the greatest development of trade unionism was among 'the employees of the National and Local Government [which was] ... entirely a growth of the past thirty years' (Webb and Webb 1920: 507). These new, specifically public service, trade unions either represented a particular department (such as the Postmen's Federation and the Tax Clerks' Association) or a particular class of employees (such as the Second Division Clerks' Association) (Clegg 1976: 377). The constituent unions which created Unison, the largest public service union – COHSE, NUPE and NALGO – could trace their origins back to the turn of the century. Despite this growth in public sector unions, national collective bargaining remained unsecured.

The breakthrough for employee representation came following the Whitley Committee of 1917, which recommended the establishment of collective bargaining and joint consultation throughout British industry. To give a lead, in 1919 the government adopted a Whitley system for its own employees: the national joint council for the civil service. In 1919 it also set up the Burnham Committee, based on Whitley principles, to deal with schoolteachers' pay and conditions. In local government collective bargaining was established at the level of regional provincial councils, with a national council to deal with disputes which could not be handled locally, although national level collective bargaining along Whitley lines was not introduced until after the Second World War, with the establishment of the national employers' body in 1948. In 1948 the creation of the National Health Service (NHS) led to new national bargaining systems for health workers based on Whitley principles.

In short, the Whitley model of joint regulation of the employment relationship predominated in the public services. Moreover, from the Second World War until the end of the 1970s, governments encouraged the development of trade unionism in the public services (apart from the police and the armed forces). As a result, union membership grew substantially, especially among white collar professionals. Unlike the private sector there was sometimes legal support for such collective organisation, as in education, where there was a statutory requirement to bargain.

The post-1945 public sector employee relations model was characterised by strong centralised and complex bargaining structures at national level; a diversity of bargaining groups and bargaining agents along sectoral and occupational lines; a commitment by both sides to conciliation and arbitration to avoid industrial conflict; and, for many public servants, a continuing emphasis upon pay comparability with the private sector. Other features (Hepple 1982) included *de facto* job security, pensions and sick pay for most public servants, effective grievance machinery, procedures for promotion and indeterminate boundaries of negotiation and consultation which often in practice worked to the advantage of the unions as the definition of the scope of collective bargaining was itself left open to interpretation and bargaining.

Indeed, some commentators have argued that up to the 1970s the government was a 'good employer' (Hepple 1982; Fredman and Morris 1989), though others have questioned this. Colling (1997: 658) comments that 'cost contraint, and its ramifications for the management of the public sector, were more prominent features of the "golden era" than is acknowledged in conventional accounts, which tend to emphasise the quest for consensus'. Moreover, as Thornley (1994) has indicated, the 'good employer' model did not stop public sector employers from keeping pay levels very low for many public servants. Nevertheless, the low paid groups in the public services, e.g. NHS ancillaries or support grades in the civil service, were usually paid better than their private sector counterparts (Low Pay Commission 1998: 45).

Be that as it may, until the early 1970s, public sector employee relations were relatively quiescent. Thus the Donovan Commission (Royal Commission 1968) had little to say about the public sector, which it saw as a haven of relatively peaceful industrial relations (coal mining apart). Furthermore, the 1960s and the first half of the 1970s witnessed a burgeoning of the welfare state, for instance the establishment of new universities, the raising of the school leaving age, the introduction of statutory maternity pay and a state earnings-related pension scheme. This expansion of public services and thus of labour in the public services led to a growth in employment costs which were largely underwritten by government (Winchester 1983).

From the mid-1960s to the 1970s, however, this peace was broken by a series of economic crises. In 1964 the Labour government made a prices and incomes policy central to its economic strategy, and new governments elected in 1970 and in 1974 first abandoned their predecessors' incomes policies and then introduced their own measures of wage restraint when faced with economic difficulties, which were exacerbated by the marked rise in oil prices from 1973. In 1976, in response to intervention by the International Monetary Fund, the Treasury introduced cash limits into the civil service and the NHS, with the result that public expenditure in these areas was no longer demand-led.

These government policies were increasingly opposed by the public sector unions, primarily because the government chose to set an example for all employers by strictly adhering to the prescribed pay limits for its own work force and, unlike the private sector, there was little, if any, collusion between the employer and unions to avoid the limits. Accordingly, from the early 1970s industrial action began to spread rapidly through the public sector as civil servants, local government workers, health workers and teachers began to exert their industrial power. This culminated in the 'Winter of Discontent' in 1978/79 which was an important factor in the fall of the Labour government.

The Conservative governments, 1979–97

In 1979 the election of a radical Conservative government under the leadership of Margaret Thatcher had profound effects on the future direction of employee relations in the public services. The slowing down of economic growth world-wide, with the less economically efficient countries such as Britain being hard hit, coincided with the new government rejecting the political consensus shared by all shades of government since the Second World War.

During the years of Conservative Party opposition in the 1970s leading right wing intellectuals and 'think tanks' developed radical critiques of the welfare state as 'under- and poorly-managed ... an unaccountable monopoly, ... professionally dominated, and lacking in client involvement' (Ferlie *et al.* 1996: 31). Building on the work of Hayek and Friedman, the New Right held that the market was the most efficient way of allocating goods and services, with contracts between suppliers and customers. Accordingly, public services should wherever possible be subjected to market disciplines or proxies for them and government services should be provided by the private sector, if that was the most cost effective form of provision.

When the Conservative party took office, although it had an overarching ideology, it proceeded cautiously and pragmatically. For instance, it adopted a step-by-step approach to competitive tendering in local government. Indeed, the government's most pronounced changes did not begin until half-way through the period 1979–97, with major reorganisations of the civil service from 1988 and of the NHS from 1990 and the privatisation of civil service agencies from 1993. There were also sub-sectoral differences. For instance, the government imposed considerable change on the civil service but relatively little change on the police. Moreover, at times political and ideological considerations did not coincide, and the former predominated. An example is the creation of a pay review body for nurses and paramedical staff in 1983 and for teachers a decade later, rather than leaving the pay of these groups to be determined purely by market forces (see chapter 4). Bearing in mind these complexities, however, developments can be grouped analytically under four headings: involvement of the private sector in the provision of public services, proxies for market mechanisms, privatisation and producer capture.

Involving the public sector

Initially the government involved the private sector in the public services through compulsory competitive tendering (CCT), under which there are rival bids by the private sector and in-house teams, with contracts being awarded to the most cost effective. From 1980 central government required local authorities to put out to tender building repair, maintenance, highways and sewage work and then, in 1983, it required the NHS to put out to tender catering, cleaning and laundry services. The government extended CCT to other local authority services: building cleaning, refuse collection, street cleansing, catering, ground maintenance, vehicle maintenance and then sports and leisure management through the Local Government Act 1988. It also required local authorities to take cognisance of commercial criteria, for instance outlawing criteria based on gender equality. The Local Government Act 1992 marked a further step in CCT: the government required local authority white collar services such as housing management, legal, personnel and computing services to be put out to tender, as well as further manual services such as security and car parking (Escott and Whitfield 1995). To be better placed to win tenders and retain in-house services, local authorities often established direct service organisations, semi-autonomous units whose managers were given freedom to seek changes in working conditions and working practices.

Meanwhile, in the civil service, market testing, as competitive tendering was called, resulted in nearly £3 billion of activities being reviewed from April 1992 to September 1995 (Cabinet Office 1995). At the same time the government took civil service tendering further with so-called strategic contracting out, whereby parts of departments or agencies were contracted out without any in-house bid being sought.

In addition, from the early 1990s the government resorted to the Private Finance Initiative (PFI). Under the PFI the private sector is a provider of both capital and services. This means that the scope of partnership is wider than under CCT/market testing. In addition, because the private sector is investing significantly, it becomes an influential partner, especially as PFI contracts are spread over many years (twenty-plus), unlike the shorter contracts (five years or less) awarded under tendering. Initially the PFI was used for transport projects but it was extended to hospitals, information technology and property. In 1994 the government announced that henceforward the Treasury would not approve any capital projects unless private finance options had been explored (Cabinet Office 1995).

Market mechanisms

Second, there were proxies for market mechanisms essentially from the late 1980s. Thus, in the civil service, executive agencies were set up following the so called Next Steps report by Sir Robin Ibbs (Efficiency Unit 1988). Separated structurally, financially and operationally from their policy-making parent departments, agencies operated semi-autonomously under a 'framework agreement', i.e. a quasi-contract, specifying their objectives, and were headed by a chief executive. By 1 April 1997 there were 110 agencies in the home civil service. In addition Customs and Excise, the Inland Revenue, the Crown Prosecution Service and the Serious Fraud Office operated on Next Steps lines, covering nearly 77 per cent of civil servants (Government Statistical Service 1998).

The mixture of ideological rationale and opportunism inherent in Conservative government policy is reflected in the changes to the structure of the NHS, as a result of the National Health Service and Community Care Act 1990. Towards the end of the 1980s there was a spate of newspaper stories about patients failing to obtain appropriate health care and there was thus political pressure on the government to reorganise the NHS. Its solution, a quasi-market, was both a pragmatic and an ideological response. In brief, the Act created an internal market where health authorities and general practitioner (GP) fundholders purchased health care from NHS hospitals, renamed trusts, each with a board of directors. Alternatively, purchasers could buy health care from private sector hospitals. In 1991 the first fifty-seven hospitals in England transferred from direct management by health authorities and became NHS trusts with certain financial and personnel 'freedoms' (NHS Management Executive 1990). By April 1997 all the hospitals in the UK had become trusts.

In education, too, there were changes designed to emulate market mechanisms and to respond to parents' concerns about the quality of schools.

Thus under the Education Reform Act 1988 and the Further and Higher Education Act 1992 further education colleges and higher education polytechnics (now new universities) and colleges, previously under local authority control, became independent corporations managed by boards of governors. As to schools, legislation in the 1980s in England led to 'local management of schools' whereby school governing bodies were given significant control over staffing and expenditure on services and head teachers became in some respects like managing directors of small businesses, having control of 85 per cent of their budget. Where schools chose grant maintained status, they could opt out of local education authority control entirely and had full freedom to determine the terms and conditions of staff, though in practice they rarely used it.

Privatisation

Third, New Right theories were used to justify privatisation. Initially privatisation centred on the nationalised industries and public utilities and not civil service agencies (Goldsworthy 1991). From 1992, however, privatisation was extended to civil service agencies, of which over a dozen had been privatised by the general election of 1997. In addition, parts of departments or agencies were privatised, for instance the information technology limb of Inland Revenue (Government Statistical Service 1998).

Preventing producer capture

A further ideological strand in the Conservative government's approach from 1979 to 1997 was public choice theory (Downs 1967): the notion that public service bureaucrats are as likely to act in their own self-interest as in the interests of citizens and that they seek status by budget maximisation and empire building. This theory of producer capture was extended by the New Right to professional bodies and public sector trade unions.

Producer capture could be obviated in a number of ways: by competitive tendering, internal markets and privatisation, as described above, by staff reduction targets for the civil service to be achieved by April 1984 (Blackwell and Lloyd 1989) and by capping local government rates from 1985. It could also be overcome by limiting the autonomy of professionals, a politically popular approach. For instance in the 1980s a national curriculum with standardised assessments in schools curtailed the professional independence of schoolteachers and the introduction of general managers and performance measures dented the power of doctors.

Perhaps the best example of the combination of ideology and opportunism is the Citizen's Charter, which sought to counteract producer capture by promoting public servants' responsiveness to their clients/customers (Cabinet Office 1991). The Citizen's Charter, launched in 1991, had six key principles: standards, information and openness, choice and consultation, courtesy

and helpfulness, putting things right and value for money. These principles, with their customer orientation, were estimable, at least superficially,
and the Citizen's Charter spanned a range of public services, including the
Inland Revenue, the prison service, the police and education (Cabinet Office
1992) It also spawned mini-charters, such as the patient's charter, the job
seeker's charter, the parent's charter. (The use of quality control systems
to control public servants and limit their autonomy is covered in detail in
chapter 8.)

As to the trade unions, their power was weakened in the economy as a
whole both by legislation (Wedderburn 1989) and by macroeconomic policies
which led to levels of unemployment in the mid-1980s of 10 per cent or
more, compared with 2–5 per cent in the 1970s (Burchill 1997). Public
service unions in particular were weakened by the fall in the number of
employees (see below) and by the government as employer adopting an anti-
union approach (see chapter 10). Examples include the exclusion of unions
from the Government Communications Headquarters (GCHQ) – the intelligence-gathering centre; the civilianisation of posts in the prison service,
designed to weaken the hold of the Prison Officers' Association; and the
removal of some 2,000 senior civil servants and half a million schoolteachers
in England and Wales and half a million nurses from collective bargaining.

New Right theories meshed with the Conservative government's desire
to constrain public expenditure. For instance, privatisation, justified on the
grounds of neoclassical economic theory, raised money for the public purse.
Similarly, staff reduction targets in the civil service and the NHS, justified
on the grounds of public choice theories, reduced the government payroll.
New Right theories also meshed with the Conservative government's desire
to make the public services more cost effective and productive.

New public management

This new managerialist approach was dubbed the 'new public management'
(Dunleavy and Hood 1994) but at least three definitions are available
(Farnham and Horton 1996: 24). First, new public management is used as
shorthand for the ideological tradition of 'managerialism' and 'neo-Taylorism'
(Pollitt 1993). Second, new public management is used synonymously with
business-centred management practices imported from the private sector
(Hood 1990). Third, it is an umbrella term covering the transformation of
bureaucratic, paternalistic and democratically passive public services into
efficient, responsive and consumer-oriented ones (Ranson and Stewart 1994).
Significantly, the rise of new public management ideas does not seem to be limited to the UK (Organisation for Economic Co-operation and Development
1992).

First, managerialism and neo-Taylorism: this emphasises the control of government spending, decentralising management, setting targets and measuring
and rewarding performance. Examples include the introduction of general

managers into the NHS, the imposition of service standards on public servants through the Citizen's Charter (Cabinet Office 1991), the financial management initiative in the civil service (which devolved financial responsibility to cost centres) and the Rayner scrutinies. Named after Sir Derek Rayner of Marks & Spencer, these involved intensive study of a particular area aimed at improving efficiency and were pioneered in the civil service and then introduced into the NHS (Harrison 1988).

There is evidence that public servants believed that they were being subjected to work intensification, which is one of the effects of neo-Taylorism. Studies have reported that employees in the NHS (Edwards and Whitston 1991; Lloyd and Seifert 1993), in schools (Sinclair *et al.* 1995) and in universities (Wilson 1991) perceived that they were working harder and for longer hours.

There are a number of examples of the second way the term 'new public management' is used: business-centred management practices imported from the private sector. For instance, in 1996 the Conservative government introduced the private sector technique of benchmarking into the civil service on a pilot basis. It entails measuring civil service agencies against the Business Excellence Model: nine criteria developed by 200 private sector organisations (Cabinet Office 1998). Individual performance-related pay (IPRP) is another example of a practice widely used in the private sector and then transposed to the public services. Casey *et al.* (1992) found IPRP to be common (nearly 90 per cent) in organisations in the private sector. It became widespread in the civil service during the 1990s, although essentially restricted to senior managers in the rest of the public services (Incomes Data Services 1997). Other private sector techniques and practices introduced into the public services include accrual accounting and outsourcing. Of course this raises the question of whether such private sector techniques are appropriate in the public services. For instance, a study by the Institute of Personnel and Development (IPD 1998) of 1,158 organisations found that over half (51 per cent) of the public sector respondents believed that IPRP was having a negative effect on staff morale, as compared with 34 per cent in the private sector (see chapter 4).

As to the third way the term 'new public management' is used, this encompasses the organisational changes outlined above as well as the adoption of the managerialist approaches which have fallen under the headings of the first two definitions.

Employment patterns

Whether or not the public services have been made more efficient, employment patterns in the public services have changed. The post-war growth in public sector employment ended in the early 1980s, and there was a general decline from that point. As can be seen from table 1.1, however, the trends in employment varied within the sector. The armed forces, for example, have seen a continuous decline in numbers, whereas the police have seen

Table 1.1 Analysis of UK work force in employment: head count, mid-year (000)

Category	1961	1971	1981	1987	1995	1996	1997
Total work force in employment	24,685	24,669	24,498	25,266	25,835	26,031	26,526
Private sector	18,826	18,042	17,313	18,907	20,602	20,905	21,469
Public sector	5,859	6,627	7,185	6,359	5,233	5,126	5,057
Public corporations	2,200	2,009	1,867	985	1,524	1,510	1,521
NHS Trusts	–	–	–	–	1,085	1,102	1,121
Other	2,200	2,009	1,867	985	439	408	400
General government	3,659	4,618	5,318	5,374	3,709	3,616	3,536
Central government	1,790	1,966	2,419	2,312	1,058	989	941
HM Forces	474	368	334	319	230	221	210
NHS	575	785	1,207	1,212	97	84	78
Other	741	813	878	781	731	684	653
Local government	1,869	2,652	2,899	3,062	2,651	2,627	2,595
Education	785	1,297	1,454	1,486	1,188	1,191	1,187
Social services	170	276	350	398	412	406	400
Police	108	152	186	191	207	207	207
Construction	103	124	143	128	83	79	65
Other	703	803	766	763	761	744	736

Source: Safford and MacGregor (1998). *Economic Trends*, Office for National Statistics, © Crown Copyright 1998.

continuous increases until recent times. Central government has seen a significant reduction from 1987 to 1997, whereas the apparent decline in local government employment can be largely explained by the statistical reallocation of some education staff to the private sector. NHS employment has remained more or less static since the early 1980s, although NHS trusts (where the majority of NHS staff now work) have been reclassified as public corporations rather than 'general government' as before.

More important, there has been a change in the occupational composition of the public services. The proportion of manual workers employed has declined, while the proportion of non-manual employment has increased. This partly reflects the steady pressure of compulsory competitive tendering on local government and NHS manual worker staffing levels and has left a primarily white-collar administrative, technical and professional work force in the public services. The gender balance has also shifted in favour of female employees, who now make up almost two-thirds of the work force in the public services, although in the economy as a whole they make up about half the work force.

This changing occupational composition of the public sector is particularly important when we make comparisons with the private sector, which retains a more balanced work force in terms of manual and non-manual occupations. In general, women tend to be better paid in the public sector, compared with the private sector, while for men it is the reverse. This largely reflects the larger numbers of female professionals and managers in the public sector (e.g. social workers, schoolteachers, nurses and professions allied to medicine), compared with the private sector. Also, the public services are more labour-intensive than the private sector, 'with labour costs approaching 80 per cent of costs' (Farnham and Horton 1996:14).

The following chapters

Unlike some other books on employee relations in the UK public services which take an organisational or sub-sectoral approach, this book adopts a thematic approach. It extracts key issues, allowing a more rigorous and coherent cross-sectoral critique than can be obtained from descriptive, organisation based texts. Nevertheless, every attempt has been made not to neglect the heterogeneity in the public services. For instance, the arrangements for determining pay vary quite widely and include pay review bodies and collective bargaining (see chapter 4) and the approach of the police and local government in respect of equal opportunities varies greatly (see chapter 5). Moreover, in some chapters a mini-organisational case study has been used to substantiate the arguments, for example accrual accounting in the NHS in chapter 2, or emphasis has been placed on a certain sub-sector where there has been most change, for example the employment status of civil servants in chapter 3.

The book's structure is separated into three parts: context, issues and players. Each chapter discusses the impact of particular sets of government policies on the employment relationship, aiming to be analytical, not prescriptive, and raises key questions. Thus a central question in chapter 2 is whether the provision of public services by the private sector is cost effective or not, particularly when the largely hidden costs of planning and monitoring are taken into account. The main question posed in chapter 3 is whether the importation of private law concepts has made public service employment indistinguishable from that in the private sector or whether there is now a new form of public employment. A key question raised by chapter 4 is whether changes in payment systems designed to make pay systems more like the private sector are reducing fairness, comparability and the 'employee voice' in pay determination. Chapter 5 asks whether equal opportunities are undermined by decentralised organisational structures because newly empowered line managers do not understand the equality dimension of their roles, or whether equal opportunities are enhanced because line managers have 'ownership'. Chapter 6 considers whether employment flexibilities are a result of public service employers seeking to contain costs or whether they are a result of employees seeking to make their work compatible with their domestic responsibilities. Chapter 7 considers whether competitive tendering has led to greater efficiency in service delivery or simply increased control by public service managers over their workers. The main question in chapter 8 is whether new quality initiatives are an attempt to improve services to the public or whether they are a technique for management control of the work force, using traditional appeals to the 'public interest' to defend a cost-cutting agenda. Chapter 9 asks whether personnel managers are adopting a strategic role or whether their role continues to be predominantly administrative. Chapter 10 considers whether union merger activity has led to a decrease in inter-union competition or exacerbated union recruitment rivalries.

The themes

In addition to the issues explored in the individual chapters, the UK public services exhibit five themes and trends which span the book:

- the blurring of the public/private sector divide;
- decentralisation;
- the growth of flexibility;
- the erosion of collectivism;
- the decline of the public service ethos.

The blurring of the public/private sector divide

'There is no absolute frontier between the public and private sectors,' the previous government said (Cabinet Office 1995: 127) and we have already shown how structural and organisational changes such as privatisation, competitive tendering and the NHS internal market have made the boundary less distinct. The Private Finance Initiative takes this further because the government retains an ongoing role in PFI projects, usually as the main purchaser of the services provided by private consortia.

This blurring of the boundary, however, extends to the importation of private sector managerial techniques into the public services and to the unions. Public service unions, having followed their members, now recruit in the private sector, while predominantly private sector unions have increasingly been seeking recruits in the public services to bolster their falling membership and, for instance, the Manufacturing, Science and Finance Union (MSF) merged with the Health Visitors' Association in 1990 (Certification Officer 1991). The legal boundaries, too, have faded. For instance, civil servants now have contracts of employment like other employees although, like other public service employees, they have a special position under European Union law (see chapter 3).

Also, people from the private sector have increasingly been brought into the public services. For instance, non-executive directors of the boards of NHS trusts and health authorities have mainly been drawn from the private sector and in the years 1994–95 to 1996–97 inclusive, seventy-four senior civil servants were appointed from the private sector (Civil Service Commissioners 1997). Although the number is small as a proportion of the 3,000 strong senior civil service, it is an innovation, as traditionally senior civil servants have been recruited almost entirely from the more junior grades.

Decentralisation

There has been widespread decentralisation in the private sector and in the public services in the last two decades, both organisationally and financially. Another important facet of decentralisation in both the private sector and the public services has been the decentralisation of collective bargaining. In the public services this has been manifested in the civil service (four central agreements replaced by some 200 agreements), in further education, to some extent in the NHS (a complex system of local pay in a national framework from 1995 to 1997), but less so in local government or higher education. There has also been decentralisation of personnel management arrangements, for instance in the civil service stemming from the Cassels report in 1983, and in the polytechnics/new universities stemming from their incorporation in 1988.

Significantly, decentralisation has provided an impetus to union amalgamations: both the merger of Unison from three partner unions essentially in health, local government and the utilities and the series of mergers of civil service unions from 1988 to 1998 which resulted in a single union, the Public and Commercial Services Union (PCS), in place of four unions. It has had an impact on the role of personnel managers, starting to turn them from administrators into operators (albeit more gradually than the rhetoric suggests – see chapter 9). It has also had an impact on equal opportunities, with central equal opportunities units in local government and the civil service, for instance, being reduced or disbanded and responsibility being handed to the line (see chapter 5).

Yet the trend to decentralisation is not straightforward and there are centripetal pressures: the centre has an interest in exerting control, for instance to ensure efficiency, quality and consistency. Thus in the private sector there are many examples of so-called tight/loose arrangements and Marginson *et al.* (1988) found that often companies did not allow their establishments any discretion in many industrial relations issues. Research by Kessler and Purcell (1996) indicates that there are still constraints on decentralisation in the public services.

In the public services the centripetal pressures are compounded. This is because in the last resort ministers are accountable to Parliament for the public services. Thus there have to be centralised structures countervailing the new decentralised forms. There are numerous examples of centripetal pressures. For instance, in the civil service although collective bargaining is carried out in a myriad of departments and agencies, the Treasury keeps tight control and managers in agencies/departments need approval of their negotiating plans and further approval if there is any deviation in any detail (e.g. even shifting 0.5 per cent of performance pay from satisfactory performers to better performers at Vehicle Inspectorate in 1996 (Corby 1998)). In the NHS, both the Conservative Health Secretary and then the Labour Health Secretary ordered so-called self-governing NHS trusts to cut their management costs (Brindle 1997). In education, central government imposed a national curriculum. It also introduced legislation to cap local authorities' tax-raising powers from 1985 and to require local authorities to put services out to competitive tender in 1988, as noted above.

Employment flexibility

Another common denominator is the growth of flexibility and again this trend is not limited to the public services. It has marked more of a departure from tradition in the public services, however, than in the private sector, as the former were characterised by hierarchy, centralism and rigidity until the1980s. Moreover, the new ideas about public management and cost pressures set the context in which flexibility has become a major objective of many in the public services (Horton 1997).

Flexibility has many aspects, including organisational structures, pay, working time and work organisation. Looking at organisational flexibility, as we have seen, traditionally the public services were organised into large bureaucracies but the Conservative government policies resulted in the fragmentation of these large organisations, such as the NHS, local government and the civil service, into semi-autonomous structures. The stated aim was that these organisations should react more sensitively and rapidly to their customers' needs. Storey (1992a) points out that the Audit Commission was influential on this front, as it repeatedly indicated that bureaucracy was no longer an appropriate organisational mode for the public services. Similarly, pay in the public services, traditionally centralised and specific, has become more flexible; for instance (as we said), no longer is there civil service-wide pay determination and the 1997 local government single status agreement has a unified pay spine but without any specified rates of pay for particular jobs. Such flexibility enables employers to respond to local labour markets, or the imperatives of their set of activities, and to reward performance (see chapter 4).

Working time flexibility takes a number of forms, including temporary and fixed term contracts, part time work and annualised hours. According to the Labour Force Survey, workers in public administration, education and health were far more likely to be on temporary contracts than other employees, with fixed term contracts being a particular feature of temporary work in these public services (Sly and Stillwell 1997: 352). Also, there are high levels of part time employment in many areas of the public services, although this varies from nearly half of all employees in the NHS to virtually none in the armed forces. The Labour Force Survey also indicates that annualised hours contracts are particularly common in higher education and in schools compared with the economy as a whole (Casey *et al.* 1997). (See chapter 6.)

It should be stressed, however, that, as far as work organisation is concerned, there is little functional flexibility in the public services. Thus in the NHS it is limited to the ancillary grades, with little functional flexibility among doctors and nurses (Corby and Mathieson 1997), and among manual workers in the direct service organisations of local authorities (White 1997).

The erosion of collectivism

Another trend is the erosion of collectivism and the growth of individualism. Again this is not limited to the public services. Nevertheless, as the public services have been characterised by extensive management/union involvement, this is a marked break with the past. Thus membership of public service unions has fallen in the last two decades, though far less dramatically than amongst private sector unions (2 per cent, compared with 40 per cent over the period 1979–96). Apart from the *cause célèbre*, GCHQ, there has been union derecognition in a few NHS trusts, particularly ambulance trusts such as Lincolnshire, Essex and Northumbria, as well as at the National Maritime Museum. Claydon (1996), comparing 1984–88 with 1989–93, found that the share of health and education in cases of union dere-cognition rose from 3.4 per cent to 9.6 per cent. This, however, must be seen in context: publishing, paper and print accounted for 22.9 per cent of cases of derecognition in 1989–93. Since Claydon's study the civil service unions have been partially derecognised in respect of 2,000 senior civil servants who have been taken out of collective bargaining and given personal contracts. These staff are now covered by the Senior Salaries Review Body.

Even where there was not derecognition, there has been an erosion of collectivism. For instance, by 1997 virtually all civil servants had at least an element of their pay determined by some form of individual performance-review and in some civil service agencies unions' views were given little or no consideration by management (Corby 1993/94, 1998). According to the Workplace Industrial Relations Survey of 1990 (Millward *et al.* 1992: 361), 'the proportion of workplaces in central government where managers said that management strongly recommended trade union membership for all employees halved between 1984 and 1990'. There are, however, signs that the 1997 Labour government may halt this trend (see below).

Nevertheless, public service unions, whatever political party is in power, are faced with managers' adoption of human resource management (HRM) and its inherent individualism. We do not set off at a tangent to discuss the competing and problematic definitions of HRM but adopt Storey's approach. He says that it is 'a set of interrelated practices with an ideological and philosophical underpinning [which] appears to align closely with prevailing ideas of enterprise, and the freeing up of managerial initiative' (Storey 1989: 3). The interrelated practices include direct forms of communication and involvement such as team briefing, staff attitude surveys and quality circles/ teams. As Guest (1989) has pointed out, HRM values are fundamentally unitarist and assume that there are no inevitable differences of interest between managers and workers.

There are many examples of HRM practices in the public services, including team briefing, staff attitude surveys, total quality management and business process re-engineering (Corby 1993/94; Colling 1997). This is supported by Storey's research (1992b), two of whose fifteen case study organisations were public services: the NHS and Bradford Metropolitan Council. He points out, however, that HRM practices in these public services typically 'carried the mantle of being "experimental" (therefore probably temporary) add-ons' (Storey 1992b: 271).

Interestingly the unions, while far from welcoming the adoption of HRM techniques by employers, have adopted a similar approach towards their own members. There are many examples from the public service unions, although the phenomenon is not limited to them. For instance, stressing the union/individual member link, the Royal College of Nursing (RCN) established a twenty-four-hour hot line to give advice to members (Brindle 1998) and under the constitution of the Public and Commercial Services Union major decisions are determined by individual member ballots rather than branch meetings or the annual conference (Public Services, Taxes and Commerce Union 1997).

The decline of the public service ethos

Finally and more nebulously there has been the decline of the public service ethos. 'Ethos' is defined by the Organisation for Economic Co-operation and Development (OECD 1996: 14) as 'the sum of ideals which define an overall culture in the public services' as opposed to ethics which are 'the rules that translate characteristic ideals or ethos into every-day practice'. The public service ethos is based on values of standardisation, probity, risk aversion and fairness, and entails detailed rules for managers. The new public management emphasises entrepreneurial characteristics such as business need, cost minimisation, innovation and flexibility for managers to deploy their resources as they think fit.

The decline in the public service ethos owes something to the fact that managers recruited from the private sector into the public services sometimes did not appreciate the political dimension. Sir John Bourn, then Comptroller and Auditor General, said that such managers often had an inadequate grasp of the importance of accountability to Parliament and were often surprised to learn that they were subject to scrutiny for their handling of public money (Willman 1994). Similarly, Trosa (1994: 38) found that agency chief executives recruited from the private sector did not realise that, on occasion, they would have to make compromises between a preoccupation with efficiency and political requirements.

Not only does the risk to the ethos arise because private sector people have come into the public service, it also arises because public servants are increasingly involved in commercial operations with the private sector. They may lack judgement or expertise and/or take risks with public money.

Several examples have been uncovered in the NHS (Wighton 1998; Brindle 1995).

Civil servants have a particular ethical dilemma. To what extent do they owe allegiance to their minister or to Parliament? Although this dilemma is not new it was thrown into relief by the trial of Clive Ponting in 1985, who deliberately leaked confidential information in an effort to expose what he considered were his minister's misleading statements to Parliament. Various attempts have been made to address such ethical issues, including a memorandum by Sir Robert Armstrong – then the Cabinet Secretary – and the Nolan Committee which recommended independent scrutiny, awareness of obligations and codes of conduct. This resulted in 1996 in a civil service code with a right of appeal to the First Civil Service Commissioner (see chapter 3).

The Labour government is taking further steps as it is seized of the need to inject an ethos of accountability and probity. Accordingly, it has said that NHS trusts will be required to open up their board meetings to the public (Department of Health 1997) and is proposing that every local authority should bring in a code of conduct, based on a national model but tailored to its circumstances. It is too early to judge how effective these measures will be. Whatever the practice, however, the language of public servants has undoubtedly become entrepreneurial. As a regional manager in the Employment Service said: 'We now use words like "business agenda" but before . . . that would have sounded not only strange, but silly' (Corby 1998).

Beyond the millennium

As we have already pointed out, the government has a central role in public service employee relations. In 1997 there was a change of government from Conservative to New Labour. To what extent did 1997 represent the end of an era? We argue that it did not: 1997 marked the end of a chapter, not a new book, as the 'plot' has continued. In particular, the new government has adopted its predecessor's stance on public expenditure controls, though perhaps influenced more by pragmatism than by ideology. In any event, this continuity can be seen in many aspects of employee relations.

First, New Labour is retaining many of the employee relations institutions bequeathed by the Conservatives. This is well illustrated by pay determination machinery such as the pay review bodies, the Police Negotiating Board and the departmental/agency bargaining units in the civil service. Pay determination arrangements may change in the NHS but the threat of equal pay claims, rather than government policy, is likely to be the driving force.

Second, when it comes to pay policy, rather than institutions, there has been little or no change as yet. Thus the government, both before and after 1997, continued to support a policy that all public sector pay increases must be funded from within existing budgets through efficiency or other savings. This policy, introduced by a Conservative Chancellor, Kenneth Clarke, in 1994, was continued by Labour Chancellor Gordon Brown until 1999.

Beyond then there are no signs that the tight constraints on public sector pay will be lifted. On the contrary, the Chancellor is adamant that he will keep a tight grip on running costs, including wages in the public services. Moreover, the national minimum wage will hardly affect pay in the public services, at least in 1999 and 2000, as it is to be set at a level below virtually all the minima applying in the public services (Low Pay Commission 1998: 45). Performance-related pay continues to apply in the civil service, though in the NHS it seems that the move to local pay, vigorously resisted by the unions, is to be replaced by a national pay system 'with appropriate local flexibility' (Incomes Data Services 1998: 127).

Third, the structures of the public services seem set to continue. David Clark, then Chancellor of the Duchy of Lancaster, said of executive agencies in the civil service that the Labour Party was happy to support them 'in opposition as well as now in government' (Cabinet Office 1998). In the NHS 'the new system will go with the grain . . . The Government will retain the separation between the planning of hospital care and its provision' (Department of Health 1997: 11). In schools, New Labour in effect is proposing to extend the Conservative government's principles of grant maintained status to all schools and give them 100 per cent delegation of their budgets (Targett 1998b).

Fourth, New Labour is continuing and taking further the strategy of involving the private sector in the provision of public services, for instance in building and running private prisons and NHS hospitals under the Private Finance Initiative started by the Conservative government (Buckby 1997). Similarly, private sector companies are to participate in some 'education action zones', government-designated failing schools in socially deprived areas (Targett 1998a). Moreover, although the Chancellor of the Duchy of Lancaster said that the privatisation of civil service agencies 'is not on the agenda' (Institution of Professionals, Managers and Specialists 1998a), the Chancellor of the Exchequer subsequently announced plans partially to sell off the Royal Mint, one of the first agencies, as well as air traffic control, the Tote and the Commonwealth Development Corporation. Furthermore, a number of buildings and land owned by civil service departments are to be sold and local government is to be expected to raise revenue from property sales (Elliott and Macaskill 1998). Meanwhile, strategic contracting-out looks set to continue: for instance, the back-office operations of National Savings. Similarly the new government is continuing with market testing in the civil service, albeit its approach 'is pragmatic, not dogmatic' (Cabinet Office 1997), and with 'best value' in local government, albeit the criteria will not revolve around cost alone (Department of the Environment, Transport and Regions 1998).

Fifth, New Labour is extending its control over public service professionals. For instance, it is proposing a range of institutions and measures to control doctors, such as a National Institute for Clinical Excellence, a Commission for Health Improvement, which will carry out spot checks and regular inspections, evidence-based service frameworks and so-called clinical governance whereby trust boards will have a duty to investigate adverse events. Similarly, there is to be a General Teaching Council to regulate teachers in England with representatives drawn not only from the teaching unions but also from local authorities, universities, school governors, parents and business (Carvel 1998).

Nevertheless, despite these continuities, the employee relations climate is different. Unions have been restored to GCHQ. Union leaders have much more access than before the general election to ministers. The public service unions, like their counterparts elsewhere, will benefit from the government's proposed statutory recognition procedure (Department of Trade and Industry 1998). In the civil service the Cabinet Office has urged departments and agencies to ensure that civil servants' letters of appointment and departmental staff handbooks state clearly that union membership is officially encouraged (Institution of Professional, Managers and Specialists 1998b). In the NHS, nationally the unions are to be involved in a task force on improving the involvement of front line staff and locally, through staff consultative committees, in dialogue about decisions affecting local health services (Department of Health 1997). The government, in its White Paper on the NHS, has said that the NHS: 'relies on the commitment and motivation of its staff . . . Involving all staff in service developments and planning change, with open communication and collaboration, is the best way . . .' (Department of Health 1997: 50, 51). This statement could apply to any part of the public services but it is still too early to assess whether it represents more than rhetoric.

Acknowledgement

The authors would like to thank David Winchester, senior lecturer at the University of Warwick, for his helpful comments on a draft of this chapter.

References

Blackwell, R. and Lloyd, P. (1989) 'New managerialism in the civil service: industrial relations under the Thatcher administrations 1979–1986' in R. Mailly, S. J. Dimmock and A. S. Sethi, (eds) *Industrial Relations in the Public Services*, London: Routledge.

Brindle, D. (1995) 'NHS trust deal lost £3.5m', *Guardian*, 6 October, p. 2.

Brindle, D. (1997) 'NHS managers' jobs targeted to provide cash for patient care', *Guardian*, 23 May, p. 5.

Brindle, D. (1998) 'Nurses get 24 hour hot line to union advice', *Guardian*, 25 February, p. 8.

Buckby, S. (1997) 'Medicine prescribed for hospital deals', *Financial Times*, 18 December, p. 10.

Burchill, F. (1997) *Labour Relations*, second edition, Basingstoke: Macmillan.

Cabinet Office (1991) *The Citizen's Charter: Raising the Standard*, Cm 1599, London: HMSO.

Cabinet Office (1992) *The Citizen's Charter: First Report 1992*, Cm 2101, London: HMSO.

Cabinet Office (1995) *Competitiveness: Forging Ahead*, Cm 2867, London: HMSO.

Cabinet Office (1997) 'Twelve guiding Principles in Using Market Testing and Contracting out', unpublished.

Cabinet Office (1998) *Next Steps Agencies in Government Review 1997*, Cm 3889, London: Stationery Office.

Carvel, J. (1998) 'Unions to be squeezed on Government's new body set up to regulate teachers', *Guardian*, 23 April, p. 7.

Casey, B., Lakey, J. and White, M., (1992) *Payment Systems: a Look at Current Practice*, Research Series 5, London: Employment Department.

Casey, B., Metcalf, H. and Millward, N. (1997) *Employers' Use of Flexible Labour*, London: Policy Studies Institute.

Cassels, J. S. (1983) *The Review of Personnel Work in the Civil Service: Report to the Prime Minister*, London: HMSO.

Certification Officer (1991) *Annual Report 1990*, London: Certification Office.

Civil Service Commissioners (1997) *Annual Report, 1 April 1996 to 31 March 1997*, London: Civil Service Commissioners.

Claydon, T. (1996) 'Union derecognition: a re-examination' in I. J. Beardwell (ed.) *Contemporary Industrial Relations: a Critical Analysis*, Oxford: Oxford University Press.

Clegg, H. A. (1976) *The System of Industrial Relations in Great Britain*, Oxford: Blackwell.

Clegg H. A., Fox, A. and Thompson, A. F. (1964) *A History of British Trade Unions since 1889* I, 1889–1910. Oxford: Clarendon Press.

Colling, T. (1993) 'Contracting public services: the management of compulsory competitive tendering in two county councils', *Human Resource Management Journal* 3 (4): 1–15.

Colling, T. (1997) 'Managing human resources in the public sector' in I. Beardwell and L. Holden (eds) *Human Resource Management: a Contemporary Perspective*, second edition, London: Pitman.

Corby, S. (1993/94) 'How big a step is "Next Steps"? Industrial relations developments in civil service executive agencies', *Human Resource Management Journal* 4 (2): 52–69.

Corby, S. (1998) 'Industrial relations in civil service agencies: transition or transformation?' *Industrial Relations Journal* 29 (3): 194–206.

Corby, S. and Mathieson, H. (1997) 'The National Health Service and the limits to flexibility', *Public Policy and Administration* 12 (4): 60–72.

Department of the Environment, Transport and the Regions (DETR) (1998) *Modernising Local Government: Improvising Services through Best Value*, London: Stationery Office.

Department of Health (1997) *The New NHS: Modern, Dependable*, London: Department of Health.

Department of Trade and Industry (1998) *Fairness at Work*, Cm 3968, London: Stationery Office.

Downs, A. (1967) *Inside Bureaucracy*, Boston MA: Little Brown.

Dunleavy, P. and Hood, C. (1994). 'From old public administration to new public management' *Public Money and Management* 14 (3): 34–43.

Edwards, P. and Whitston, C. (1991) 'Workers are working harder: effort and shop floor relations in the 1980s', *British Journal of Industrial Relations* 29 (4): 593–601.

Efficiency Unit (1988) *Improving Management in Government: the Next Steps* (the Ibbs report), London: HMSO.

Elliott, L. and Macaskill, E. (1998) 'Brown's £12 bn sale', *Guardian*, 12 June, p. 1.

Escott, K. and Whitfield, D. (1995) *The Gender Impact of CCT in Local Government*, Manchester: Equal Opportunities Commission.

Farnham, D. and Horton, S. (1996) *Managing People in the Public Services*, Basingstoke: Macmillan.

Ferlie, E., Pettigrew A., Ashburner, L. and Fitzgerald, L. (1996) *The New Public Management in Action*, Oxford: Oxford University Press.

Fredman, S. and Morris, G. (1989) *The State as Employer*, London: Mansell.

Goldsworthy, D. (1991) *Setting up Next Steps*, London: HMSO.

Government Statistical Service (1998) *Civil Service Statistics 1997*, London: Government Statistical Service.

Guest, D. (1989) 'Human resource management: its implications for industrial relations and trade unions' in J. Storey (ed.) *New Perspectives on Human Resource Management*, London: Routledge.

Harrison, S. (1988) *Managing the National Health Service: Shifting the Frontier?* London: Chapman & Hall.

Hepple, B. (1982). 'Labour law and public employees in Britain' in W. Wedderburn and J. T. Murphy (eds), *Labour Law and the Community: Perspectives for the 1980s*. London: Institute of Advanced Legal Studies, University of London.

Hood, C. (1990) 'Beyond the Public Bureaucracy State? Public Administration in the 1990s', inaugural lecture, London School of Economics.

Horton, S. (1997) 'Employment flexibilities in the public services: concepts, contexts and practices', *Public Policy and Administration* 12 (4):1–13.

Incomes Data Services (1997). *Pay in the Public Services: Review of 1996; Prospects for 1997*, London: Incomes Data Services.

Incomes Data Services (1998) *Pay in the Public Services: Review of 1997; Prospects for 1998*, London: Incomes Data Services.

Institute of Personnel and Development (1998) *IPD 1998 Performance Pay Survey*, London: Institute of Personnel and Development.

Institution of Professionals, Managers and Specialists (1998a) 'No more privatisation plans, says Clark', *IPMS Bulletin* 3/98, 1 April.

Institution of Professionals, Managers and Specialists (1998b) 'A higher profile for training', *IPMS Bulletin* 3/98, 2 April.

Kessler, I. and Purcell, J. (1996) 'Strategic choice and new forms of employment relations in the public service sector: developing an analytical framework', *International Journal of Human Resource Management* 7 (1): 206–29.

Lloyd, C. and Seifert, R. (1993) 'Restructuring the NHS: Labour Utilisation and Intensification in four Hospitals', paper given at the eleventh annual Labour Process Conference, Blackpool, April.

Low Pay Commission (1998) *The National Minimum Wage: First Report of the Low Pay Commission*, Cm 3976, London: Stationery Office.

Marginson, P., Edwards, P. K., Martin, R., Purcell, J. and Sisson, K. (1988) *Beyond the Workplace*, Oxford: Blackwell.

Millward, N., Stevens, M., Smart, D. and Hawes, W. R. (1992) *Workplace Industrial Relations in Transition*, Aldershot: Dartmouth.

NHS Management Executive (1990) *NHS Trusts: a Working Guide*, London: HMSO.

Organisation for Economic Co-operation and Development (1992) *Public Management Developments Update 1992*, Paris: OECD.

Organisation for Economic Co-operation and Development (1996) *Ethics in the Public Service: Current Issues and Practice*, Public Management Occasional Papers 14, Paris: Organisation for Economic Co-operation and Development.

Pollitt, C. (1993) *Managerialism and the Public Services,* second edition, Oxford: Blackwell.

Public Services, Tax and Commerce Union (1997) *PCS: the Final Rules for a new Union*, London: PTC.

Ranson, S. and Stewart, J. (1994) *Management for the Public Domain*, Basingstoke: Macmillan.

Royal Commission on Trade Unions and Employers' Associations (1968) (the Donovan report) Cmnd 3623, London: HMSO.

Safford, J. and MacGregor, D. (1998) 'Employment in the public and private sectors', *Economic Trends* 532 (March).

Sinclair, J., Seifert, R. and Ironside, M. (1995) 'Market driven reforms in education: performance, quality and industrial relations in schools' in I. Kirkpatrick and M. M. Lucio (eds) *The Politics of Quality in the Public Sector*, London: Routledge.

Sly, F. and Stillwell, D. (1997) 'Temporary workers in Great Britain', *Labour Market Trends*, September: 347–54.

Storey, J. (1989) 'Introduction: from personnel management to human resource management' in J. Storey (ed.) *New Perspectives on Human Resource Management*, London: Routledge.

Storey, J. (1992a) 'Human resource management in the public sector' in G. Salaman (ed.) *Human Resource Strategies*, London: Sage.

Storey, J. (1992b) *Developments in the Management of Human Resources*, Oxford: Blackwell.

Targett, S. (1998a) 'Teachers attack business involvement in schools', *Financial Times*, 9 April, p. 11.

Targett, S. (1998b) 'State schools may gain autonomy', *Financial Times,* 30–1 May, p. 6.

Thornley, C. (1994) 'Nursing Pay Policy: Chaos in Context', paper presented to Employment Research Unit annual conference 'The Contract State: the Future of Public Management', Cardiff Business School, September.

Trosa, S. (1994) *Next Steps: Moving On*, London: Office of Public Service and Science.

Webb, S. and B. (1920) *The History of Trade Unionism*, second edition, London: Longmans.

Wedderburn, W. (1989) 'Freedom of association and philosophies of labour law', *Industrial Law Journal* 18 (1): 1–38.

White, G. (1997) 'Employment flexibilities in local government', *Public Policy and Administration* 12 (4): 47–59.

Wighton, D. (1998) 'NHS chief to face MPs' grilling over clinical codes', *Financial Times*, 12 March, p. 9.

Willman, J. (1994) 'Private managers of public services "surprised at scrutiny"', *Financial Times*, 2 February, p. 8.

Wilson, T. (1991) 'The proletarianisation of academic labour', *Industrial Relations Journal* 22 (4): 250–62.

Winchester, D. (1983) 'The public sector' in G. S. Bain (ed.) *Industrial Relations in Britain*, Oxford: Blackwell.

Part II
Context

2 The economic and financial context

The shrinking state?

Jean Shaoul

> Public Expenditure is at the heart of Britain's economic difficulties.
> Over the years public spending has increased on assumptions about
> economic growth which have not been achieved. If this continued our
> economy would be threatened with endemic inflation and economic
> decline.
>
> (Treasury 1979: 1)

The central policy of shrinking the public sector was introduced and justified as an economic necessity in 1979 and was not repudiated by the incoming
Labour government in 1997. This chapter provides a brief exposition of the
economic, financial and managerial changes by which this policy was implemented to show the context against which employee relations in the public
services must be considered. It examines the changing levels and composition of public expenditure and the cost structure of the different functional
programmes of the state; the various attempts to control expenditure and
costs and to increase outputs; and the recent reconfiguration of the entire
public sector into business units delivering services. This is illustrated by a
study of the NHS acute hospital trusts. The chapter concludes by drawing
out the significance of some of these changes for employee relations.

Trends in public expenditure

State expenditure encompasses revenue expenditure by central government,
local authorities and public corporations (state enterprises and other bodies)
on goods and services; transfer payments such as pensions, unemployment
and housing benefit, sick and disability allowances, and subsidies; capital
formation; and debt interest and net lending. While this appears relatively
straightforward to specify, interpretation of the relevant data is difficult as
a result of conceptual, definitional and measurement problems (Heald 1983).
Partly this is because government can choose methods other than state
expenditure to achieve the same objectives. For example, child tax
allowances, investment grants and housing subsidies may be substituted for
child benefits, capital allowances and mortgage interest relief, and reflected

in lower tax revenues. Thus some public expenditure may be 'hidden' or subsumed within the revenue stream, making it difficult to assess accurately the 'real' extent of public expenditure. Indeed, some have described tax concessions as the 'hidden welfare state' (Field *et al.* 1977). At the very least, public expenditure totals, showing only one side of the account, can give a very incomplete picture.

Such difficulties notwithstanding, the usual starting point is to examine the way public expenditure has altered over time, using the ratio of total public expenditure to Gross Domestic Product (GDP), which corrects, to some extent at least, for inflation. The widely used measure General Government Expenditure (GGE) includes central and local government expenditure on goods and services, capital formation, transfers, subsidies and grants, as well as that of the public corporations such as the nationalised industries, Post Office, etc.

At the beginning of the twentieth century, total GGE/GDP was about 10 per cent, increasing hugely during the First World War to 45 per cent, falling to about 27 per cent in the inter-war period, and rising again to 61 per cent during the Second World War. After falling sharply in the immediate aftermath of the war, it fell fairly continuously till the early 1960s. It grew in the 1960s and early 1970s, peaking at 49 per cent in the mid-1970s as expenditure rose faster than GDP. Attempts to rein it back in the second half of the decade were more successful than in the early 1980s. GGE/GDP fell in the boom years of the late 1980s and rose again during the recession of the 1990s. In general, expenditure varied inversely with the state of the economy, rising in recession and declining in the economic upswings. But, over the whole post-war period, public expenditure grew at the same rate as GDP. Despite the privatisation of most of the state enterprises and determined efforts to restrain public expenditure, particularly since 1987, GGE/GDP was still about 43 per cent in the 1990s (table 2.1). It was, however, expected to fall to 40 per cent or below by the end of the decade.

The widespread misconception that public expenditure in the UK in the mid-1970s was unusually large arose because of the manipulation of the figures by the Labour government in order to provide support for the International Monetary Fund (IMF) imposed cuts in public spending in 1976 (Treasury 1976a). (The following year, the government manipulated the figures in the opposite direction (Treasury 1977) to show the success of its policies.) However, a comparison using the United Nations (UN) standardised system, which is accepted as being the most reliable, shows that the UK experience was in fact an international phenomenon. In the economies of both the advanced capitalist and the developing countries in the post-war period there has been growth in expenditure by the state. In 1970, however, UK public expenditure was not significantly different from that of the other large European countries (table 2.2). But by the 1990s, as a result of a number of measures taken by the Conservative government, GGE/GDP in the UK was considerably lower than in its European counterparts, although higher

Table 2.1 Trends in UK public expenditure

Year	Total GGE/ GDP	GGE goods and services/ GDP	Capital expenditure/ GDP	Transfers/ GDP	Other/GDP
1948	0.37	0.16	0.04	0.11	0.07
1950	0.34	0.16	0.03	0.09	0.05
1955	0.33	0.17	0.03	0.08	0.06
1960	0.35	0.16	0.03	0.08	0.07
1965	0.37	0.17	0.04	0.09	0.07
1970	0.40	0.18	0.05	0.10	0.08
1975	0.49	0.22	0.05	0.13	0.09
1980	0.45	0.22	0.02	0.14	0.07
1985	0.44	0.21	0.02	0.16	0.05
1990	0.39	0.20	0.02	0.13	0.04
1995	0.43	0.21	0.02	0.16	0.05
1996	0.41	0.21	0.01	0.15	0.04

Source: *UK Economic Trends*, Annual Supplement (various years).

Table 2.2 International comparison of public expenditure trends: total outlays of general government expenditure as a % of nominal GDP

Country	1960	1970	1980	1990	1995	1998[a]
USA	27.0	31.7	33.7	32.8	33.2	33.3
Japan	17.5	19.4	32.6	31.3	35.4	36.0
Germany	30.4	38.6	48.3	45.1	49.5	48.1
France	34.6	38.5	46.1	49.8	53.7	52.8
Italy	30.1	34.2	41.7	53.4	51.8	50.6
UK	32.2	38.8	44.7	39.8	43.3	40.1
Canada	28.6	34.8	40.5	46.0	46.5	43.7

Source: *OECD Economic Outlook* (various years).

Note
a Projected.

than in the United States and Japan. Many of those countries which had in an earlier period spent a smaller proportion of GDP on public goods and services increased their expenditure.

It is instructive to break public expenditure down into its constituent parts in order to understand how and why it has risen in the post-war period and why successive governments, committed to its curtailment, appear to have been relatively unsuccessful. Table 2.3 shows how general government expenditure on goods and services, capital formation and transfers has changed since the war. The largest single component is expenditure on goods and services, accounting for approximately half of all expenditure by the state, although varying over the post-war period. The smallest item of government expenditure is capital formation, including road, school, hospital and house building, etc. But the most striking factor is the huge growth in transfer payments.

Table 2.3 The changing composition of general government expenditure in the UK (£ million)

Year	Goods and services	Capital	Transfers	Other[a]	Total
1946	2,348	58	1,118	1,060	4,584
	(51)	(1)	(21)	(23)	(100)
1951	2,522	798	1,255	796	5,371
	(47)	(15)	(23)	(15)	(100)
1956	3,531	764	1,543	1,203	7,041
	(50)	(11)	(22)	(17)	(100)
1961	4,570	928	2,419	1,839	9,756
	(47)	(10)	(25)	(19)	(100)
1966	6,671	1,691	3,432	2,680	14,474
	(46)	(12)	(24)	(19)	(100)
1971	10,552	2,585	5,667	4,725	23,529
	(45)	(11)	(24)	(20)	(100)
1976	27,698	5,424	16,441	9,088	58,651
	(47)	(9)	(28)	(15)	(100)
1981	56,512	4,579	38,080	17,930	117,101
	(48)	(5)	(31)	(15)	(100)
1986	80,911	7,272	57,988	16,260	162,431
	(50)	(4)	(36)	(910)	(100)
1991	124,105	12,294	76,365	15,661	228,425
	(54)	(5)	(33)	(7)	(100)
1996	155,732	10,465	112,644	27,376	306,217
	(51)	(3)	(37)	(8)	(100)
Increase 1946–96 as % 1946	650	1,790	1,000	250	690
Increase 1976–96 as % 1976	420	120	500	200	390

Source: *UK Economic Trends* (various years).

Notes
a Including public corporations.
b Figures in parentheses are %.

Transfers have grown from 21 per cent in 1946 to 37 per cent of total expenditure in 1996, with most of the increase occurring after 1976. It is now, as a result, the second most important element of public expenditure. Some of these payments, pensions and child benefits, depend on demographic factors; while some, such as benefits to those without work, are highly dependent upon the level of economic activity and the business cycle. The relationship of these different forms of expenditure to GDP is brought out more clearly in table 2.1.

Several points should be noted. First, these figures are interesting because they show relative stability between the years, irrespective of the political party in government. Second, there was relatively little variation despite the change in governments until the end of the long boom in the 1970s. The year 1976, not 1979, was the watershed. Third, the overall increase in public expenditure, cited earlier, disguises significant changes in the composition of expenditure. Finally the relative inability to roll back the state beyond 40 per cent of GDP is in part at least a function of the changing composition of expenditure and a reflection of changes in the wider economy.

The distinctions between the different types of expenditure are important from the perspective of controlling and managing public finance. They also help to explain, to some extent at least, why successive governments have not been able to reduce public expenditure as much as they would have liked. Expenditure on goods and services, known as exhaustive expenditure, is a function of previous legislation placing obligations upon the state to carry out certain activities, such as educating schoolchildren. While the budget is determined annually, it is in practice difficult for governments to alter it by more than one or two percentage points while at the same time maintaining the volume and quality of services. But it is this area which is most directly amenable to internal managerial control to secure increased value for money. The significance of this will be developed later. The capital budget is the most directly amenable to short term variation, particularly since its effects may not be felt immediately. However, its relative size is small, and, although large in absolute terms, it now leaves the government little room to manoeuvre. The 'other' expenditure, including debt servicing and public corporations, is largely dependent upon wider government policy and is therefore less amenable to direct control. Transfer payments, the category which has seen the most rapid growth, are made on the basis of strict rules of entitlement and all who claim and qualify must be paid. Thus attempts to reduce this entail changing eligibility and the size of payments.

But not all public sector activities, which range from the armed forces, overseas embassies, state enterprises run on commercial lines such as the Post Office to food inspections, parks, libraries and schools, are public services. Government expenditure is classified into fourteen major functional programmes, in accordance with UN methodology (*UK National Accounts* 1997). Within this there are four major groups:

- *general government services* comprising general public services, i.e. executive and legislative organs, financial and fiscal affairs, external affairs, foreign aid and economic aid; defence; public order and safety, including the police, fire services, law courts and prisons;
- *community and social affairs*, comprising education, health, social security and welfare, housing and community amenity, and recreational and cultural;
- *economic services*, comprising fuel and energy; agriculture, forestry and fishing; industry; transport and communications, and other economic services;
- other functions, including public debt.

Thus, since we are primarily interested in the public services, it is the second and first groups which are particularly relevant. We therefore examine next the different expenditure programmes, their size and how they have changed.

Table 2.4 shows the total spend (including capital, transfers, etc.) on each of these fourteen functions from 1977 to 1996, a period for which there is a consistent reporting methodology. Community and social affairs as a whole accounted for more than half of total expenditure, while general government services took about 25 per cent in 1977. By 1996 community and social services had increased their share to 66 per cent, while general government services had decreased to 17 per cent. Between them, these two functions accounted for 75 per cent of total expenditure. The big spending programmes in 1977 were: social security, education, defence, health, public order and housing. These six accounted for 77 per cent of all spending. By 1996 just three programmes – social security, health and education – accounted for 62 per cent. Thus the biggest spending departments are the public services. While expenditure as a whole grew by 400 per cent over the period, that on public order, social security and health grew even faster. On the other hand, housing was particularly badly hit.

Table 2.5 shows the operational costs of each programme: expenditure on labour, goods and services, but excluding capital and transfers, over the twenty year period, as well as the total costs. A number of points emerge. Community and social services accounted for more than half of all operating costs, while general government services accounted for more than one-third in 1977. By 1996 community and social services were taking an even greater share of the total operating budget. While total expenditure as a whole had risen by 400 per cent by 1996, operating costs had risen by 440 per cent. There was enormous variation between the cost of running different programmes. Some had very low operating costs in relation to total expenditure, with social security, housing and agriculture, for example, made up largely of transfer payments, capital costs and payments to farmers and food producers respectively. Others had a very high proportion of operating costs: defence, public order and safety, health and education. Evidently all defence expenditure, including military hardware, is classified as an operating cost, whereas comparable plant and equipment in the case of hospitals and universities are classified as capital, making them vulnerable to cuts in the capital budget. Fuel and energy is an anomaly in that it provided income to the government in the form of revenues and, more latterly, privatisation proceeds. In general, operating costs rose as a percentage of total costs as capital, subsidies and grants declined. In 1977 the most expensive programmes to run were defence, health and education, and in 1996 health, education and defence. But by far the largest increases were in social security and public order.

If we consider operating costs in more detail, we can see from table 2.6 that in most areas, labour was the major cost. Only in defence, of all the major spending programmes, is procurement more costly than manpower. Because wage costs for health were under-reported in 1996, as employees of the hospital trusts are recorded separately, operating and wage costs, with and without health, are presented in various ways in order to establish a more

Table 2.4 Analysis of total government expenditure by function (£ million)

Function	Total expenditure			
	1977	*1986*	*1996*	*Increase (%)[a]*
General government services				
General	3,213	6,326	13,223	340
	(5)[b]	(4)	(4)	
Defence	6,863	19,066	23,018	240
	(11)	(12)	(8)	
Public order	2,132	6,826	15,458	630
	(3)	(4)	(5)	
Total	12,208	32,218	51,699	323
	(19)	(20)	(17)	
Community and social affairs				
Education	8,341	19,271	39,133	370
	(13)	(12)	(13)	
Health	6,823	19,164	43,199	500
	(11)	(12)	(14)	
Social security	15,013	49,947	106,958	610
	(24)	(31)	(35)	
Housing and community	5,446	8,066	9,513	80
	(9)	(5)	(3)	
Recreational and cultural	811	2,446	4,579	470
	(1)	(2)	(1)	
Total	36,434	98,894	203,382	458
	(59)	(61)	(66)	
Economic services				
Fuel and energy[c]	−1,058	−1,174	−2,978	180
	(< 1)	(< 1)	(< 1)	
Agriculture	1,059	2,088	5,395	470
	(2)	(1)	(2)	
Industry	1,579	1,906	679	−60
	(3)	(1)	(1)	
Transport	2,425	3,728	8,366	250
	(4)	(2)	(3)	
Economic	1,691	4,128	6,285	270
	(3)	(3)	(2)	
Total	5,696	10,677	17,477	207
	(13)	(8)	(7)	
Other				
Debt	7,462	20,643	33,369	350
	(12)	(13)	(11)	
Total	61,800	162,431	306,217	400
	(100)	(100)	(100)	

Source: UK National Income Blue Book (various years).

Notes
a Increase in total expenditure since 1977 as % of 1977.
b Figures in parentheses are %.
c Fuel and energy affected by trading revenue and receipts from privatisation.

Table 2.5 Analysis of operating expenditure by function

Function	1977 Total exp.	Op costs (% total)	1986 Total exp.	Op costs (% total)	1996 Total exp.	Op costs (% total)	Increase (%)[a] Total exp.	Total op costs
General	3,213	1,803 (58)	6,326	4,050 (64)	13,223	9,412 (71)	340	430
Defence	6,863	6,762 (99)	19,066	18,613 (98)	23,018	23,108 (100)	240	230
Public order	2,132	1,929 (90)	6,826	6,401 (94)	15,458	14,301 93)	630	620
Education	8,341	6,301 (76)	19,271	16,755 (87)	39,133	32,396 (83)	370	390
Health	6,823	6,375 (93)	19,164	17,956 (94)	43,199	42,272 (93)	500	530
Social security	15,013	1,851 (12)	49,947	5,253 (11)	106,958	14,661 (14)	610	670
Housing and community	5,446	906 (17)	8,066	2,599 (32)	9,513	3,972 (41)	80	360
Recreational and cultural	811	615 (76)	2,446	1,737 (71)	4,579	3,410 (74)	470	450
Fuel and energy[b]	−1,058	98 (−9)	−1,174	304 (28)	−2,978	161	180	60
Agriculture	1,059	262 (25)	2,088	552 (26)	5,395	1,169 (22)	470	350
Industry	1,579	166 (11)	1,906	437 (23)	679	364 (54)	60	120
Transport	2,425	823 (34)	3,728	1,895 (51)	8,366	2,970 (36)	250	260
Economic	1,691	539 (32)	4,128	1,776 (43)	6,285	3,883 (62)	270	620
Debt	7,462	11 (< 1)	20,643	2,583 (13)	33,369	3,653 (11)	350	–
Total	61,800	28,441 (46)	162,431	78,328 (48)	306,217	152,079 (50)	400	440

Source: UK National Income Blue Book (various years).

Notes
a Increase in total expenditure and total costs since 1977 as % of 1977.
b Fuel and energy, affected by trading revenue and receipts from privatisation.

accurate position. Wage costs rose less than either operating or total costs over the twenty year period. They fell from 64 per cent of operating costs in 1976 to 54 per cent in 1996 as the government moved to external procurement via market testing, compulsory competitive tendering (CCT) and the Private Finance Initiative (PFI), etc. Or, to put it another way, procurement rose from £10.2 billion in 1976 to £71 billion in 1996, while wage costs rose from

Table 2.6 Analysis of cost structure by function (£ million)

Function	1977 Purchases	Wage costs	1986 Purchases	Wage costs	1996 Purchases	Wage costs	Increase (%)[a] Purchases	Wage costs
General	−247[b]	2,050	−498	4,548	2,303	7,109	1030	246
	(−0.14)[c]	(114)	(−0.12)	(112)	(24)	(76)	–	
Defence	3,681	3,081	11,278	7,335	12,606	10,502	242	240
	(54)	(46)	(61)	(39)	(55)	(45)		
Public order	382	1,547	1,343	5,058	3,913	10,386	924	241
	(20)	(80)	(21)	(78)	(27)	(73)		
Education	1,412	4,889	4,828	11,927	15,088	17,308	969	577
	(22)	(78)	(29)	(71)	(47)	(53)		
Health	2,731	3,644	8,013	9,943	19,872	3,560[d]	628	
	(43)	(57)	(45)	(55)	(47)			
Social security	718	1,133	1,939	3,314	6,994	7,667	874	515
	(39)	(61)	(37)	(63)	(48)	(52)		
Housing and community	382	524	1,143	1,456	2,677	1,295	601	577
	(42)	(58)	(44)	(56)	(67)	(33)		
Recreational and cultural	193	422	720	1,017	2,166	1,244	1022	147
	(31)	(69)	(41)	(59)	(64)	(36)		
Fuel and energy[e]	36	62	285	19	161	–	347	195
	(37)	(63)	(94)	(6)	(1.00)			
Agriculture	128	134	360	192	631	538	393	−100
	(49)	(51)	(65)	(35)	(54)	(46)		
Industry	98	68	325	112	177	187	81	301
	(59)	(41)	(74)	(26)	(49)	(51)		
Transport	429	394	1,355	540	1,788	1,182	317	175
	(52)	(48)	(72)	(28)	(60)	(40)		
Economic	206	333	571	1,205	2,592	1,291	1,158	200
	(38)	(62)	(32)	(68)	(67)	(33)		
Debt	11	–	–	2,583	–	3,563	–	288
				(1.0)		(1)		
Total	10,160	18,281	31,662	46,666	70,968	65,832	598	260
	(36)	(64)	(40)	(60)	(52)	(48)		
If exclude all health expenditure					51,096	62,272		
					(46)	(53)		
If include health wages[d]					70,698	81,112		
					(46)	(53)		

Source: *UK National Income Blue Book* (various years)

Notes
a Increase in purchases and wage costs as a % of 1977.
b Negative values indicate net revenues.
c Figures in parentheses are %.
d The data for health are affected by the fact that the trusts are classified as public authorities for employment purposes although their operational costs are listed in general government expenditure. A guestimate of £22.4 billion seems reasonable here at 53% of operating costs.
e Fuel and energy, affected by trading revenue and privatisation.

Table 2.7 Changes in the cost structure of public and social services (£ million)

	1977		1986		1996	
	Purchases	Wage costs	Purchases	Wage costs	Purchases	Wage costs
General government and social services	5,571	14,209	17,488	34,680	49,360	57,023
As % of operating costs	28	72	34	66	51	48
% increase 1977–86					214	144
% increase 1986–96					182	66
% increase 1977–96					786	303

Source: UK National Income Blue Book (various years).

Note
A high estimate of £22.4 billion for health wage costs has been used.

£18 billion to £81 billion. If we consider only the public and social services, excluding defence, economic and other functions, then the change in cost composition is even starker: wages fell from 72 per cent in 1977 to 54 per cent in 1996, and procurement rose from 28 per cent to 46 per cent. This growth in procurement means that many services are now paid for but not provided by the government.

An examination of the trend in public sector employment sheds some light on this phenomenon. Total employment in the public sector rose until the late 1970s, remained fairly constant during the 1980s and then declined quite substantially in the 1990s (table 2.8). There were 5.1 million government employees in 1996, 12 per cent fewer than in 1961 but 29 per cent fewer than in 1977. At the peak, in 1980, some 29 per cent of the work force were employed in the public sector. That is, the rate of decline was sharper than the earlier rate of growth.

The public sector work force is made up of two groups – public corporation and general government employees – who are, in the main, public service workers. If we consider them both separately, the picture becomes clearer. First the public corporations, which include the nationalised industries, organisations such as the BBC, Post Office and latterly the trusts. They employed about 2 million in the 1960s, about one-third of all public employees. This number began to decline in the 1970s, with about 250,000 jobs lost. It accelerated in the 1980s, with about 1 million jobs lost as a result of the preparation for and the privatisations themselves, until only 0.874 million were employed in 1991. Although it has since risen to 1.5 million, this increase is probably due to the classification of NHS trusts as public corporations. Turning next to general government employment, we again see the number of employees rising until the mid-1980s and then declining. Only 3.6 million were employed in the public services in 1996, 6 per cent fewer than in 1961 and 32 per cent fewer than in 1977. Some

Table 2.8 Trends in public sector employment (000)

Year	Total employed	Total govt emp.	Public corps	General govt emp.	Total govt/ total emp. (%)	General govt/ total emp. (%)	General govt/ total govt (%)
1961	24,457	5,859	2,200	3,659	24	15	62
1966	25,355	6,063	1,962	4,101	24	16	68
1971	24,533	6,627	2,009	4,618	27	19	70
1977	24,866	7,302	1,980	5,322	29	21	73
1981	24,498	7,186	1,756	5,319	29	22	74
1986	24,739	6,534	1,187	5,347	26	22	82
1991	26,343	5,849	847	5,125	22	19	88
of which NHS Trusts			124				
1996	25,881	5,130	1,512	3,618	20	14	71
of which NHS Trusts			1,102				
Increase 1961–96 as % 1961	6	−12	−31	−6			

Source: *UK Economic Trends* (various years).

Note
General government employment excludes those employed by the public corporations.

250,000 jobs were shed between 1986 and 1991 and 500,000 after 1991 in the public and social services, after adjusting for the transfer of 1.1 million health workers to the public corporations.

Finally we consider what has happened to wage levels in the public sector at the aggregate level. Clearly such an analysis is very limited, as it masks the differences within and the changing composition of the work force, and chapter 4 deals with this in depth. Nevertheless it provides some contextual information on employee relations in the public services. Table 2.9 shows the wage bill, including National Insurance and pension costs, for general government employees in the fourteen functional areas, excluding the public corporations and the NHS trusts. The wage bill rose very significantly in the 1970s, but less so in the 1980s as the rate of inflation declined. After 1991 the wage bill fell for the first time as the number employed dropped sharply with job shedding and the transfer of workers to the trusts, etc. Average wage costs per employee followed a similar pattern until 1991, after which they continued to rise to £17,200. Nevertheless, in 1996 average annual wage *costs* were lower than the average *full time* public service *earnings*, which were £18,500 (*New Earnings Survey* 1996: table 1), despite the fact that wage costs are usually 20–30 per cent higher than earnings. Such a discrepancy suggests that a significant minority of the public sector work force are part time. (It is, however, possible that the timing of the New Earnings Survey, which is carried out in April, when some workers receive backdated wage settlements, may have introduced some distortion into the annualised figures.)

Table 2.9 Trends in average wages costs

Year	General govt emp. (000)	Growth rate (%)	Wage costs (£ million)	Growth rate (%)	Ave wage costs per employee (£)	Growth rate (%)
1961	3,659		2,538		693	
1965	3,970	6	3,418	35	883	27
1971	4,618	19	6,583	93	1,425	61
1976	5,282	14	18,281	1.78	3,461	1.43
1981	5,319	1	33,608	84	6,318	83
1986	5,347	1	46,666	39	8,727	38
1991	5,125	−2	68,552	47	13,065	50
1996	3,618	−29	62,271	−9	17,211	32
Change 1961–96 as % 1961	−1		23		24	

Sources: UK Economic Trends (various years); UK National Income Blue Book (various years).

But as wage settlements have been cash limited since 1992 (Treasury 1992), the increase in wage costs since 1991 probably reflects the changing composition of the work force, from manual to non-manual. Or, to put it another way, the 500,000 jobs lost were chiefly those of the lower paid manual workers in cleaning and catering and resulted in a saving of approximately £6 billion, equivalent to an average cost per worker of about £12,000. But this in turn raises questions about value for money, since, as we have shown earlier, external procurement rose much faster than wages. Recalculating public expenditure for 1996, assuming the purchase/wage split of 1986 and up to a 12 per cent wage increase on 1991 levels for those workers who left the public sector, indicates that public expenditure would have been lower without external procurement. While clearly not definitive, this does mean that the extent of cost 'savings' is therefore unclear, as other more detailed studies have shown (Cutler and Waine 1994). In general, the labour costs of the firms which won the contracts for service provision under CCT, were lower than their public sector comparators (Treasury 1986, Bargaining Report 1990) as a result of re-specifying the work and reducing the number of staff employed and the conditions of service (sick pay, payment by results, holiday entitlement, etc.) But this in turn suggests that external procurement not only has not saved money but has also resulted in a redistribution of income away from the work force to the employers.

Taken together, these findings show considerable changes in the scale and composition of public expenditure in the post-war period. Public expenditure has risen, although less markedly in the recent period. A major change has been the increase in transfer payments, as a result of Britain's declining economic position. Moreover attempts to contain the growth of expenditure have concentrated thus far on reducing capital spending and the operational costs of delivering public services, with the concomitant implications for government employees. In particular the last twenty years have seen outsourcing, job shedding, part time and flexible working, and cash limited wage settlements between 1979 and 1986 and then again after 1992 when pay increases were often achieved at the expense of jobs (White 1996). Most of the downsizing in public services occurred under the Major rather than under the Thatcher administration. Despite this, the Conservative governments were largely unable to reduce the relative weight of public expenditure in the economy, although their policies did affect its composition. But that in turn means that over the last twenty years it is the public services which have borne the brunt of tight expenditure control.

Controlling public expenditure

Alongside the nominal and relative increase in public expenditure in the post-war period has gone a three-pronged attempt to roll back the state: first, measures to cap its activities and size; second, a series of institutional measures to control public expenditure as a whole; and third, a whole raft of financial, organisational and managerial measures to increase outputs and reduce costs through greater efficiency at the point of service delivery. Each of these will be very briefly summarised in order to indicate how they have affected the work force and the delivery of services.

The scope of public sector activities was curtailed first by various forms of privatisation whose purpose was to take the activities and services, and their associated revenues, out of the public sector altogether. But the sale of state assets at prices well below their depreciated historic book value without the burden of debt and liabilities such as clean-up costs, decommissioning, etc., meant that these assets not only provided huge revenues for their new owners but also deprived the government of a revenue stream which was to contribute to subsequent financial and social problems (Shaoul 1997). Second, continuing from a policy initiated under Labour in 1968 (Ascher 1987), many low paid manual services, such as cleaning, catering and refuse collection, within the local authorities and hospitals, were subject to competitive tender by outside contractors, although an in-house team could also bid (Cutler and Waine 1994; Walsh 1995). (See chapter 7.) The range of activities was subsequently extended to the higher paid professional services such as legal and information technology functions. Third, there was increasing emphasis on the Private Finance Initiative: the financing of new investment in hospitals and schools by the private sector, which would build and lease the facilities back to the public sector (Treasury 1993a; Public Services Privatisation Research Unit 1997).

Second, institutional measures aimed at curbing public expenditure were introduced. But, before outlining these, it is necessary to understand how public expenditure had been determined in the post-war period. The Plowden report (Plowden 1961), written at a time when the GGE/GDP was at its post-war low (table 2.1), recommended the separation of the planning of government expenditure from the annual parliamentary supply process. Henceforth government expenditure would largely be determined as an executive process by setting five year volume based expenditure plans. The plans were to be explicitly linked with projected growth in the economy which, as we have seen, usually failed to live up to expectations after the mid-1960s. Volume based planning meant that expenditure programmes were compensated for any increase in costs, chiefly wages, which after 1970 grew faster than in the private sector, particularly in the nationalised industries, after years of pay restraint. It represented an attempt to plan expenditure on a more rational basis.

But the financial crisis in 1976 led to the Labour government abandoning this in favour of annual cash limits for departmental expenditure on goods and services in order to apply greater financial discipline (Treasury 1976b, c). The international intervention by the IMF marked the end of the post-war system of the welfare state and Keynesian demand management to regulate the economy. After the 1979 election the object of Conservative government policy was to introduce the concept of a 'bottom line', comparable with the profit and loss criteria of the private sector, and the private sector management techniques that go with the concept, into the public sector – in other words, to run government services as a business. Volume planning was formally abandoned in 1982–83 in favour of planning in cash terms based on Treasury assumptions about inflation (Treasury 1982). Wages, the chief operational cost, were controlled by cash limited wage settlements from 1979 to 1986 and then again after 1992. Wage rises were largely dependent upon productivity bargaining, which meant wage increases at the expense of jobs and intensified work effort for those who remained. In the 1990s further changes were launched to control public expenditure. First the planning of public expenditure was changed with the introduction of the New Control Total (Treasury 1992). This meant setting an annual ceiling on public expenditure based on the assumption that real growth in central government expenditure would not exceed 2 per cent a year. Second the Conservative government introduced a unified budget to ensure that spending proposals would be considered alongside taxation (Treasury 1993b). However, the incoming Labour government reverted to the old system in 1998.

These changes in the institutional arrangements were accompanied by a series of measures to reduce costs and increase output and a culture that soon became known as the 'new managerialism' or the 'new public sector management' (Pollitt 1990). The 'new managerialism' took a variety of forms. Some services were required to make a return on assets, as in the direct labour organisations of the local authorities. The nationalised industries were required to make a rate of return on capital based on the current replacement cost of the ageing assets, which provided the financial ratchet to drive costs down. Management was reorganised along private sector lines with the emphasis on management's responsibility to achieve a balanced budget limited in cash, not volume, terms at a time of high inflation, with all that it meant for industrial relations. Devolved budgets and cost and profit centres leading to decentralised decision making and internal payments between units and departments were introduced. More explicit procedures for capital budgeting and project appraisal based on the financial methods of private sector corporations seeking finance from the capital markets rather than social objectives were prescribed. Other measures included tighter financial control of defence procurement, with a move to end cost-plus contracts, various value for money initiatives under the Rayner scrutiny programmes, and increasing emphasis on audit techniques through the establishment of the Audit Commission to audit and monitor local authorities and the NHS and the National Audit Office for central government. While this list is not exhaustive or very detailed, it does give some idea of the wide range of measures introduced by the government.

The chief characteristic of all these financial and organisational measures was that these were the techniques used by the private sector to generate profit out of the production of commodities for distribution to the providers of finance. Henceforth state services were to be organised on a similar basis. Above all there was an emphasis on financial management as a pro-active tool to manage the public services and administrative functions in order to achieve objectives, not simply as a passive tool to record income and expenditure – its role in the past. It represented a break with the past tradition of attempting, in principle at least, to organise services on the basis of social need.

There followed a series of reports which introduced changes based on this agenda into most activities of the state such as the Financial Management Initiative for the civil service (Cmnd 8616 1982), the Griffiths report on the NHS (Griffiths 1983) and the Jarrett report on the management structures in the universities (Committee of Vice Chancellors and Principals 1985). The Next Steps initiative, launched in 1988, transferred many of the executive functions of central government departments and trading units to semi-autonomous agencies (Efficiency Unit 1988). Some of the agencies, such as Her Majesty's Stationery Office (HMSO), were subsequently privatised. By April 1996 more than 70 per cent of all civil servants were working in Next Steps agencies or in departmental units organised on similar lines. In 1990 the NHS was reorganised into an internal market with health authorities and general practice (GP) fundholders purchasing health care services from hospitals and community health centres organised in self-governing trusts (Department of Health 1989).

The various reports aimed at introducing new organisational structures and managerial methods were characterised by their generality. They contained little sector-specific information about the service they purported to be improving. Indeed, the government initiated the proposals for creating an internal market in health care with a purchaser/provider split after a report from a visiting US economist which was prefaced by 'I do not pretend to be a well-informed observer of the NHS . . . And I have had no opportunity to verify independently much of the information I read or heard'

(Enthoven 1985: 5). As far as the authors themselves were concerned, the primary issue was the style of management adopted. The activity itself and the appropriateness of the form of management to the service concerned was not an issue. But all these measures resulted in the increasing fragmentation and decentralisation of public sector functions.

This approach was accompanied by an emphasis on the 'three Es' – economy, efficiency and effectiveness – and the growth of performance measures which attempted to capture and compare the performance of public sector providers and thereby ratchet up output or throughput (see chapter 8). Underpinning almost all these measures was the assumption that the toolkit of private sector management could improve output and thereby resolve or at least contain the 'problem' of the rising cost of the public sector. It represented a very real change in the way that the public sector was managed in two significant respects: from planning on the basis of perceived need to managing by financial numbers; and from decision making and control by the service professionals to decision making and control by managers.

Reorganisation of the public services into business units

What remained of the old public sector was required to take a 'more business-like approach' (Cm 2626 1994: iii) and adopt the accounting practices of the private sector. The Chancellor of the Exchequer introduced the reform as 'probably the most important reform of civil service accounting and budgeting arrangements this century' (Cm 2626 1994: iii). The introduction of private sector forms of accounting, accrual accounting, across the entire public sector is tantamount to reconstituting its activities as business units, analogous to the old nationalised industries. The changes have largely been ignored as technical and incomprehensible, with few operational consequences. But they are being implemented and will have dramatic implications for public service employees, the provision of public services, the physical infrastructure and even the constitutional position of Parliament and the relationship of the nation state to the world economy.

Accrual accounting is the method used by private sector corporations to report on the generation and distribution of profit to their shareholders. The same framework is now being used by government departments which discharge administrative functions and provide services such as benefits, education and housing, etc. All these departments and sections are to be reconstituted as business units within the public sector and operate as if they were PLCs, with the government as shareholder and creditor. They must account for capital, as well as record income and expenditure (Cm 2929 1995). The local authorities (Chartered Institute of Public Finance and Accountancy 1989), Next Steps agencies (Efficiency Unit 1988) and the NHS hospitals (Department of Health 1989) have already been operating this system for several years. The practical implications for employee relations and service provision can therefore be illustrated by showing the workings of a seemingly technical and neutral system within the NHS.

Accrual accounting, or capital charging, as it became known in the NHS, means first that the trusts, as health care providers, have to charge their purchasers a price which not only includes the cost of capital and a charge for depreciation but also does not contain any element of cross-subsidisation between services. Second they have to take responsibility for the repayment of past capital and the future maintenance and enhancement of their infra-structure and equipment. Capital charges are represented in the financial accounts as the charge for depreciation (for the consumption of productive capital), interest on the debt which has been assigned to the trusts as a result of past capital expenditure, and dividends to the government on the Public Dividend Capital (PDC), the equivalent of the government's shares in the trusts. Trusts must make a surplus, after covering all the operating expenses, including a charge for depreciation, in order to finance the interest and dividends, a sum equivalent to at least 6 per cent of the value of their asset base.

Previously the capital for new buildings and equipment came in the form of a government grant with no dividend or repayment obligations, in a separate allocation. The proponents of capital charging, even those who opposed the present system, argued that, as it was a 'free' good, hospitals had no incentive to use capital efficiently (Perrin 1978; Lapsley 1981; Association of Health Service Treasurers 1985; Mayston 1990). Therefore charging for capital would make the trusts more efficient and managers more aware of the cost of capital, and would enable comparisons to be made between different parts of the NHS and between the NHS and the private sector (Department of Health 1989).

Implicit in all this was the assumption that the NHS was inefficient in its use of capital and less efficient than the private sector, and that this was the cause of the NHS's problems, not inadequate funding. But the Conser-vative government provided little evidence either to support the validity of these assumptions and assertions or to examine the outcomes and hence evaluate the claims and promises that were made. However, it is possible to examine these claims and the outcomes by briefly summarising research which analysed the impact of capital charging in the NHS, based on the annual accounts of all the acute care hospital trusts in England and inter-views with hospital finance directors (Shaoul 1998). It should be noted that the Labour government's White Papers on the NHS propose to extend these measures to the primary health care sector (Department of Health 1997; Scottish Office 1997).

The first point to consider is the importance of capital to the hospitals. The accounts showed that the capital charges (the sum of depreciation, interest and dividend on the PDC) in the years to 1995 constituted 9 per cent of total income received, whereas external purchases constituted 28 per cent and labour 63 per cent. Thus the most important operating cost to control was not capital but labour, as the analysis of public service expenditure shown earlier in table 2.5 confirmed. Yet the government introduced capital charging because capital was assumed to be a major cost. Although it is small as a percentage of total income, it is a significant item in a cash-strapped service where income is essentially static, if not declining, in real and demographic terms. Since it is a charge that must be met, and external sourcing is already low at 28 per cent, then labour must be squeezed to provide the surplus to cover the capital charges or revenues must be increased. This is its real significance.

The justification for capital charging was to put the public hospitals on to a similar footing to that of the private hospitals and thereby to permit comparisons of efficiency to be made (Department of Health 1989). But such comparisons are not straightforward. Three major private hospital groups account for 50 per cent of the beds in the private hospital sector: BUPA, General Healthcare (part of the BMI group), and Nuffield. BUPA, part of a mutual insurance group and the largest of the private sector groups, pays no dividends or interest charges and has a policy of reinvesting the surplus. Nuffield is a charity, a non-profit-making organisation, which therefore pays no dividends. Thus first these two hospitals do not pay the full cost of capital and their capital is, to some extent, a free good. Only the General Healthcare hospitals operate on a 'for profit' basis and pay the full cost of capital. Second, although private companies value their assets at the original or historical cost, the government required the trusts to value their assets at current replacement cost, which is much higher than the original cost. The significance of this will be developed later.

The private hospitals are much smaller, having typically fewer than 100 beds. Their (rising) income is derived largely from their patients' insurance policies. They have the commercial freedom to charge those patients whose bills are not covered by insurance on any basis they like. Even though they operate at less than full capacity, they do not normally seek NHS work, as their charges are higher. Private hospitals do not carry out a full range of medical and surgical treatments, but concentrate on elective surgery and acute care, usually of the less complex variety. They perform fewer services 'in house' and buy in more goods and services, often from the public hospitals. Thus comparisons are bedevilled by the fact that the private sector hospitals differ from the trusts in terms of their income base and ability to charge premium prices, their patients and their activity mix as well as in their accounting and financial regime.

The relevant efficiency measures for comparison purposes are asset and labour utilisation. Asset utilisation is typically measured as income divided by total fixed assets or, as is preferable because it corrects for bought-in goods and services, value added or net output divided by total fixed assets. The larger the ratio, the higher or better is the asset utilisation. Table 2.10 compares the trusts with private sector hospitals despite their different mix

Table 2.10 Asset utilisation (value added/tangible fixed assets)

Organisation	1989	1990	1991	1992	1993	1994
Hotels						
QMH (hotel)	0.14	0.14	0.07	−0.09		0.23
Forte (hotel)		0.37	0.29	0.27	0.32	0.26
Ladbroke Hotels	0.10	0.10	0.10			
Retailers						
M&S (retail food and clothing)		0.57	0.56	0.52	0.53	0.56
Tesco (retail food)		0.46	0.41	0.38	0.37	0.34
Sainsbury (retail food)		0.48	0.48	0.46	0.44	0.38
Hospitals						
General Healthcare Group (hospital)		0.66	0.87	0.74	0.78	
BUPA hospitals			0.42	0.39	0.38	
NHS trusts				0.74	0.75	0.73

Sources: *Annual Report and Accounts* (various) from Health Information Service (1996), MicroExstat (1994).

of activities; with hotel groups, because most hospitals are hotels for the ill; and with the giant retailers, because they use expensive space to deliver a service and are considered to be models of private sector efficiency. Despite the triple handicap of low income per case, high asset valuations and no commercial freedom of manoeuvre, the publicly run hospitals are not inferior. Contrary to the assumptions of the Conservative government's white paper, asset utilisation is superior to that in private sector organisations like Marks & Spencer, Forte and the supermarkets. The comparison with private sector hospitals is particularly interesting; asset utilisation in the trusts is nominally the same as in General Healthcare and twice as good as in BUPA hospitals, despite the private sector advantage of lower asset valuations.

The private hospitals spend less on labour, at around 40 per cent of income, than the trusts, which spend 62 per cent. Their wage costs per employee are slightly lower than the public hospitals', since they employ few or no senior medical staff, as patients pay their consultants and anaesthetists direct via insurance. But the chief reason why their labour costs are lower is that they employ far fewer staff, albeit with a higher staff/patient ratio per comparable case. Their lower staffing levels are achieved not via different and more efficient work practices but by concentrating on activities which maximise throughput with conveyor belt treatments and cases with a lower labour content. Thus their lower labour costs depend upon their ability to choose their case mix – like the privatised buses – not upon technically superior efficiency.

But despite cost management which is not inferior to that of the giant retailers, universally acknowledged to be efficient (Shaoul 1997), in two out of four years the NHS trusts simply could not achieve the required rate of return (table 2.11). In 1995, sixty-three trusts (27 per cent) did not make the 6 per cent rate of return and forty-one had a cumulative deficit; the situation has since deteriorated. Table 2.12 compares three groups of trusts: those with below average capital charges, those with average charges and those with high charges. The above average group have the lowest income and a high proportion of their assets in equipment which carries a higher depreciation charge than buildings. But the really interesting point is the surplus to income figure. This reflects their ability to manage costs: the higher the ratio the lower their costs and the more 'efficient' or economical they are. The hospitals with the highest charges are the most cost efficient. But because of capital charges they have the lowest surplus and accumulated reserves and are the least able to meet their financial targets. But the accounts showed that BUPA could not break even if it had to pay interest and dividends on its capital and General Healthcare could not make an adequate profit if its assets were valued on the same basis as the trusts'. Thus the system of capital charging imposed on the public hospitals puts them at a disadvantage and particularly penalises the specialist, the small and the most efficient hospitals. The source of the problem is the low income relative to their high asset base.

Table 2.11 Relationship between the trusts' income, surpluses and assets ($\pounds$ 000)

	1992	*1993*	*1994*	*1995*
No. of acute trusts in England	42	92	168	234
Total income from all sources, including transitional subsidies, education, research and training, etc.	2,591,883	5,571,561	10,563,464	15,419,242
Total tangible assets	2,525,153	5,397,164	10,337,767	14,039,088
Total surplus after operating expenses	192,282	312,784	645,467	812,778
Surplus/income	0.074	0.056	0.061	0.053
Actual financial target performance (FTP)	0.076	0.058	0.062	0.058
Required surplus to meet 6% FTP	151,509	323,830	620,266	842,345
Actual surplus less required surplus	40,773	−11,046	25,201	-29,567
Possible financial 'solutions' for the sector as a whole				
Increase income to		6,476,597		16,846,906
Reduce asset base to		5,213,067		13,546,300
Reduce number of trusts by		15		22

Source: Health Care Information Services (1996).

Table 2.12 Comparison of capital charges in 1995 (averages, £ 000)

| | Capital charges as % income 1995 | | | |
	Below average (4–7%)	About average (8–10%)	Above average (11%+)	All trusts
No. of trusts	72	131	31	234
Income	63,281	68,657	60,183	15,419,242
Depreciation	1,949	2,835	3,096	2,806
Capital charges	4,014	5,704	6,621	5,765
Surplus/income	0.04	0.05	0.07	0.05
Equipment/fixed assets	0.05	0.10	0.09	0.10
Income/assets	0.73	1.05	0.85	0.91
Net surplus for the year	477	898	681	3,473
Cumulative surplus/deficit	1,125	1,013	320	514

Source: Health Care Information Services (1996).

It can be explained quite simply. The trusts are required to make a surplus equal to at least 6 per cent on their capital employed, after meeting all their operating costs and depreciation charges on the assets, to pay their finance charges. This can be expressed as:

$$6 \text{ per cent surplus} = \frac{\text{Income} - (\text{Operating costs} + \text{Depreciation})}{\text{Assets}}$$

The absolute amount required to achieve this is therefore affected by the value of the assets, which are valued at current replacement cost and therefore set to rise with inflation; the level of income, which is set to decline for the hospital sector as a whole; and the cost of staff, who are, in the main, already low paid. In principle there are three ways of achieving the required surplus: by increasing income, but at the expense of neighbouring hospitals; by reducing costs, meaning labour, by improving flow, altering the activity mix to improve throughput via conveyor belt treatments which minimise the need for labour or reducing labour costs via new wage structures and conditions of employment; or by reducing their asset base by closing wards and selling land and buildings. In practice, they must do all three. Table 2.11 demonstrates the scale of the problem facing the trusts: the acute hospital sector as a whole was underfunded relative to its asset base by £1.43 billion in 1995, a level of underfunding which has since increased. Unless they are bailed out by the government, some trusts must sell their buildings and land and/or close to bring their income into line with their assets.

It is the logic of these financial relationships, set in place by accrual accounting, which take no account of the actual health needs of the population, that is driving so many trusts to 'rationalise' their activities and drive a hard bargain with their staff. While such measures may be represented as efficient solutions for the trusts, they are socially perverse. Yet this same accounting regime, which is analogous to that of a PLC, is being imposed on the rest of the public services with little or no public debate and even less understanding of its consequences.

Conclusion

The financial analysis of government spending, so rarely undertaken, has been a revealing exercise. Measures such as competitive tendering, supposedly introduced to cut costs, have in reality simply created new sources of profit for the private sector, albeit dependent upon the very state the government claimed it wanted to roll back. The analysis has shown that the rationale of government policies is based on dubious assumptions and that policies themselves do not necessarily produce the desired consequences. If the stated reasons do not match the results it is perhaps because they are part of a hidden agenda: to ensure that a greater proportion of general taxation is spent in the private sector by reducing taxation and opening up the provision of public and social services for private profit. Service provision is now dependent upon whether the services can be made to yield the desired rate of return on capital to the government, as provider of capital. It signifies that the public services and the activities of the state, previously outside the realm of private exploitation, have been transformed into commodities to be produced for profit, not use, and that public service employees are the source of that profit.

These changes mark a very definite transformation of social relations in a number of important respects. First, the relations of production in the public sector are being realigned so that they match those of the private sector. Second, government units must now make a surplus over and above the operational costs of the services provided by its work force in order to pay for capital. Third, services, funded by the public through taxation, are organised by the state to serve the financial interests of private corporations, not the public. Fourth, the public is being reconstituted as the customer for the goods and services so produced. Fifth, these changes are part of an ongoing process whereby the social and public services pass into the private sector through buy-outs, subcontracting and sale and lease back operations such as the PFI. Finally such services, following the path of the former nationalised industries before them, are then integrated into the wider international economy as they are taken over by the transnational corporations. In other words the social welfare functions of the nation state are being integrated into the world economy, for the benefit of capital, not labour.

From the perspective of public service employee relations, these findings are important. A financial regime (business units which account for capital and charge for their services) has been set in place which is analogous to running the public services as private sector operations in the public sector. Like privatisation, this adds a new set of stakeholders and another dimension to conflict as these stakeholders have claims on the surplus for the physical replacement and improvement of the capital infrastructure and the repayment of finance capital which must be met. But in the context of declining resources for the public services, this means that management can balance the books only by some combination of drastically reducing the number of staff, wages, conditions of employment, the range and quality of services offered and the physical infrastructure used to deliver the services. It means more direct control by management over the work of service professionals and a greater intensification of work effort. It presages increasing conflict between the government and public service workers over jobs, pay and conditions.

References

Ascher, K. (1987) *The Politics of Privatisation: Contracting out Public Services*, Basingstoke: Macmillan.

Association of Health Service Treasurers (1985) *Managing Capital Assets in the National Health Service*, London: Chartered Institute of Public Finance and Accountancy.

Bargaining Report (1990) *Compulsory Competitive Tendering: the Effect on Wages and Conditions*, pp. 5–11.

Chartered Institute of Public Finance and Accountancy, Capital Accounting Steering Group (1989) *Capital Accounting in the Local Authorities: the Way Forward*, London: CIPFA.

Central Statistical Office (various years) *Economic Trends*, London: HMSO.

Central Statistical Office (various years) *Economic Trends: Annual Supplement*, London: HMSO.

Cmnd 2626 (1994) *Better Accounting for the Taxpayer's Money: Resource Accounting and Budgeting in Government*, London: HMSO.

Cmnd 2929 (1995) *Better Accounting for the Taxpayer's Money: The Government's Proposals: Resource Accounting and Budgeting in Government*, Report by the Comptroller and Auditor General, HC Session 1994–95, London: HMSO.

Cmnd 8616 (1982) *Efficiency and Effectiveness in the Civil Service*, London: HMSO.

Committee of Vice Chancellors and Principals (1985) *Report of the Steering Committee for Efficiency Studies in Universities* (the Jarrett report), London: Committee of Vice Chancellors and Principals.

Cutler, T. and Waine B. (1994) *Managing the Welfare State: The Politics of Public Sector Management*, Oxford and Providence RI: Berg.

Department of Health (1989) *Working for Patients: The Health Service–Caring for the 1990s.* (includes the White Paper Cmd 555 and nine working papers), London: HMSO.

Department of Health (1997) *The New NHS: Modern, Dependable*, Cmd 3807, London: Stationery Office.

Efficiency Unit (1988) *Improving Management in Government: The Next Steps* (the Ibbs report), London: HMSO.

Enthoven, A. C. (1985) *Reflections on the Management of the National Health Service: an American looks at Incentives to Efficiency in Health Service Management in the UK*, Occasional Paper 5, London: Nuffield Provincial Hospitals Trust.

Field, F., Meacher, M. and Pond, C. (1977) *To Him who Hath: a Study of Poverty and Taxation*, Harmondsworth: Penguin.

Griffiths, R. (1983) *NHS Management Inquiry*, London: DHSS.

Heald, D. (1983) *Public Expenditure: its Defence and Reform*, Oxford: Martin Robertson.

Health Care Information Services (1996) *The Fitzhugh Directory of NHS Trusts: Financial Information*, fourth edition, London: Health Care Information Services.

Lapsley, I. (1981) 'A case for depreciation accounting in UK health authorities', *Accounting and Business Research* 12 (4): 21–29.

Mayston, D. (1990) 'Managing capital resources in the NHS' in A. Culyer, A. Maynard and J. Posnett (eds) *Competition in Healthcare*, London: Macmillan.

New Earnings Survey (1996) London: HMSO.

Organisation for Economic Co-operation and Development (various years) *OECD Economic Outlook*, Paris: OECD.

Perrin, J. (1978) *Management of Financial Resources in the National Health Service*, Royal Commission on the National Health Service, Research Paper 2, London: HMSO.

Plowden, E. (chairman) (1961) *Control of Public Expenditure*, Cmnd 1432, London: HMSO.

Pollitt, C. (1990) *Managerialism and the Public Services: The Anglo-American Experience*, Oxford: Blackwell.

Public Services Privatisation Research Unit (1997) *Private Finance Initiative: Dangers, Realities and Alternatives*, London: Public Services Privatisation Research Unit.

Scottish Office (1997) *Designed to care*, Cm 3811, Edinburgh: Stationery Office.

Shaoul, J. (1996) *BSE: for Services Rendered. The Drive for Profit in the Meat Industry*, Public Interest Report, Manchester: Department of Accounting and Finance, University of Manchester.

Shaoul, J. (1997) 'A critical financial analysis of the performance of privatised industries: the case of the water industry in England and Wales', *Critical Perspectives on Accounting* 8 (5): 479–505.

Shaoul, J. (1998) 'Charging for capital in the NHS: to improve efficiency?' *Management Accounting Research* 9: 95–112.

Treasury (1976a) *Public Expenditure to 1979/80*, Cmd 6393, London: HMSO.

Treasury (1976b) *Cash Limits on Public Expenditure*, Cmd 6440, London: HMSO.

Treasury (1976c) *Control and Presentation of Public Expenditure*, Economic Progress Report 80, London: HMSO.

Treasury (1977) *The Government's Expenditure Plans*, Cmnd 6721 I–II, London: HMSO.

Treasury (1979) *The Government's Expenditure Plans 1980–81*, Cmnd 1746, London: HMSO.

Treasury (1982) *The Government's Expenditure Plans 1982–83 to 1984–85*, Cmnd 8494 I–II, London: HMSO.

Treasury (1986) *Using Private Enterprise in Government: Report of a Multi-departmental Review of Competitive Tendering and Contracting for Services in Government Departments*, London: HMSO.

Treasury (1992) *Autumn Statement*, Cmd 2096, London: HMSO.

Treasury (1993a) *Breaking New Ground*, London: HMSO.

Treasury (1993b) *Financial Statement and Budget Report 1994–95*, HC 31, London: HMSO.

Walsh, K. (1995) *Public Services and Market Mechanisms: Competition, Contracting and the New Public Management*, Basingstoke: Macmillan.

White, G. (1996) 'Public sector pay bargaining: comparability, decentralisation and control', *Public Administration* 74 (1): 89–111.

UK National Accounts Blue Book (various years) London: HMSO.

UK National Accounts Blue Book: Supplementary Information (1997), London: Stationery Office.

3 The legal context

Public or private?

Sandra Fredman

The transformation of the public services during the Thatcher and Major years had, as its central motif, the belief that, while 'public' was good, 'private' was better. Most of the changes of the period were therefore aimed at reshaping the public sector in the image of the private, complete with markets, consumers, contracts and profit incentives. For public sector employees the changes have been fundamental. Central to the project of 'rolling back the state' was a commitment to reducing the number of public sector employees, a commitment systematically put into effect. The overall drop in numbers from 7.4 million in 1979 to 5.2 million in 1996 (Safford and MacGregor 1997) demonstrates that, for many, the changes have meant redundancy or the transfer of their employment relationship to the more precarious private sector. This raises the central question to be addressed in this chapter: to what extent have these intensely political developments been reflected in the law governing the state as employer? Has the legal framework changed to resemble more closely that of the private sector, or have the changes instead created a new public employment law?

This chapter argues that the importation of private law concepts has not made public employment indistinguishable from that in the private sector. As Freedland has powerfully argued, the result of two decades of change has been to create a different kind of public sector rather than a new distribution between public and private (Freedland 1997). This is reflected in the legal framework: instead of privatising the legal framework, newly introduced private law elements have themselves been reshaped by the forces of public law, creating a new form of public employment. This argument is elaborated in three parts: first by considering changes in the employment relationship, particularly those in the civil service; second, by examining the interaction between constitutional law and the private sector ethic; and finally by describing the influence of EU law, which has endorsed the distinctive public law position of public employees. This approach is likely to be further reinforced when the Human Rights Bill, incorporating the European Convention on Human Rights, becomes law.

Background and context

The past two decades have witnessed fundamental changes in the attitude to the public sector. Central to this vision was the notion that the public service was 'inefficient', largely because of its centralised and hierarchical structures of authority. The answer appeared to lie in the introduction of market discipline, where competition and budgetary constraints would create the necessary incentives to efficiency, replacing a public service ethic of political accountability. These changes were achieved in a wide variety of ways. In the NHS, the internal market necessitated the creation of new entities, such as NHS trusts, and the reorganisation of budgetary responsibility, for example in respect of fund holding general practitioners. For nationalised industries and public utilities, it led to break-up and sale to the private sector. Throughout the public services, and in particular in local government and the health service, the emphasis on competition was translated into an obligation to put services out to competitive tender and contract out to the private sector on commercial grounds.

Possibly the most dramatic were changes in the civil service. Although some aspects of the changes were presaged in the report of the Fulton Committee, which recommended the subdivision of departments on a functional basis, the market-oriented ideology of the Thatcher and Major governments gave them life in a new and radical form. The 'Financial Management', 'Next Steps' (Efficiency Unit 1988) and 'New Public Management' initiatives were based on the theory that efficiency would be achieved by devolving power for operational decisions and budget management to 'cost centres'. This involved a fundamental shift in structures of accountability. Instead of a public service culture, in which the constraints on power derived from the responsibility of civil servants to their ministers, who were in turn responsible to Parliament, the idea was to introduce private sector criteria of managerial efficiency, in which managers' accountability derived from their response to 'market' constraints as reflected in their ability to produce services for lower cost. The notion of market-led accountability necessitated too the introduction of personal financial incentives for public service actors to replace a public service ethic based on promotion and reputation (see chapter 4). This of course raises the clear risk of a conflict between politically accountable public sector styles and private sector criteria of management efficiency, which create incentives to adopt strategies which have immediately visible effects on reducing expenditure.

These principles were quickly put into practice through the Next Steps programme. Central to this was the break-up of the traditional unitary and hierarchical civil service into semi-autonomous agencies, headed by chief executives with personal budgetary responsibility and whose relationship to the minister and central government depended on quasi-contractual arrangements. By 1997, nearly 387,000 civil servants, 76 per cent of the total, worked in the 138 agencies and four departments[1] working along Next Steps lines.[2] Moreover, the change continues to proceed apace. In its two major policy statements on the civil service (Cmd 2627 1994; Cmd 2748 1995) the Major government reiterated its belief in the success of these reforms, and went on to propose the creation of a new senior management group, with recruitment to senior posts by open competition rather than internal promotion. Known as the Senior Civil Service, the latter began to be established from April 1996, after senior management reviews in all departments.

These changes inevitably had major effects on the employment status of public employees. Outside the civil service, where public employees were already considered to be employed under contracts of employment, the employment status itself did not need adjustment. But other crucial legal responses were required. A change in the nature of the employer, as in the NHS, required statutory adjustment, deeming employees to have transferred to the trust as employer.[3] Particularly complex have been the legal consequences of the contracting-out programme, a topic which is dealt with in chapter 7. It is striking too that none of these changes has been amenable to a wholly private law solution. In the NHS, for example, it has been impossible wholly to sustain the fiction of separate employers competing in an 'internal market'. In particular, it has become necessary to use the law to recreate aspects of the unified service. Thus for redundancy purposes the NHS is treated as a single employer. This means that although the NHS is in fact and in law made up of many separate units, a move from one NHS employer to another does not breach continuity for the purposes of redundancy.[4] Since 1996 the same principle has been applicable to other rights, including the right to return to work after maternity leave, the right not to be unfairly dismissed and the right to notice periods.[5]

Of all these legal responses, the most complex has been in respect of civil servants. This is because historical and constitutional forces have given civil servants a specific status, traditionally believed to exclude the possibility of a contract of employment. While in many respects the move to contract is a valuable modernisation of the employment relationship, it will be argued that, instead of a private law result, it has created a new kind of contract, with a crucial public law dimension. The public law dimension is reinforced when the constitutional law aspects of the relationship are considered. The second part of this chapter considers the changes in the employment status of civil servants, while the third part considers their constitutional position. The focus in these two parts is on the civil service, because of the uniqueness and complexity of their legal position.

Prerogative and contract: the status of civil servants

The legal framework governing civil service employment is a particularly salient example of the unusual nature of our constitution, a constitution in which the formal law is overlaid with non-justiciable and often unwritten norms derived from practical experience. Thus, in formal legal terms, the source of power to employ civil servants is the royal prerogative, a power deriving directly from a prior constitutional order, where the monarch as executive head of government had the power to employ. The anachronistic form of the power, however, masks its real nature, which is that, in the modern state, it is vested in the hands of the executive without the need for express parliamentary sanction.[6] The prerogative gives the executive the formal legal power to dismiss civil servants at will, and for many years appeared inimical to the possibility of a binding contract of employment between the Crown and civil servants. These formal legal rules, however, bore little relation to the reality. Instead of the precarious employment which the prerogative appeared to create, the firm set of understandings inherited by the Thatcher government was based on lifetime tenure for civil servants and a stable and established system of collective bargaining over terms and conditions.

The Next Steps programme inevitably had major effects on these inherited understandings. Centralised setting of terms and conditions was considered inimical to the flexibility necessary to gain efficiency and cut costs within the agency structure. Instead, it was claimed, chief executives should have the power to set terms and conditions of employment appropriate to the needs and budgetary constraints of the agency. The result was the enactment of the Civil Service (Management Functions) Act 1992, which gave the Minister for the Civil Service the power to delegate the discretion to set terms and conditions. Prior to this statute, employment management functions had been exercised under the prerogative (shared by the Treasury and the Office of the Minister for the Civil Service) and, crucially, were non-delegable, under the general public law principle that a delegate cannot further delegate powers.[7] The significance of the Act was that it made these functions delegable to any Crown servant, without the usual safeguards of parliamentary legislation or even secondary legislation which have always been thought necessary to authorise the transfer of functions even between ministers. Indeed, no formality is required by the statute in exercising these powers of delegation.

The results of such delegation are found in the Management Code, which sets out the wide range of personnel matters over which office holders have authority as of 1 April 1997. These include the prescription of terms and conditions of employment of home civil servants in so far as they relate to the classification of staff, remuneration,[8] allowances, expenses, holidays, hours of work and attendance, part time and other working arrangements, performance and promotion, retirement age and redundancy, and redeployment of staff within and between departments.[9] The full range of disciplinary functions is similarly delegated. The presumption is that the functions will be exercised by agency chief executives.[10] Notably, the precise extent to which ministers and office holders to whom the power has been delegated wish to allow chief executives to exercise such power is declared to be a matter for them to determine.

Traditionally, terms and conditions of civil service employment have been set out in the Civil Service Terms and Conditions Code. The change in name, to the Civil Service Management Code (issued under the Civil Service Order in Council 1995) is highly symbolic. Although the introduction to the code makes a gesture towards the public service ethic by reminding departments and agencies that 'the Government is committed to maintaining the reputation of the Civil Service as a good employer', the criteria stated for determining terms and conditions for civil servants have a decidedly private sector flavour, referring as they do to 'the general practice of large employers'; and 'value for money'.[11] This is reflected too in the formulation of framework agreements. Thus a typical framework agreement between an agency and its core department states that the chief executive's delegated responsibility for grading arrangements and pay bargaining is expressly aimed at instituting structures which best suit the 'business needs of the agency'. To this end, the chief executive has the power to introduce such changes as 'are necessary to maximise the agency's efficiency and effectiveness'. Notably, the chief executive is generally required to consult staff and recognised trade union representatives, but 'appropriate consultation on matters wholly or primarily affecting the agency will be a matter for the agency'.[12] In most cases, agencies operate performance-related pay schemes (see chapter 4).

These changes necessitated too a reappraisal of the employment status of civil servants. The market ethic is inextricably bound up with reliance on contract as the basic legal form of interaction. It was inevitable therefore that the uncertain status of civil servants should require clarification in the direction of the introduction of a contract of employment. Yet the courts had for decades refused to produce an authoritative statement as to civil servants' contractual status (Fredman and Morris, 1989). Moreover, the Civil Servants' Pay and Conditions Code declared explicitly that 'a civil servant does not have a contract of employment enforceable in the courts'.[13] Pressure for change, it should be acknowledged, did not arise solely from the ideological commitment to emulating private sector employment. Thus it is arguable that the introduction of a contract for civil servants was in any event long overdue, in order to bring civil servants into line not only with private employees but also with other parts of the public services, such as local government and the NHS, whose employees have always been employed under contracts. Also of importance to a government committed to introducing severe legal constraints on industrial action was the fact that liability for unlawful industrial action depends on establishing the tort of inducing breach of contract. Indeed, frustrated with the courts' uncertain response to attempts to assert the existence of a contract,[14] the Conservative government used legislation to deem the existence of a contract for the purposes of attracting liability in tort in the context of industrial action.[15]

But the most important pressure for change, at least so far as the judiciary was concerned, came from a series of cases in which civil servants and other public employees sought to assert their uniquely public law character in order to have access to public law procedures and remedies which were superior to those available in contract or under statute. The public law remedy of *certiorari* is potentially equivalent to reinstatement, a remedy which is in practice very difficult to obtain in private law. In addition, public law grounds of review include rights to procedural fairness which are usually unavailable in contractual claims (Fredman and Morris 1991, 1994). These applicants found the courts and government in unexpected agreement that, in its role as employer, the state should be considered to be acting purely within a private law framework. For public sector employees (such as those in local government and the NHS) who were unequivocally employed under a contract of employment the courts had a straightforward means to express this view. As the Court of Appeal held in the important case of *ex p. Walsh*, the relationship was governed solely by the private law of contract and therefore judicial review was inapplicable.[16] In the case of civil servants, however, the contract was not available to the judges to justify a refusal to permit access to public law remedies. To the contrary, civil servants were inevitably prompted to argue that the absence of a contract of employment for civil servants left the option of judicial review open to them. Thus, in order to sustain their view that the civil service relationship was not a public one, the courts were propelled towards a finding that a contract of employment existed, and, after much equivocation, they did so. In *R. v. Civil Service Appeal Board ex p. Bruce*, the Divisional Court held that there was no constitutional bar to a contract: the only obstacle was the paragraph in the code which indicated a lack of intention to be legally bound.[17] This last hurdle was finally cleared in *R. v. Lord Chancellor's Department ex p. Nangle*.[18] In this case, Stuart Smith LJ felt able to conclude that it was 'plain beyond argument that the parties intended to create legal relations', the paragraph in the Civil Service Code being merely a mistaken expression of what the government believed to be the case.

As a result of this line of cases civil servants generally now believe themselves to be employed under contracts, the contract being found in the staff handbook. The judicial approach also appeared to strip away the public dimension from the employment relationship of civil servants, by shutting the door on the availability of public law remedies except in unusual circumstances. Indeed, in the most recent case on the subject, the Court of Session in Scotland declared that 'there is no room for judicial review where there are contractual rights or obligations which can be enforced'. This was held to apply to contractual relationships whether they occur in the public or in the private sector without distinction. The result was to preclude even a genuinely public law claim, namely that the decision to suspend a local government employee was *ultra vires* the council.[19]

Opening the door to contractual status gives the impression of a rationalisation of the employment relationship of civil servants, from the untrammelled exercise of prerogative power to the constraints of a binding contract.

In practice, however, prerogative remains the driving force behind moves towards contract. The result has been to increase the power of the executive with little constraint from parliament and diminishing restraint from collective forces. Until this period, prerogative powers had been exercised in accordance with accepted non-legal rules, or conventions. Although conventions were usually regarded as binding norms, they could not, by definition, be judicially enforced. It was this malleable structure which permitted the Thatcher and Major governments to achieve dramatic changes with little publicity and scarcely any parliamentary or judicial scrutiny. The utility of the prerogative to the government is perfectly illustrated in the 1995 White Paper *Taking forward Continuity and Change* (Cmd 2748, para. 2.14). The White Paper begins by reiterating that the 'Royal Prerogative denotes the constitutional authority which rests with the Crown . . . It follows that it is for Ministers to issue instructions concerning the management of the Civil Service, and they do not require Parliamentary authority to do so.' Parliamentary control via statute is expressly rejected, because, it is asserted, 'special legislation relating to terms and conditions of employment might obscure the fact that the basis of employment of civil servants is contractual'. Even more striking is the open acknowledgement of the expedience of prerogative: 'A new Code could also be promulgated as soon as it had been agreed, without waiting for a legislative opportunity' (Cmd 2748, para. 2.14). Finally, and most extraordinarily, having firmly located its power to act without parliamentary approval in constitutional law, the White Paper immediately goes on to equate it with private power. Thus: 'the Prerogative in this context resembles the power of other employers to employ without special legislative authority'.

In effect, however, the move to contract has not created a private law relationship. Agency employees remain formally civil servants. Chief executives are not their employers, and cannot therefore be the other party to the contract of employment. Instead, the power to set terms and conditions rests with the chief executive because of a public law legal framework, in the form of a combination of statute and delegated discretions. Similarly, the function of the code has been transformed, but not necessarily in the direction of a private sector model. The Civil Service Pay and Conditions Code, despite eschewing contractual status, in practice created a stable set of conditions which were treated as if they were binding. Its successor, the Management Code, cannot perform such a function because of the delegation of powers to chief executives. It therefore is required to state its own function in terms of an intrinsically public law notion of constraint of discretion and delegated powers. Thus, according to the second paragraph, 'the Code sets out the rules and principles which must be adhered to in the exercise of these discretions. It does not of itself set out terms and conditions of service'.[20] Ironically, therefore, the earlier code, despite its express refusal to embrace contractual status, was in practice almost universally binding, whereas the newer Management Code does no more than guide the exercise of discretion.

The continued public law dimension, despite an apparently private sector ethic, is illustrated particularly graphically in relation to prison officers. Despite moves to privatise the prison service, the government was not prepared to accord prison officers rights to take industrial action equivalent to those in the private sector. The Criminal Justice and Public Order Act 1994, while extending employment protection and freedom of association rights to prison officers, also removed their freedom to take industrial action. Prison officers taking industrial action commit a special statutory tort against the Home Secretary, a tort for which there can be no immunity for action in contemplation and furtherance of a trade dispute[21] (Morris 1994).

It is notable that these restrictions extend too to 'private sector' custody officers. Indeed, it has been impossible to treat even the latter in the same way as other private employees. Private sector prison staff must be certified by the Secretary of State, a certificate which can be withdrawn if the person is not deemed a 'fit and proper person' to perform the statutory functions. Conditions of employment, such as disciplinary and equal opportunities procedures, are subject to approval by the Secretary of State, and pay and conditions must be as favourable as those in the public sector. Only public sector prison staff are restricted in their political activities, but it is possible that the power to withdraw certification could be used to achieve a similar result in the private sector.

Constitutional position of civil servants

It has been argued thus far that the introduction of private legal forms, such as the contract of employment, has not privatised the law of public sector employment. Instead, the combination of the contract with uniquely public law powers, such as the prerogative, has resulted in a different type of public employment, characterised by greater *de facto* power in the hands of the state as employer over its employees. This section considers how attempts to recast public employment law in the image of the private sector have affected the constitutional position of civil servants. In its two major policy statements on the civil service (Cmd 2627 1994; Cmd 2748 1995) the government of John Major asserted that the traditional public characteristics of the civil service, namely its integrity, political impartiality, objectivity and accountability through ministers to Parliament, would remain central within the reformed, market-oriented civil service. It has become clear, however, that the basic constitutional principles underpinning civil service employment cannot be guaranteed under a purely private law regime. There have certainly been fundamental changes in the constitutional understandings of civil servants' position. But the result has not been the creation of a relationship analogous to that in the private sector. Instead, what has emerged is a new set of constitutional arrangements.

Traditionally, the prerogative has been exercised in accordance with three major conventions (Fredman and Morris 1989: 209): first, that the civil service is permanent, remaining in office even when governments change; second, that civil servants are politically neutral, carrying out decisions of the government of the day whether they agree with them or not; and finally that civil servants remain anonymous, protected from both public criticism and public praise. These conventions are held together by the fundamental principle of ministerial accountability: civil servants are accountable to their departmental ministers; it is the minister who is in turn accountable to Parliament. All these conventions have been reshaped, some more explicitly than others. External recruitment into fixed term posts inevitably puts pressure on the notion that the civil service is permanent, and clearly raises the risk that an incoming administration might take the opportunity to recruit into the civil service individuals who are perceived to support its policies. This in turn raises questions about the political neutrality of the civil service. While neither of these pressures has produced a formal change in the conventions, the third convention, that of anonymity, has been decisively punctured. Devolution of responsibility for operational decisions made it inevitable that the responsible civil servants should be accountable for their decisions directly to Parliament. Civil servants may now appear before departmental select committees of the House of Commons. Although they officially appear on behalf of the minister and not as individuals, it is inevitable that they should become public figures in their own right. This is particularly true of accounting officers, who may be called to answer directly to the Public Accounts Committee for the administrative management of their departments. Moreover, the chief executive's replies to parliamentary questions will be published in the official report.

One possible consequence of these developments is the risk that civil servants will be caught up in a tussle between parliamentary select committees, searching for information, and ministers keen to conceal such information. The Liaison Committee, in its first report, noted some cases of named officials being prevented from giving evidence to a select committee when invited to do so. There was even greater reluctance on the part of government to allow former civil servants to give evidence about their previous responsibilities. The Liaison Committee considered that it was unacceptable that committees should be denied access to civil servants whose knowledge of and involvement in government activity was essential to a committee of inquiry. It therefore concluded that all civil servants should be required to attend upon committees when invited, and the departments should assist in identifying their former staff where requested. It was only when the personal conduct of a civil servant was at issue and he or she might be subjected to disciplinary proceedings that an exception could be made.[22] The Head of the Civil Service has now affirmed that when named civil servants are summoned to appear they have a duty to do so, although ministers can suggest that other civil servants also give evidence. This understanding is now reflected too in agency framework documents, which typically state that MPs are encouraged to communicate directly with the chief executive on day-to-day operational matters.

Moreover, while the power to decide who should represent the Secretary of State at departmental select committee hearings formally remains with the latter, it is stated that in practice, where a committee's interest is confined to the day-to-day operations of the agency, the Secretary of State will 'normally' regard the chief executive as the best person to answer on his or her behalf.[23]

Perhaps most controversial has been the operation of the convention of loyalty to the government of the day, particularly in cases in which civil servants have perceived themselves to be the instruments of political manoeuvring which borders on abuse of ministerial power. This throws into relief the potential conflict between loyalty to the government, on the one hand, and loyalty to Parliament and some wider notion of the 'public interest' on the other. To what extent should civil servants in such a position be permitted to 'speak out', particularly by revealing information to Parliament itself? During the 1980s the well known cases of Ponting and Westland were acute examples of the problems raised. Such conflicts are unavoidable even within a public law framework. But they are cast in a different light by the attempts to incorporate market-type solutions into public sector problems. The 'new public management' philosophy emphasises market incentives as the solution to the problems of waste and inefficiency in the public sector. It has little to say, however, about the standards of personal conduct which should be expected of civil servants because of their role in public life. Some reformers justify this by arguing that entrepreneurial public management, because of its claimed contribution to economic growth, is more important than the preservation of traditional standards of open, honest and account-able government.[24] Yet a parliamentary report in 1994[25] highlighted the fact that the new enterprise culture significantly increased the risk of dishonesty, unethical conduct and poor control of public funds. The report drew attention to several examples of inadequate financial controls, and deficient stewardship of public money and assets was directly associated with the fundamental changes in government.

In the publication *Taking forward Continuity and Change* (Cmd 2748 1995) the Major government emphatically rejected claims that a decline in standards had resulted from the devolution of authority within the civil service. It did, however, recognise that, with greater delegation and more movement in and out of the civil service, there was a need for increased vigilance about standards in the civil service. Subsequent events triggered the need for even more extensive inquiry into standards of public life. The 'arms for Iraq' scandal and the allegations of impropriety among MPs and ministers led to two major inquiries into standards of public life, the Scott inquiry and the Nolan Committee. Both revealed serious concerns about the standards of conduct of some civil servants, MPs and ministers. The Nolan Committee's[26] restatement of the general principles of public life demonstrate clearly the gulf between the demands on public employees and the private sector profit-oriented ethic. The former include selflessness, integrity, objectivity, accountability, openness, honesty and leadership, principles clearly at odds with private sector managerialism. As the British Council points out: 'These developments are a reminder that good government is not only about efficiency and enterprise; it must also be seen to be honest and accountable if it is to enjoy a stable and productive relationship with its own citizens.'[27]

Such serious episodes of misconduct and unethical behaviour have meant that the moves to inject 'private' legal and institutional forms into the public services have had to coexist with a wide-ranging examination of essentially public approaches to the maintenance of standards in public life. Partly in response to such episodes, the Civil Service Select Committee of the House of Commons demanded a new Civil Service Code and recommended that it should have statutory backing.[28] Similarly, the Nolan Committee proposed a range of measures, including a revised code of conduct for both ministers and civil servants, and a statutory offence of misuse of public office, which would apply to ministers, civil servants, councillors, judges, local government officers, police and magistrates. The Nolan Committee also recommended that better arrangements should be made within departments for the confidential investigation of staff concerns about propriety.

The Major government vehemently denied the need for legislation. It did, nevertheless, accept the need for a code, and the Civil Service Code duly came into force on 1 January 1996, forming part of the terms and conditions of every civil servant. Its major thrust is emphatically public. Thus it reaffirms the duty of civil servants loyally to carry out the decisions of the government, and restates the public law duties of civil servants, including the duty to give honest and impartial advice to ministers; to refrain from deceiving or knowingly misleading ministers, Parliament or the public; to deal with the affairs of the public sympathetically, efficiently, promptly and without bias or equivocation; and to ensure the proper, effective and efficient use of public money. Civil servants are enjoined to comply with restrictions on their political activities; not to misuse their official position or information acquired in the course of their official duties to further their own private interests or those of others; and to refrain from unauthorised disclosure of confidential official information.

What safeguards, then, are provided for cases in which a civil servant believes that a minister or other civil servant is acting wrongfully? The primary method, according to the code, is to issue a similar injunction to ministers to follow the Ministerial Code,[29] which was itself tightened up following recommendations of the Nolan Committee. Published in July 1997 to replace the Code of Conduct on Procedures for Ministers, the Ministerial Code includes the duties not to deceive or knowingly mislead Parliament, not to use public resources for party political purposes, to uphold the political impartiality of the civil service, and not to ask civil servants to act in any way which would conflict with the Civil Service Code. The Civil Service Code does nevertheless envisage the possibility of a situation arising in which a civil servant believes he is she is being required to act in a way which is illegal, improper or unethical; is in breach of constitutional convention or a professional code; may involve maladministration; or is otherwise inconsistent with the code. In such cases the civil servant is not permitted simply to act in accordance with his or her conscience. Instead, the matter should first be reported in accordance with departmental procedures. In probably the only real innovation in the code, an external appeal is established for the first time. This is an important development: under the Armstrong memorandum, which previously governed conscience matters, the right of appeal to the Head of the Home Civil Service had yielded only one case in nine years. This must at least raise the suspicion that individuals would have used the procedure more frequently if they had been able to appeal to a genuinely independent figure. The current code establishes a right of external appeal to the Civil Service Commissioners, who are not civil servants and are appointed by a separate procedure. Nevertheless, such an appeal is available only if internal procedures have been exhausted; in the meantime the civil servant should continue to carry out the demands of the minister. If a matter cannot be resolved to the civil servant's satisfaction, the code states that the only remaining option is to resign from the civil service; and even then the duty of confidentiality must continue to be observed.

These codes of conduct must of course be read against the background of the Official Secrets Act 1989, which continues to make it a criminal offence for civil servants to make damaging disclosures without lawful authority (Fredman and Morris, 1989). Although the 1989 Act relaxed some of the most draconian aspects of its predecessor, the Official Secrets Act 1911, it remains highly restrictive. Most important is the absence of a defence of disclosure in the public interest, an absence which was justified by the government at the time by pointing to internal procedures for bringing attention to misconduct or abuse of power. However, as we have seen, such procedures may not always be sufficient. The result is an Act which gives overwhelming weight to the right of the state to expect loyalty from its employees, entirely submerging the value of individual freedoms such as free speech and access to information.

The Blair government has made some moves to address these concerns, although the impact in practice on civil servants faced with a conscientious dilemma may be severely limited by the proposed exemptions. There are three sources of such protection. First, the promise of a new ethic of 'open government' should change the climate of secrecy and make it more difficult and less tempting for ministers to require civil servants to act in ways which breach the code of conduct. The proposed Freedom of Information Act will cover a wide range of public bodies, including government departments, executive agencies, the NHS, local authorities, the armed forces and administrative functions of the police and police authorities. In its White Paper *Your Right to Know* (Cmd 3818 1997), the government proposed a right of access by individuals to a wide range of records or information, as well as a duty on public authorities to make certain information routinely available, including facts and analysis on which major policy proposals and decisions are based, reasons for administrative decisions and operational information about how public services are run, how much they cost, and the expected standards and results. However, while the exclusions permitted by the proposed legislation are narrower and more clearly defined than those presently operating, they inevitably leave open the possibility that a politically motivated decision to conceal information will fall within one of the permitted exceptions yet raise serious conflicts of conscience for civil servants. Moreover, the White Paper makes it clear that the Freedom of Information Act is not intended as an aspect of public sector employment law. It draws a distinction between the rights of individuals as members of the public to official information and the different relationship between public sector employees and their employers and argues that it would be unacceptable to give civil servants and other public sector employees a right of access to their personnel files when such a right is denied to private employees. Thus the Act will not cover access to the personnel records of public authorities by their employees.

The second source of protection is the Public Interest Disclosure Act, which aims to protect individuals who make certain disclosures of information in the public interest. The Act, a private member's Bill which had government backing, protects employees (both public and private) in respect of disclosure information which, in the reasonable belief of the worker making the disclosure, tends to show, for example, that a criminal offence has been committed, that a person has failed to comply with any legal obligation to which he is subject, that the health or safety of any individual has been, is being or is likely to be endangered, that the environment has been, is being or is likely to be harmed, or that information tending to show one of these matters is being deliberately concealed. However, the Act does not protect a person who commits an offence by making a disclosure: thus any disclosure falling within the Official Secrets Act 1989 will be outside the scope of the new legislation. For matters outside the Act, it protects disclosure only if the employee has already made the disclosure to his or her employer, or genuinely believes that such disclosure will cause detriment to himself or herself or would precipitate the destruction of the relevant information.

The third potential source of protection for public employees facing such dilemmas arises from the incorporation of the European Convention on Human Rights, which includes the protection of free speech rights[30] (Vickers 1997). However, although public employers may well be directly bound by the newly enforceable rights (see below), Article 10 (the free speech right) includes a series of derogations permitting restrictions on freedom of speech if they can be shown to be 'necessary in a democratic society' for a range of reasons, including restrictions aimed at preventing the disclosure of information received in confidence. The extent to which these provisions will protect civil servants who disclose information believed to be in the public interest, or who actively enter into political debate, depends on the way in which the courts weigh the interest in free speech against the other specified interests, including the issue of confidentiality in the public sector.

The public nature of the state as employer: the role of EU law and the European Convention on Human Rights

It has been argued thus far that attempts to remould the public service to emulate private employment have led only to a new kind of public employee. While this is most apparent in relation to the civil service, it remains true of the public sector as a whole. Pressures to maintain a distinct identity for public employees have been reinforced by European Union (EU) law and the European Convention on Human Rights. This section begins with a brief explanation of EU law and its effect on the employment position of public employees, and then considers the possible impact of incorporation of the Convention.

The distinction between public and private employees in EU law arises largely as an unexpected off-spin of the particular way in which the relationship between EU law and domestic law has been structured. Responding to member states' recalcitrance, the European Court of Justice has developed the doctrine of direct effect, whereby EU law can be enforced directly in domestic courts even if domestic legislation requires otherwise. While some treaty articles, notably Article 119 on equal pay for equal work, can be enforced both against private and public defendants, most directives cannot bind private individuals. According to the European Court of Justice, direct effect is justified against the state because the state should not be allowed to rely on its own failure to perform the obligations which a directive entails.[31] This rationale clearly does not permit enforcement against private individuals. The result of this principle is that, in some important contexts, state employees can rely on EU law in situations not available to private employees. For example, in the seminal case of *Marshall*[32] an NHS employee could rely on the Equal Treatment Directive to claim that she was entitled to an equal retirement age as a man in comparable employment, even though the domestic legislation at that time specifically precluded any claims relating to death or retirement. A private employee could not have used EU law in this way. More recently, teachers made redundant by the governing body of a voluntary aided school were able to rely directly on the EU Business Transfers Directive,[33] which requires consultation before redundancy, even though at that time the UK Transfer of Undertakings Regulations[34] precluded claims in cases where the undertaking was 'not in the nature of a commercial venture'.[35] In both cases the legislation was later amended to extend the rights to private employees, but there was a significant time lag.

The EU law definition of the 'state' is therefore of crucial importance, especially at a time when the boundaries of the state and the private sector are continually shifting. The case law of the European Court has consistently revealed a broad approach to this question. As a start, and in direct contrast with the assumption domestically, the Court has refused to take the view that in its role as employer the state is indistinguishable from private employers. Instead the Court has held that, where a person involved in legal proceedings is able to rely on a directive against the state, he or she may do so regardless of the capacity in which the latter is acting, whether employer or public authority.[36] In the seminal case of *Foster v. British Gas*[37], the European Court went on to define the state broadly, to encompass any body which has been made responsible for providing a public service under the control of the state and has for that purpose special powers beyond those which result from the normal rules applicable in relations between individuals. It is clear from this that Next Steps agencies, and indeed the whole of the civil service, are covered. In addition, case law has established that public employers such as the NHS[38] and the governors of a voluntary aided school[39] are emanations of the state for this purpose.

The notion that the responsibilities of the state as employer have a distinctively public law character is reinforced by the new Human Rights Act, which incorporates the European Convention into domestic law. Human rights obligations, according to the Act, attach only to public bodies or bodies carrying out public functions.[40] While private employers and their employees are clearly outside the scope of the Act, it is clear that public employees do enjoy the protection of its human rights guarantees. How then is 'public' defined for this purpose? The familiar notion that a state in its role as employer is no different from a private employer has been raised before the European Court of Human Rights but emphatically rejected (Hepple forthcoming). Instead, the Court has stated unequivocally that, at least as far as Article 11 is concerned, the Convention is binding upon the state as employer, whether its relations are governed by public or private law.[41] The Lord Chancellor has accepted that the Crown, the police and local authorities will be bound in respect of all their acts.

This leaves open the question of how useful the Convention rights may be to public employees. The Convention guarantees, among others, the rights to freedom of association, privacy, freedom of expression, freedom of thought, conscience and religion and the right to a fair and public trial. The usefulness of some of these guarantees has already been demonstrated: in the case of Alison Halford, the European Court of Human Rights held that the Merseyside Police had breached her privacy by intercepting calls from her office telephones for the purpose of gathering material to sustain their defence against her sex discrimination claim.[42] So far as freedom of expression is concerned, the major issue concerns the restrictions placed on the political activities of civil servants and senior local government employees. A complaint that the freedom of speech guarantee was violated by restrictions on senior officers in local government from speaking in public, canvassing or supporting political parties[43] has recently been held to be admissible by the European Commission.[44] However, as we have seen, the usefulness of these rights is limited by the permissible derogations, which in most cases allow a state to justify restrictions on a right by showing that the restriction is necessary in the interests of a democratic society for a range of reasons including national security and the protection of public health and morals. The derogation in respect of freedom of association goes even further, stating that 'this Article shall not prevent the imposition of lawful restrictions on the exercise of these rights by members of the armed forces, of the police or the administration of the state'.[45] It was this exception which led the European Commission on Human Rights to declare inadmissable the case brought by civil servants at GCHQ claiming that their freedom of association had been breached.[46] It remains to be seen how strict the standard of justification set by the courts is likely to be, but it is on this that the substantive value of the rights depends.

Conclusion

As the above discussion has demonstrated, there have been two conflicting visions of the nature of public service employment, each of which has had an important influence on the legal framework. The first, epitomised by the Thatcher–Major governments, considers that the conditions of public employment should be as close as possible to those in the private sector. This view has been reinforced by the domestic courts, which have consistently stressed that in its role as employer the state should be treated in the same way as private employers, and therefore that judicial review should generally be inappropriate for public employees. According to the contrasting vision, the state in its role as employer is unique and essentially public. This vision, which informed the traditional legal framework governing public sector employment, has been kept alive by constitutional imperatives and political realities, which make it impossible to ignore the public nature of civil service employment. It has also been reinforced by EU law, which in the context of direct effect has taken it for granted that the state remains public even in its role as employer, and by the incorporation of the European Convention into UK Law.

What direction does the new Labour government appear to be taking? According to press reports, in its forthcoming proposals for a White Paper on 'better government', the government will reaffirm its belief in a modern and professional public service which combines the most modern standards of efficiency with a public service ethos. Stressing the public dimension, its themes are to include transparency, accountability and integrity as well as strong leadership at the centre allied to local delivery that gets the best from the delegation of authority. How this modernised reaffirmation of the public nature of the civil service will be reflected in the legal framework remains to be seen.

Acknowledgement

I am indebted to Professor Mark Freedland for his comments on a draft of this chapter.

Notes

1 HM Customs and Excise, Inland Revenue, Serious Fraud Office and Crown Prosecution Service.
2 Figures taken from information issued by the Press Office of the Cabinet Office and the Office of Public Service at www.open.gov.uk/.
3 National Health Service and Community Care Act 1991, s. 20.
4 Redundancy Payments (National Health Service) Modification Order 1993 (SI 1993/3167).
5 Employment Protection (Continuity of Employment of NHS Employees) (Modification) Order (SI 1996/1023); see also SI 1983/1160, which deems local government to be a single employer for redundancy purposes.
6 The prerogative is exercised in the form of orders in council, of which the most recent is the Civil Service Order in Council 1995.
7 For a valuable discussion of this Act, on which this paragraph relies, see Freedland (1994).
8 With respect to classification and remuneration the Senior Civil Service is exempted.
9 See Management Code, para. 3.
10 Management Code, para. 5.
11 Management Code, para. 4.
12 See for example the Ordnance Survey Framework Document s. 5, and Planning Service Framework Document s. 6 at www.open.gov.uk/.
13 Paragraph 14.
14 *R. v. Civil Service Appeal Board ex p. Bruce* [1988] ICR 649 upheld on different grounds by the Court of Appeal.
15 Trade Union and Labour Relations (Consolidation) Act 1992, s. 245.
16 *R. v. East Berkshire Area Health Authority ex p. Walsh* [1984] IRLR 278 CA.
17 *R. v. Civil Service Appeal Board ex p. Bruce* [1988] ICR 649, upheld on different grounds by the Court of Appeal.
18 [1991] IRLR 343.
19 *Blair v. Lochaber District Council* [1995] IRLR 135 (CS).
20 Management Code, para. 2.
21 Criminal Justice and Public Order Act 1994, ss. 127(1) and 127(8).
22 Select Committee on Liaison, First Report, printed 18 February 1997.
23 See e.g. Ordnance Survey Framework Agreement, ch. 2.
24 British Council, 'The Evolution of the UK Civil Service 1848–1997', *Governance and Law* at www.open.gov.uk/.
25 Committee of Public Accounts, Eighth Report, *The Proper Conduct of Public Business*.
26 Constituted in October 1994 as a standing body to examine current concern about standards of conduct among all holders of public office, including civil servants. It is now under the chairmanship of Lord Neill.
27 British Council, 'The Evolution of the UK Civil Service 1848–1997', *Governance and Law* at www.open.gov.uk/.
28 House of Commons, Session 1993–1994, Treasury and Civil Service Committee, Fifth Report, *The Role of the Civil Service*, HC 27–I.
29 In July 1997 this succeeded 'Questions of Procedure for Ministers'.
30 Human Rights Bill 1997, schedule 1.

31　Case 152/84 *Marshall v. Southampton and South West Area Health Authority* [1986] IRLR 140 ECJ.
32　Ibid.
33　EC Business Transfers Directive, Council Directive 77/187/EEC.
34　UK Transfer of Undertakings (Protection of Employment) Regulations 1981 (SI 1981/1794).
35　*NUT v. Governing Body of St Mary's Church of England (Aided) Junior School* [1997] IRLR 242 CA.
36　Case 152/84 *Marshall* [1986] IRLR 140 ECJ.
37　Case 188/89 [1990] IRLR 353 ECJ.
38　Case 152/84 *Marshall* [1986] IRLR 140 ECJ.
39　*NUT v. Governing Body of St Mary's Church of England (Aided) Junior School* [1997] IRLR 242 CA.
40　Clause 6(1).
41　European Court of Human Rights, Series A 20, para. 37 (1980); Series A 21, para. 33 (1980).
42　European Court of Human Rights, judgement 25 June 1997; noted in [1997] EHRLR 540.
43　Local Government (Political Restrictions) Regulations 1990.
44　*Ahmed v. United Kingdom*, App. No. 22945/93, [1997] HRCD 620.
45　Article 11(2).
46　*Council of Civil Service Unions v. United Kingdom*, App. No. 11603/85, (1987) 10 EHRR 269.

References

Cmd 2627 (1994) *The Civil Service: Continuity and Change*, London: HMSO.
Cmd 2748 (1995) *The Civil Service: Taking forward Continuity and Change*, London: HMSO.
Cmd 3818 (1997) *Your Right to Know*, London: HMSO.
Efficiency Unit (1988) *Improving Management in Government: the Next Steps* (the Ibbs report), London: HMSO.
Fredman, S. and Morris, G. (1989) *The State as Employer*, London: Mansell.
Fredman, S. and Morris, G. (1991) 'Public or private? State employees and judicial review', *Law Quarterly Review* 107: 298–316.
Fredman, S. and Morris, G. (1994) 'The costs of exclusivity: public and private re-examined', *Public Law*, pp. 69–85.
Freedland, M. R. (1994) 'Civil Service (Management Functions) Act 1992', *Industrial Law Journal* 32.
Freedland, M. R. (1997) 'Public service, the state and citizenship – a case for a public service Act?' Paper presented at St John's Seminars on Law and Public Administration, Oxford, November.
Hepple, B. (forthcoming) 'The impact of incorporation of the European Convention on Human Rights on labour law' in B. S. Markesinis (ed.) *The Effect of the European Convention on English Law*.
Morris, G. S. (1994) 'The new legal regime for prison officers', *Industrial Law Journal* 23 (4): 326–31.
Safford, J. and MacGregor, D. (1997) 'Employment in the public and private sectors', *Economic Trends* 520: 22–33.
Vickers, L. (1997) 'Whistle blowing in the public sector and the ECHR' *Public Law*, pp. 594–602.

Part III

Issues

4 The remuneration of public servants

Fair pay or New Pay?

Geoff White

The last two decades have seen major changes in the way in which public sector pay is determined. In some respects these changes reflect wider policies of public sector reform and in other respects they reflect the broader trends of UK private sector remuneration practices, in particular the language of the 'New Pay'. Despite this convergence between public and private sectors, however, the public services are still distinct in several aspects of their pay practices. In this chapter we describe the main trends in public sector pay since 1979 and set them in the context of the organisational changes in the public sector and the wider trends in pay practices. The chapter takes a thematic approach, rather than a sector by sector analysis. In particular we concentrate on government policy on public sector pay, in terms of both the ideology and its outcomes; the relative position of public servants' pay in comparison to the private sector; changes in the level of pay determination; changes in pay structures and grading systems; and changes in pay progression systems. Finally we discuss the degree of change in public service pay determination and the prospects under New Labour.

Background

Until 1979 methods of determining pay for the public sector were characterised by several key features, including strong national pay structures organised along both sectoral and occupational lines; a commitment to joint regulation of pay through national level collective bargaining with a large number of both public sector-specific and general and craft trade unions (see chapter 10); and lastly (for substantial numbers of public servants) a continuing emphasis on pay comparability with private sector pay movements and levels. Indeed, highly centralised national pay and grading structures have existed in the public services for most of the post-war period (Clegg 1976). In the civil service, a national collective bargaining forum was established at the end of the First World War, whilst in local government a similar national framework was finally agreed upon in 1948. In the public health sector, a comparable national structure was established with the formation of the NHS in 1948. In education, a national collective bargaining forum for schoolteachers was established as early as 1919.

In all of the four sectors considered here (civil service, NHS, local government and education) highly institutionalised systems of national collective bargaining, supported by elaborate conciliation and arbitration procedures, were the norm until 1979. This system of pay determination reinforced the view that each sector was a national service with uniform grading structures and pay levels, the only exception being the payment of London allowances to those working in the capital. Thus, while variations might exist between different sectors (e.g. the civil service and local government) and between occupational groups (e.g. between civil service professional, scientific and technical and civil service clerical and administrative staff), there were no geographical differences in basic pay setting arrangements and there was little scope for negotiation at local level (except in the case of incentive pay schemes for manual workers).

The other major feature of post-war public sector pay determination has been the commitment to comparability of pay levels with those prevailing outside the public sector. The earliest attempt to link public service pay to external comparators was in the civil service. In 1931 the Tomlin Royal Commission on the Civil Service asserted that: 'broad general comparisons between classes in the Service and outside occupations are possible and should be made' (quoted in Kessler 1983: 89). However, no systematic method for making comparisons was established until the Royal Commission on the Civil Service (the Priestley Commission) of 1955, which stated that the pay of civil servants should be based on 'fair comparisons with the current remuneration of outside staffs employed on broadly comparable work, taking account of differences in other conditions of service' (quoted in Clegg 1976: 380). This recommendation led to the creation of a specialist and independent Pay Research Unit to collect pay data for the negotiators.

Whilst other public service groups have occasionally had the benefit of a national enquiry into their pay and conditions, several key groups have had special comparability arrangements for many years. The arrangements have been of two types: independent pay review bodies; and pay indexation to national movements in earnings in the case of the police and fire services. Before 1979 pay review bodies covered NHS doctors and dentists; the armed forces; and the Top Salaries groups of public servants (the judiciary, senior armed forces officers and senior civil servants). As we discuss later, two other groups have since been given pay review bodies. The review bodies, whose members are appointed by the government, take evidence from interested parties, collect information for comparative purposes and produce recommendations which the government is then free to accept or reject. The review bodies are generally concerned only with recommendations on pay levels and other monetary allowances. Other conditions of service, such as holiday entitlement and sickness benefit, are still subject to collective bargaining (except in the case of the armed forces and judiciary, which have no employee representation).

Influences upon government pay policy

Since 1979 there have been major changes in the way in which public sector pay is determined. The overarching concern has been the control of public expenditure, and successive Conservative governments (and now Labour) have adopted various strategies to control public sector pay (Bach and Winchester 1994; Bailey 1994; White 1996). In the section following this one we look at the stages of government policy. First, however, we consider the origins of the ideology which the government has followed in its reform of public sector pay practices. Many of the new ideas on pay systems design adopted by the government in the 1980s and 1990s have their origins in the American 'New Pay' literature.

The term 'New Pay' was first used by the US management writer Edward E. Lawler III (1990), and later developed by Jay Schuster and Patricia Zingheim in their book of that title (1992). The concept has been taken up by British writers such as Armstrong and Murlis (1994) and Hewitt Associates (1991). More important, these ideas were peddled extensively by US-based management consultancies operating in the UK public services during the 1980s and 1990s.

Schuster and Zingheim (1992) argue that the traditional pay concepts of job-evaluated grading structures – payment by time; seniority-based pay progression and service-related benefits – are the product of Taylorist, manufacturing-based industries operating in stable and predictable business conditions. 'New Pay' concepts, in contrast, are seen as more suitable for the nimble, fast-moving and performance-driven business organisations of the late twentieth century. The New Pay draws on a number of themes, but central to the paradigm is the objective of increasing control over pay at company level by allowing pay levels and composition to fluctuate according to business circumstances. The design of pay systems must therefore be contingent upon business strategy and culture, and hence 'strategic'. As Lawler (1995: 14) states, 'The new pay argues in favour of a pay-design process that starts with business strategy and organisational design. It argues against an assumption that certain best practices must be incorporated into a company's approach to pay.' As Heery (1996) comments, 'For Lawler, and other new pay writers, discrete business strategies require particular behaviours and attitudes from employees and strategic pay management involves selecting pay policies which will secure these behaviours and attitudes.'

This contingency approach to pay systems design, argue the New Pay writers, is facilitated by a shift from traditional 'job-related pay' to new 'person-related pay' structures (Lawler 1990; Schuster and Zingheim 1992; Gomez-Mejia and Balkin 1992). As Moss Kanter (1989: 231) explains:

> Traditional pay scales have reflected, largely, such estimated charac-
> teristics of jobs as decision-making, responsibility, importance to the

organisation, and number of subordinates. People's pay has been largely a function of the social and organisational positions they occupy . . . In traditional compensation plans, each job came with an assigned pay level, relatively fixed regardless of how well the job was performed or the real value of the performance produced for the organisation . . . The surest way – often the only way – to increase the paycheck was to change employers or get promoted.

To support such 'job-related' pay systems, argue the New Pay writers, elaborate job evaluation schemes have been created to ensure an equitable correlation of job responsibilities and rewards. Mahoney (1992: 338) argues that 'the concept of job was the unifying concept in the Scientific Management approach to organisation and management'. Moreover, such payment systems led to 'the development and application of a concept of job ownership expressed in the labor movement and collective bargaining' (Mahoney 1992: 339). While not really dealt with as a major concern in the New Pay literature, partly reflecting the different context within which the American literature is located, this last point also indicates that part of the New Pay philosophy involves the rejection of any concept of joint regulation of pay or collective bargaining. The new pay literature takes a fundamentally unitarist standpoint, although, as Heery (1996) suggests, some of the writers stress the value of employee involvement in the design and operation of pay systems (for example, Schuster and Zingheim 1992 and Lawler 1995).

In contrast to these traditional 'job-related' pay systems, the New Pay is distinguished by its emphasis on 'person-related' pay systems. Lawler (1990: 153) states that strategic pay systems must emphasise the person-related forms of reward – 'Paying people according to their value in the market pays . . . After all, it is people who move from job to job and from company to company, it is people who develop skills, and it is people who are the important organisational assets.' New Pay therefore implies a more individual approach to pay – most obviously manifest in the use of individual performance-related pay (IPRP) but also evident in new skills-based or competence-based pay systems, where employees are individually rewarded for the acquisition of new skills, competences or qualifications. Linked with this is the concept of more individualised choice in the range of benefits provided – the so-called flexible or 'cafeteria' approach to benefits.

Lastly, New Pay involves much more variability in the pay package. Heery (1996) identifies three aspects of variable pay. The first is that the amount of pay which is contingent on performance should increase. New Pay writers emphasise that the balance of fixed to variable remuneration must shift towards more variable or 'at risk' pay components. In the words of a CBI report on variable pay, the great attraction of variable pay systems is that pay 'can go up and, crucially, down in line with individual, group and company performance' (CBI/Wyatt 1994: 5). Moreover, indirect compensation, in the form of benefits, should be reduced so as to free up more money for incentive pay. Second, the scope of variable pay should be expanded so that employees' total remuneration reflects a range of measures of corporate performance – at individual, group and organisation levels. Lastly, base pay should reflect individual market worth rather than the content of the job. In place of rigid, job-evaluated structures, employers are encouraged to adopt simple, broad-banded grading structures within which managers have discretion to appoint and reward employees according to their achievements and market value.

Government pay policy, 1979–98

Government policy in respect of the pay of public servants from 1979 to the present has been episodic, with three main periods. These were from 1979 to 1986; from 1986 to 1992; and from 1993 to the present. First, in the early 1980s, the government imposed strict controls through a system of cash limited 'pay provision' figures, which were gradually reduced in level from 14 per cent in 1989 to 3 per cent in 1985. These cash limits were abandoned as the economy recovered from the recession of the early 1980s and skill shortages began to affect the public services. From 1986 (i.e. the second period) the government attempted to make these national agreements in the public services more flexible and responsive to local circumstances through the adoption of pay policies based on 'merit, skill and geography' (Incomes Data Services 1988: 1). These attempts were, however, only partially successful.

The Conservative government had some success in meeting its first objective – merit. The first groups to have IPRP were in the civil service, where government had direct control. The existing system of pay comparability through the Pay Research system mentioned above was ended unilaterally by the government and, following a period of industrial action, new pay agreements with each civil service union were negotiated over a period of years so that all groups became subject to IPRP. Moves were also made in the NHS to introduce forms of IPRP for senior managers (hospital consultants had had a system of merit awards on top of their salaries for some years before). In local government there was no national initiative to introduce IPRP, mainly because political control of the majority of councils was in the hands of the Labour and/or Liberal Parties, whose many councillors were often uneasy with IPRP, especially for more junior staff. A significant number of local councils, however, decided to introduce it, at least for senior managers.

The government also had some success in meeting its second objective – skill. The tight labour market generated by the economic boom of the mid to late 1980s, especially in the south-east, had created skill shortages in particular geographical areas and in particular occupations. To resolve these shortages, special pay additions and new types of employee benefits were targeted at those in short supply to attract and retain staff. The government, however, had little success in meeting its third objective – the decentralisation of public sector pay determination.

Perhaps this failure to achieve decentralisation was because there were contradictions within the Conservative government's public sector pay policy from the start. Despite strong rhetoric against nationally determined pay structures and any form of comparability linkage with external pay movements, on two occasions the government decided to introduce new independent pay review bodies, in 1983 for the NHS nurses, midwives and professions allied to medicine (chiropodists, radiographers, occupational therapists, etc.) and in 1991 for schoolteachers in England and Wales. (Scottish teachers have retained national collective bargaining.)

The establishment of the pay review body for nurses and the professions allied to medicine in 1983 followed large scale industrial action over pay by the NHS trade unions and was a political expedient, as was the establishment of the School Teachers' Review Body in 1991 which followed a four year period in which collective bargaining had been suspended unilaterally by the government after industrial action and the failure of negotiations over a new national pay structure.

Despite the government's objective, the severe economic recession of the early 1990s led, in 1992, to a major U-turn in government policy. In November 1992, in the face of increased trade union militancy and rising public sector pay settlements, the Chancellor of the Exchequer announced a return to a centrally imposed pay limit for the public services, with a 1.5 per cent ceiling for increases in 1993. This was followed by a freeze on pay budgets for the next three years, with any pay increases having to be self-financing.

Despite this return to explicit pay limits for public servants, the organisational restructuring of the public services continued apace, nevertheless, with quasi-autonomous bodies being established in the civil service (executive agencies), the NHS (trusts) and education (local management of schools and grant maintained status) (see Chapter 1). In 1994 the government sought to make these new organisational structures consistent with pay arrangements. It announced the ending of national pay bargaining for the civil service (with local bargaining in place from April 1996) and instructed all NHS trusts to have local bargaining machinery established by February 1995. This devolved or decentralised pay determination was designed to force public service organisations to behave in a much more market-driven manner and to introduce more contingent pay systems.

The election of a Labour government in May 1997 did not, at least immediately, herald a major change in public sector pay policy, as the government committed itself to the Conservative government's public expenditure plans prior to the general election. We consider the possible direction of the new government's policy in the conclusions to this chapter. Table 4.1 summarises the stages in government policy on public sector pay from 1979 to 1997.

Table 4.1 Government pay policy 1979–98

May 1979: Conservative government elected

May 1979–January 1980	No limit.
January 1980	14% limit for public services.
November 1980	6% limit for local govt from November 1980.
February 1981	6% limit for central government. A separate pay provision figure set for the first time. Limit to cover settlements from 1 November 1980 to 31 March 1982
September 1981	4% limit from due settlement dates 1982–83
October 1982	3.5% limit for central government 1983–84
September 1983	3% limit for central government 1984–85
February 1984	3% policy tightened. No offsetting of manpower savings
November 1986–November 1992	No formal limits. Policy of 'merit, skill and geography'
November 1992–November 1993	Chancellor announces 1.5% limit for the public services for the year from November 1992 to November 1993
November 1993–November 1996	Three year pay 'freeze' for the public services. All increases to be self-financing
November 1996	Chancellor announces continuation of pay 'freeze' for the public services

May 1997: Labour government elected

May 1997	Chancellor committed to Conservative government's spending limits. 'Freeze' on public sector pay continues
June 1998	Chancellor reiterates tight control of public sector current account. Any increase in public spending to go on capital expenditure.

Outcomes of public sector pay policy

The outcomes of government public sector pay policy since 1979 have varied from year to year and from group to group, although overall there has been a decline in earnings relative to the private sector for almost all groups. A common feature of national pay movements is the tendency for public sector pay to exhibit a counter-cyclical pattern, with large 'catching up' awards tending to come at times when private sector real earnings are declining with the onset of a recession (CBI 1994; Trinder 1994). The pay of most public servants, relative to the private sector, declined in the 1980s, before being slightly arrested in 1991 and 1992 (Elliott and Duffus 1996). Since 1993 public sector pay in general has tended to decline in relative terms again.

There are some statistical problems in comparing public and private sector pay movements over the entire period since 1979, not least because of the government's redefinition of certain public servants as employees of private non-profit-making organisations (e.g. the new universities, further and higher education college staff and sixth form colleges). This makes long term comparisons of public/private sector earnings difficult. The employment composition of the two sectors has also changed radically. As mentioned in the opening chapter, the large fall in public sector employment is largely due to the transfer of large numbers of public corporation and nationalised industry employees to the private sector, although there has also been a decline in the size of central government. This transfer of staff to the private sector has left the public services as overwhelmingly a sector of non-manual employment, whereas the private sector continues to exhibit a much more varied work force of manual and non-manual employees. This means that when we compare the private and public sectors we are looking at different employment compositions for the two sectors. This is reflected in the annual New Earnings Survey figures, which show that in overall terms the public sector's weekly average earnings are behind the private sector (£379.4 per week in the public sector, compared with £386.9 per week in the private sector at April 1998). If we disaggregate these figures into separate figures for manual and non-manual employees, in both cases the public sector is behind the private sector.

The public sector also contains a much larger proportion of female managers and professionals than the private sector, and this weights the average earnings of women within the overall national picture. In other words the public sector provides some key areas of better paid employment for women (e.g. schoolteachers, local government managers, social workers, nurses, etc.) and there has been much more movement of women into higher paid managerial positions than in the private sector. This explains the very large differential between public sector female non-manuals (£349.6 per week in April 1998) and their private sector counterparts (£315.7 per week).

Table 4.2 Public sector earnings at April 1998 (average gross weekly, £)

Sector	Males		Females		Males and females		
	Manual	Non-manual	Manual	Non-manual	Manual	Non-manual	All
Public sector	311.2	465.1	229.7	349.6	293.9	399.8	379.4
Public services	289.1	445.6	222.3	347.7	272.7	393.4	376.6
Central govt	287.2	414.6	220.8	308.7	275.3	361.8	355.2
Local govt	289.5	461.2	222.5	363.8	272.3	407.8	385.4
Public corporations	333.0	552.5	240.5	354.5	316.5	420.0	386.4
Private sector	332.5	521.8	208.3	315.7	311.5	438.3	386.9
Private not-for-profit	259.5	466.2	192.3	353.2	233.6	405.0	375.4
All industries and services	328.5	506.1	210.8	330.1	307.3	425.2	384.5

Source: *New Earnings Survey*, April 1998, Part A, table A1. *New Earnings Survey*, Office for National Statistics, © Crown Copyright 1998.

For males the picture is reversed – private sector male non-manuals average £521.8 per week, compared with £465.1 for their public sector counterparts.

There is also variation between different parts of the public sector and between different occupational groups. In general, local government average earnings have tended to remain ahead of central government and the NHS over the period. Again, however, the reclassification of NHS trusts, universities, and schools and colleges in the national statistics in 1995 makes longer term examination of pay comparisons difficult. Currently the highest earnings are found in public corporations (£386.4 per week in April 1998), followed by local government (£385.4 per week) and lastly central government (£355.2 per week).

A longitudinal study of public service pay from 1970 to 1992 by Elliott and Duffus (1996) suggests that certain public sector groups have consistently done better than other public servants. These groups include doctors, nurses, schoolteachers and the police, who all received the largest increases in real earnings and among the largest pay settlements in real terms over the period from 1980 to 1992. What all these groups have in common is the fact that their pay is no longer determined by collective bargaining, although nurses and schoolteachers were not covered by pay review bodies for all the period analysed. They suggest that these groups have always had more bargaining power than other groups of public servants and hence have been able to command higher increases than others. This stronger bargaining power is based on particular characteristics, such as the essential nature of the services they provide, strong employee organisations which articulate a good case in defence of their members' interests and the public sympathy which such groups can generate. Elliot and Duffus consider that the absence of collective bargaining is indicative of the power that these groups hold.

Movements in the average earnings index have, until recently, not shown the difference in movement between the public and private sectors but recent improvements in the index now allow this. In May 1998, for the first time, separate private sector and public sector average earnings indices were published. Figure 4.1 shows that there has been a clear widening of the rate of growth in average earnings for the two sectors since January 1993. The index is a rather crude measure of changes in public and private sector pay because changes in the composition of the two sectors (e.g. more part time employees or more overtime working) can produce quite significant changes, but even so it does give an indication of the effects of the government's 'freeze' on public sector pay since 1993.

Pay determination levels

This section examines changes in the level at which public service pay determination is carried out in the four main sectors. The changes in the public sector have to be seen within the broader context of changes in pay

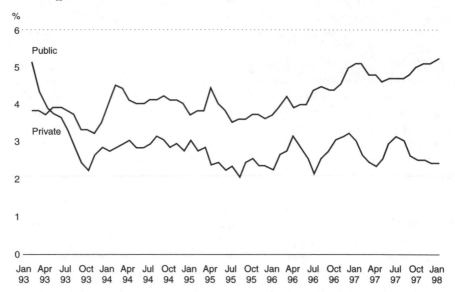

Figure 4.1 Public and private sector increase in UK average earnings (annual change averaged over three months), seasonally adjusted, 1993–98.
Source: *Labour Market Trends*, May 1998, p. 262. *Labour Market Trends*, Office for National Statistics, © Crown Copyright 1998.

determination. A key development since 1979 has been the decline of collective bargaining as the major method of determining pay. A minority of employees now have their pay determined in this manner and figures from the 1996 Labour Force Survey suggest that collective bargaining covers only around 37 per cent of the total work force (Cully and Woodland 1997). The last major survey of pay determination methods – the Workplace Industrial Relations Survey 1990 – showed that collective bargaining coverage had fallen from around 71 per cent in 1984 to 54 per cent in 1990 (Millward *et al.* 1992) although, within the public sector, collective bargaining remained the most common method of pay determination. It had declined over the period 1984–90 from 91 per cent to 78 per cent for manual workers and from 98 per cent to 84 per cent for non-manual employees. This decline in collective bargaining was largely explained by a fall in coverage in local government and the withdrawal of the nurses and professions allied to medicine and the schoolteachers from such arrangements, with the establishment of the independent pay review bodies. The 1996 Labour Force Survey indicated that in the public sector 79 per cent of employees in larger workplaces (defined as employing twenty-five or more) were covered by collective bargaining and 59 per cent of those employed in smaller workplaces (defined as employing fewer than twenty-five). Coverage was highest in public administration, at 78 per cent. In health it was 52 per cent.

Even where collective bargaining has been retained there has been a shift in the locus of pay bargaining. In the private sector there has been a marked shift away from industry-wide collective bargaining and towards more company level or divisional arrangements. This trend has been noted by several writers, including Millward *et al.* (1992), Jackson *et al.* (1993), Marginson *et al.* (1993) and Purcell and Ahlstrand (1994). In the public sector, the shift to decentralisation was only slight. Nationally determined pay arrangements (either through collective bargaining or through some form of independent review) remained the major method of pay determination until the 1990s. According to the Workplace Industrial Relations Survey of 1990 (Millward *et al.* 1992), 58 per cent of manual and 67 per cent of non-manual employees in the public sector had their pay determined through multi-employer collective bargaining in 1990.

There is clear evidence of a shift to decentralised bargaining within some parts of the public services in the 1990s (Kessler and Purcell 1996). The main change has been in the civil service, with pay delegation to departments and agencies. A survey in 1996 (Incomes Data Services 1997a) found that there was increasing variety and differentiation in pay settlements within the various civil service departments and agencies and some were developing their own pay structures.

In the NHS each trust is, at least in theory, able to design its own pay systems to match its own needs. Unlike the civil service, where many agreements remain 'national' in scope (i.e. the departments and agencies largely operate throughout the UK), within the health sector the geographical fragmentation of pay bargaining is also possible, as each trust is located in a specific part of the country. An agreement reached in 1995 established a complex new two-tier pay determination system for the NHS: 'local pay in a national framework', with provision for review body recommendations, local top-up bargaining at trust level and an uprating mechanism. In 1997 the nurses' pay review body stepped back from this system and recommended only a national increase, with no recommendation of an average local increase.

In local government pay determination has always been more flexible than elsewhere in the public services. Individual local authorities can choose whether to follow the national agreements which cover a wide range of employee groups, and most choose to do so. There are around thirty-four local councils in England which have opted out of the national agreement for non-manual staff. Most of these opt-outs date back to the late 1980s and reflect particular labour market pressures in south-east England in that period. They also reflect the then political control of these councils by largely Conservative majorities and the wish to introduce performance-related pay (Bryson *et al.* 1993). There have been no opt-outs in recent years and some councils have rejoined the national negotiations. The major development in local government is the harmonisation of the two agreements for manual and non-manual employees into a single agreement covering around 1.5 million workers. This new 'single status' agreement, concluded in May

1997, introduced a common pay spine and harmonisation of working hours, among other things (White 1997).

Lastly, decentralised pay determination in education is much less developed. Schoolteachers' pay remains subject to pay review body recommendations and grading systems remain national in scope, albeit with London locational allowances. Individual schools, however, which must follow national scales unless they have opted out of local government control, have new powers of control over the staffing mix (e.g. more lower paid and fewer higher paid teachers). While opted-out schools have the power to set their own scales, only one has actually done so. In further education, where colleges are now independent corporations with the power to determine their own pay systems, attempts have been made to impose a new national contract on staff. This effort, however, has led to fragmentation and many local agreements. Both the employers' body and the main union agree that around 80 per cent of lecturing staff are now on local contracts, with the remainder still refusing to move from their existing nationally agreed contracts (IDS 1997b). Out of 356 further education colleges in England and Wales, 194 have locally agreed contracts.

In higher education (i.e. the universities and colleges of higher education) national agreements continue, for the most part, although some merit pay has been introduced for senior staff. One of the two unions representing academic staff in the sector, the Association of University Teachers, has been calling for a pay review body for academic staff for some years. The Dearing Committee of Inquiry into Higher Education also recommended the setting up of an independent committee to review the framework for determining pay and conditions of service in the sector. This was set up in January 1998 and includes representatives of employers, trade unions and independent members. Whether this committee argues for greater decentralisation of pay bargaining to individual universities remains to be seen.

Changes in grading and pay structures

The second major change in pay systems in the private sector is the development of new grading structures. This draws on New Pay ideas and is reflected in the shift from traditional job-related pay systems, with detailed job descriptions to ensure equitable treatment of employees, to much more flexible 'person-related' pay systems in which employees are assessed against competences and grouped into 'job families' with broadly banded grades. In these broad-banded structures each employee may be on a separate salary point according to the perceived value to the organisation of the individual employee. Whilst there is little evidence of any decline in the use of job evaluation in Britain – indeed, there is evidence of some increase – there are signs that some organisations are moving to much more flexible grading schemes, especially in the financial services sector (CBI 1995). This suggests increased individualisation of the pay relationship.

In the public services there have also been moves towards more flexible grading systems. Pay structures remain relatively traditional in the main, and largely based on national systems, but there are signs of change. Certainly, individual market worth can now be accommodated more easily within pay structures, but many public services continue to use traditional incremental scales (in some cases still service-related). Signs of a shift to more 'open' grading systems are emerging, however, especially in those parts of the public services with the greater degree of management discretion. On the other hand, there is countervailing pressure to ensure that grading structures comply with 'equal value' legislation, which essentially entails job evaluation. One of the major objectives of the new local government 'single status' agreement is to deal with equal value issues.

The pace of change is fastest in the civil service. By January 1998 most agencies and departments had introduced their own pay and grading structures. However, freedom to establish new pay systems is subject to strict central government controls, under which all changes must be cleared by the Treasury. Even pay offers must be cleared before negotiation with the unions commences. There has also been a requirement on all units to implement a performance-related pay system, although there is no central dictat on how it should be designed. The Treasury must also approve all changes in grading systems in each agency and department. This is done through a voluminous set of regulations entitled *Pay and Grading Delegation – Guidance for Departments, Agencies and Non-departmental Public Bodies*. This stipulates that each delegated unit must produce a detailed account of how the review and negotiations with unions will be conducted; a delegation plan, a control framework and an annual negotiating remit (Talbot 1997: 12). According to research (Incomes Data Services 1996: 19):

> New pay and grading structures have been tailored to the individual requirements of agencies and departments, but many of them share a number of common features. Typically the new structures involve a move away from the central civil service performance-related pay arrangements [to] . . . systems which allow a greater degree of control over the payroll costs.

The range of grading systems varies from four broad bands at several departments and agencies to forty at the royal household (IPMS 1997). Job evaluation has been used to allocate staff to the new structures in about four-fifths of the delegated units. While most have used the civil service job evaluation scheme, some have used other systems.

Moves towards new local pay structures in the NHS have been more conservative, and a major obstacle to the spread of new grading systems is the continued existence of nationally determined Whitley Council grades for most NHS staff. In particular, the Pay Review Body for Nurses continues to exert a strong influence on the pay of all groups of staff, despite increased flexibility. In the case of doctors and dentists, and the nurses and professions allied to medicine, there has been no real challenge in the continuation of national scales updated each year by the pay review body recommendations. Research suggests that moves to new local pay structures have been limited. Corby's (1992) analysis of the first wave of fifty-seven trusts set up in 1991 found only half a dozen that had introduced a local pay structure, whilst later surveys by Industrial Relations Services (1993) and the NHS Management Executive (1993) confirmed this view. The latter survey found that only eight out of sixty-eight trusts had adopted local pay determination, with a further eleven planning to do so. All NHS trust staff have the right to remain on national terms and conditions, unless they change employer or change jobs, so that local agreement is necessary for a change in local conditions. According to Incomes Data Services (1998), fewer than twenty trusts have local grading structures that are different from the national grades. Most of them are NHS ambulance trusts, which have a limited number of discrete groups of staff, compared with the wide range of occupational groups employed in hospitals.

There have been limited changes in grading structures at local level in local government. A survey by the local government employers' body in 1989 found greater use of flexible entry scales, more linkage of career progression to ability rather than seniority, selective pay enhancement, extended salary scales and flatter grade structures (Local Authorities Conditions of Service Advisory Board/Local Government Training Board 1990), but overall there were no major changes until the recent harmonisation agreement for manual and non-manual workers. The new 'single status' agreement is considerably less prescriptive than the previous agreements and allows councils to vary local conditions to a much greater degree than before. While a new job evaluation scheme has been agreed, councils are not duty bound to use it and this opens the potential for considerable variation in grading systems (White 1997).

National grading structures continue to apply to the police and fire services. In education the main national grading systems continue, with the School Teachers' Pay Review Body still a major influence. Unlike other public service groups, schoolteachers' pay remains subject to statutory control.

Changes in pay composition

The third major area of change in pay systems is the shift to more variable pay. Variable pay is about making more of the total pay package 'at risk', or unconsolidated, so that employees must re-earn a certain proportion of their pay each year. Such 'at risk' components may be based on individual, group or company measures or targets. In general, this has meant a shift to more performance-related pay systems and a growth in financial participation schemes (such as employee share ownership schemes and profit-related pay). However, a recent survey of pay practices found that there was little sign of any significant change in the balance of guaranteed to variable pay (CBI 1995).

Whilst variable pay has existed for manual workers in the public services for many years in the form of incentive bonus schemes, such variable components are relatively new for non-manual staff. In the public sector the main form of pay variability currently on offer is individual performance-related pay. There was a significant growth in IPRP in the public sector in the 1980s (Incomes Data Services 1989), especially in the civil service, where all staff are now covered by such schemes. Nevertheless, a survey by the Institute of Personnel and Development (IPD 1998: 6) found that 'public sector respondents make less use of nearly all forms of performance pay than respondents in the private sector'. The survey also found significant differences between the public and private sectors in terms of the perceptions of success with such schemes. Public sector respondents were 'much less likely to feel that their schemes are generating beneficial outcomes for their organisation on virtually every indicator' (IPD 1998: 6). Some 51 per cent of public sector respondents saw IPRP as having a negative effect on staff morale, compared with 34 per cent of the private sector respondents. Seventeen per cent of public sector organisations were actually considering abandoning IPRP for management staff, compared with only 5 per cent in the private sector.

Research into the performance-related pay system in the Inland Revenue also suggests that it is not without its problems. Marsden and French's (1997) study of employees' views suggests that staff see the scheme as about increasing the amount of work done, rather than about the rhetoric of improving quality, teamwork and empowerment. There had been a considerable decline in motivation since an earlier study (Marsden and Richardson 1991), the major culprit being identified by staff as the performance management scheme.

Progress has been slower in the NHS, where IPRP is largely concentrated among senior administrative staff and managers, but some research suggests that there has been more success than elsewhere in the public services. A study by Dowling and Richardson (1997) of the attitudes of NHS managers towards IPRP found the scheme to be 'modestly successful'. There were clear indications that IPRP had raised motivational levels and induced more effort, albeit for a minority of managers. Nevertheless, the survey discovered that 'motivational and behavioural change was less likely among those who thought that certain aspects of the objective-setting process were done badly, or that assessments were conducted inappropriately, or that the subsequent rewards were unattractive' (Dowling and Richardson 1997: 1).

In local government some local councils have introduced IPRP for all staff and others just for managers. According to research by the Local Government Management Board (1994), about 40 per cent of local authorities have IPRP for at least some staff. In education, IPRP has been steadfastly resisted by schoolteachers, despite urging from central government. The

School Teachers' Pay Review Body has also resisted the idea, except in the case of head and deputy head teachers, although the new grading structure for classroom teachers introduced in 1993 does allow 'excellence points' to be awarded on the pay spine for 'performance in all duties but with particular regard to quality of classroom teaching' (IDS 1996: 114). Evidently, few schools have awarded such excellence points. In his evidence to the School Teachers' Review Body for the 1998 award the Secretary of State for Education and Employment proposed a new 'super-teacher' grade with a separate pay spine at higher pay levels.

In the case of heads and deputy heads there is no automatic progression up the pay spine. Governing bodies of schools must review the salary of the head and any deputies annually and write to them setting out their salary, the basis on which it has been set and the grounds on which it will be reviewed in the future. Criteria for determining the pay of heads and deputies include the responsibilities of the post; the social, economic and cultural background of the pupils attending the school; whether the post has been difficult to fill; and whether there has been a sustained high quality of performance by the head or deputy in the light of performance criteria previously agreed between the relevant body and the head or deputy (School Teachers' Review Body 1997: 29).

In terms of other forms of variable pay, such as group or team bonuses and organisational bonuses, there is little evidence of their presence in the public sector, although some local government contracting organisations (such as refuse collection and building maintenance) have introduced forms of gain sharing bonuses related to efficiency gains. There have also been some examples in the civil service, where at least a dozen agencies have adopted group or organisation-wide bonuses, including Companies House and the Central Office of Information (Corby 1993/94: 56). Most public service organisations are expressly prohibited from taking part in any of the government's tax advantageous financial participation schemes, a major difference from the private sector. Universities are considered to be private sector 'not for profit' organisations and this has allowed at least one to adopt a PRP scheme.

Conclusion

The degree of change in pay practices and systems in the public sector has been significant since 1979 but there are clear sectoral differences, for example between the civil service and local government. The spread of New Pay practices in the public services is summarised in Appendix 4.1. Collective bargaining still remains relatively important as a major method of pay determination, despite increasing decentralisation. Even where collective bargaining has either been ended or never been present in the public services (e.g. the police, senior salaries/pay review body groups and the school-teachers), pay determination is still largely based on concepts of national grades and annual increases in grade rates. However, there are signs that this centralised system is beginning to break down.

The civil service is probably the sector closest to adapting to New Pay practices. The organisational restructuring which has happened there has most in common with private sector developments towards multi-divisional, product market based pay systems. The shift to delegated pay bargaining has broken the traditional linkage between different parts of the civil service and also limited the use of external comparability in setting national pay levels. In the NHS the continuing presence of strong trade unions and two independent pay review bodies means that some form of national pay determination will continue for the foreseeable future, and progress to local pay systems remains slow (Corby and Higham 1996). In local government the flexibility traditionally present in the national pay arrangements (and extended in the new single status agreement) means that new pay ideas may have more opportunity to develop, but the political dimension may mean that local politicians are reluctant to move to such local pay flexibility (White and Hutchinson 1996). Local authority employers recognise that variable pay systems carry within them a very real threat of pay drift and loss of control of pay costs. In education, whilst national collective bargaining was ended in the 1980s, pay determination remains national in scope and pay variability based on the performance of individual teachers remains unpopular. This is also true of many other public sector professional groups with a strong culture of collegial working practices.

Nevertheless, it would be wrong to underestimate the effect of such changes as have occurred in pay practices. There has been a clear attempt by management to individualise payment systems and to reduce the effect of collective representation, notably where individual performance related pay has been introduced. There has also been some movement away from service-based progression systems towards more performance or productivity based systems. It might be argued that the 'employee voice' in pay determination has been diminished through the process of individualisation but, in comparison with the private sector, union involvement in pay setting remains strong.

The change of government in 1997 led to some changes in the approach to public sector management, notably compulsory competitive tendering of services in local government. The new government, in its pre-election rhetoric, also showed support for public servants or at least public services. Clearly health and education are to be the major focus of government policy. In terms of public sector pay policy, however, little has changed to date. The government's own evidence to the pay review bodies in 1997 made clear its decision to abide by the previous Conservative government's spending targets. Moreover, in June 1998 the Chancellor announced that current government expenditure growth would be kept at 2.25 per cent a year in real terms from 1999 to 2002 (*Financial Times*, 12 June 1998). He also announced, however, a doubling over the lifetime of the Parliament in the ratio of public sector investment – in infrastructure and buildings – to gross domestic product. This implies that any increase in public sector spending will be used for capital projects, leaving public sector pay tightly controlled.

There is no suggestion that there will be any return to central pay determination in the civil service and no sign of any rapid change in the approach to NHS pay arrangements, although, speaking to the Royal College of Nursing conference in the aftermath of the general election in 1997, the Health Secretary announced that the new government would be developing proposals for 'a revised approach to NHS pay . . . a system which combines national pay determination with appropriate local flexibility' (IDS 1998: 129). There has also been talk of more private sector involvement in the running of failing schools and increased separation of schools from local authority control. The local authority employers, for their part, have called for the abolition or at least the reform of the School Teachers' Pay Review Body, arguing that the government's continuing failure to fund the recommended increases (which the government has approved, even if staged) has put unbearable pressure on local government finances (LGA/LGMB 1998). The local government employers argue for either a return to free collective bargaining or the reform of the teachers' pay review body so that the employers and unions would nominate some of its members.

In short, the new government appears keen to follow the example of its predecessor in maintaining central control of public sector pay while at the same time demanding increased savings and improvements in productivity. This dilemma is not new. Public sector pay has been subject to government limits for much of the period from 1979 to 1998, and only in the period from 1986 to 1992 was there a degree of freedom from cash limited pay controls. This period coincided with a number of pressures upon the public services which made recruitment and retention a key management concern. Since 1993 the screw has continued to be tightened and delegated or devolved pay determination has allowed local bargaining to take most of the strain. This has been most true in the civil service, where national pay determination has been abolished by diktat, but it has also been true of local government at the local level. As shown earlier in this chapter, the pay of many groups of public servants has fallen behind the private sector since the early 1990s and overall earnings have grown much faster in the private sector. Unions appear to have been prepared to engage in efficiency or productivity bargaining but the continued 'freeze' on pay budgets means that pressure is building again. Recruitment and retention problems are beginning to re-emerge and there is little 'fat' left in the system for efficiency gains. Expectations have also risen among public sector employees and their representatives with the change of government. The next few years may see a resurgence of public sector union confidence and with it the possibility of conflict over pay. Whatever the government may wish, pay comparability will not go away.

Appendix 4.1. 'New Pay' in the public services

Element of change	Civil service	National health service	Local government	Education
Change in method of pay determination. Decentralisation of collective bargaining.	Yes. All civil service agencies and departments are now separate bargaining units. In a state of flux from old national structures to new structures.	Yes. All NHS trusts able to determine their own pay and conditions but limited changes. Few staff yet on new local conditions, as existing staff retain existing terms and conditions.	Some forty councils operating their own pay structures, but large majority following nationally agreed rates. New single status deal allows more local variation.	No. Pay review body sets national levels for schoolteachers. Mixed position in further education but still national agreements in higher education.
Pay contingent on local circumstances.	Yes. New pay structures being designed to reflect the circumstances of each unit. Some examples of broad-banded grading.	Yes. Individual trusts instructed to set up own pay arrangements. But limited by pay review bodies' nationally recommended rates for doctors and nurses.	To some extent. Those councils with own agreements have tried to reflect local circumstances but to a limited degree. Some experiments with benefits.	No. Teachers' pay set by Pay Review Body. Individual schools, colleges and universities can control the mix of staffing and hence paybill.
More variable pay (e.g. IPRP).	Yes. IPRP for all staff groups below senior manager (covered by pay review body).	Yes, but limited. IPRP for most managers and senior administrative staff. Merit pay for doctors. Some new pay structures.	Yes, but limited. Some councils have IPRP for all staff while others have it only for managers. Some local incentives for manual workers.	In general, no. Encouragement of 'excellence' points in schools but no IPRP at present except for heads and deputies. Some universities have small amounts of IPRP for senior staff.

Source: Updated from White (1997).

92   *Geoff White*

References

Armstrong, M. and Murlis, H. (1994) *Reward Management: a Handbook of Remuneration Strategy and Practice*, third edition, London: Kogan Page.

Bach, S. and Winchester, D. (1994) 'Opting out of pay devolution? The prospects for local pay bargaining in UK public services', *British Journal of Industrial Relations* 32 (2): 263–82.

Bailey, R. (1994) 'Annual review article 1993: the British public sector', *British Journal of Industrial Relations* 32 (1): 113–36.

Bryson, C. Gallagher, J. Jackson, M. Leopold, J. and Tuck, K. (1993) 'Decentralisation of collective bargaining: local authority opt-outs', *Local Government Studies* 19 (4): 558–83.

CBI/Wyatt (1994) *Variable Pay Systems*, London: Confederation of British Industry.

Confederation of British Industry (1995) *Trends in Pay and Benefits Systems 1995: CBI/Hay Survey Results*, London: CBI.

Clegg, H. A. (1976) *The System of Industrial Relations in Great Britain*, Oxford: Blackwell.

Corby, S. (1992) 'Industrial relations developments in NHS trusts', *Employee Relations* 14 (6): 33–44.

Corby, S. (1993/4) 'How big a step is "Next Steps"? Industrial relations developments in civil service executive agencies', *Human Resource Management Journal* 4 (2): 52–69.

Corby, S. (1997) 'Industrial relations in the civil service' in P. Barberis (ed.) *The Civil Service in an Era of Change*, Aldershot: Dartmouth.

Corby, S. and Higham, D. (1996) 'Decentralisation in the NHS: diagnosis and prognosis', *Human Resource Management Journal* 6 (1): 49–62.

Cully, M. and Woodland, S. (1997) 'Trade union membership and recognition', *Labour Market Trends* 105 (6): 231–40.

Dowling, B. and Richardson, R. (1997) 'Evaluating performance-related pay for managers in the National Health Service', *International Journal of Human Resource Management* 8 (3): 348–66.

Elliot, R. and Duffus, K. (1996) 'What has been happening to pay in the public-service sector of the British economy? Developments over the period 1970–92', *British Journal of Industrial Relations* 34 (1): 51–85.

Gomez-Mejia, L. and Balkin, D. (1992) *Compensation, Organizational Strategy and Firm Performance*, Cincinnati, Oh.: South Western.

Heery, E. (1996) 'Risk, Representation and the New Pay', paper for the BUIRA/EBEN conference 'Ethical Issues in Contemporary Human Resource Management', Imperial College, London, April.

Hewitt Associates (1991) *Total Compensation Management: Reward Management Strategies for the 1990s*, Oxford: Blackwell.

Incomes Data Services (1988) *Public Sector Pay 1988: Review of 1987, Prospects for 1988*, London: Incomes Data Service/KPMG Peat Marwick McLintock/Public Finance Foundation.

Incomes Data Services (1989) *Paying for Performance in the Public Sector: a Progress Report*, London: IDS Public Sector Unit/Coopers & Lybrand.

Incomes Data Services (1996) *Pay in the Public Services: Review of 1995, Prospects for 1996*, London: Incomes Data Services.

Incomes Data Services (1997a) 'Civil service: delegated pay bargaining in departments and agencies 1996', *IDS Report* 729: 25–30.

Incomes Data Services (1997b) *Pay in the Public Services: Review of 1996, Prospects for 1997*, London: Incomes Data Services.

Incomes Data Services (1998) *Pay in the Public Services: Review of 1997, Prospects for 1998*, London: Incomes Data Services.

Industrial Relations Services (1993) 'Local bargaining in the NHS: a survey of first and second wave trusts', *Employment Trends* 537.

Institute of Personnel and Development (1998) *IPD 1998 Performance Pay Survey*, Executive Summary, London: Institute of Personnel and Development.

Institute of Professionals, Managers and Specialists (IPMS) (1997) 'Future pay policy for the Civil Service', policy paper for the Institution of Professionals, Managers and Specialists (IMPS) annual delegate conference, pp. 1–11.

Jackson, M., Leopold, J. and Tuck, K. (1993) *The Decentralization of Collective Bargaining*, London: Macmillan.

Kessler, I. and Purcell, J. (1996) 'Strategic choice and new forms of employment relations in the public service sector: developing an analytical framework', *International Journal of Human Resource Management* 7 (1): 206–29.

Kessler, S. (1983) 'Comparability', *Oxford Bulletin of Economics*, February: 85–104.

Lawler, E. E. (1990) *Strategic Pay*, San Francisco: Jossey-Bass.

Lawler, E. E. (1995) 'The new pay: a strategic approach', *Compensation and Benefits Review*, July–August: 46–54.

Local Authorities Conditions of Service Advisory Board/Local Government Training Board (1990) *Recruitment and Retention Survey 1989*, London: LACSAB/LGTB.

Local Government Association/Local Government Management Board (1998). *Consultation Paper on the Future of School Teachers' Pay Determination*, London: LGA/LGMB.

Local Government Management Board (1994) *Performance Management and Performance-related Pay*, Luton: LGMB.

Mahoney, T. A. (1991) 'Multiple pay contingencies: strategic design of compensation', in G. Salaman (ed.) *Human Resource Strategies*, London: Sage.

Mahoney, T. A. (1992) 'Multiple pay contingencies: strategic design of compensation' in G. Salaman (ed.) *Human Resource Strategies*, London: Sage.

Marginson, P., Armstrong, P., Edwards, P., Purcell, J. and Hubbard, N. (1993) *The Control of Industrial Relations in Large Companies: Initial Analysis of the Second Company-level Industrial Relations Survey*, Warwick Papers in Industrial Relations 45, Coventry: Warwick: University of Warwick Industrial Relations Unit.

Marsden, D. and French, S. (1997) 'Taxing performance: performance pay at the Inland Revenue', *CentrePiece* 2 (2): London: Centre for Economic Performance, London School of Economics.

Marsden, D. and Richardson, R. (1991) *'Does Performance-related Pay Motivate?'* London: Centre for Economic Performance, London School of Economics.

Millward, N., Stevens, M., Smart, D. and Hawes, W. R. (1992) *Workplace Industrial Relations in Transition*, Aldershot: Dartmouth.

Moss Kanter, R. (1989) *When Giants learn to Dance*, London: Routledge.

NHS Management Executive (1993) *Human Resource Survey: Final Results Report*, Leeds: NHS Management Executive.

Purcell, J. and Ahlstrand, B. (1994) *Human Resource Management in the Multi-divisional Company*, Oxford: Oxford University Press.

Schuster, J. R. and Zingheim, P. K. (1992) *The New Pay: Linking Employee and Organizational Performance*, New York: Lexington Books.

School Teachers' Review Body (1997) *Sixth Report*, Cm 3536, London: Stationery Office.

Talbot, C. (1997) 'UK civil service personnel reforms: devolution, decentralisation and delusion, *Public Policy and Administration* 12 (4): 14–34.

Trinder, C. (1994) 'Public and Private Sector Pay Convergence? The overall earnings distribution in the public and private sectors compared and contrasted', Public Finance Foundation conference paper, October.

White, G. (1996) 'Public sector pay bargaining: comparability, decentralization and control', *Public Administration* 74 (1): 89–111.

White, G. (1997) 'Pay flexibilities in the UK's public services', *Review of Public Personnel Administration* 17 (3): 34–45.

White, G. and Hutchinson, B. (1996) 'Local government' in D. Farnham and S. Horton (eds) *Managing People in the Public Services*, London: Macmillan.

White, G. (1997) 'Employment flexibilities in local government', *Public Policy and Administration* 12 (4): 47–59.

5 Equal opportunities
Fair shares for all?

Susan Corby

This chapter covers equal opportunities on grounds of gender, race and disability. Inevitably, however, there is more emphasis on gender, because it has had a higher profile for a longer period of time in terms of research and practice. Because this chapter's focus is employment, it does not cover the steps unions are taking to involve their female and ethnic minority members in union activity. (This is covered in chapter 10.)

There are two main arguments in this chapter. First, it is argued that the public services can be conceived of as a continuum as far as action on equality is concerned. At one end there is local government, which is generally held to be in the forefront, followed by the civil service. These have what Cockburn (1989) would call a long agenda on equal opportunities. Moving along the continuum, the National Health Service (NHS) has begun to devise equality measures, as has higher education. At the other end of the continuum are the uniformed services (armed forces, police, fire services) where there are well publicised instances of sexism and racism and which, to use Cockburn's phrase, have a short agenda on equal opportunities (Cockburn 1989). In other words, it is misleading to bracket all the public services together. (See Figure 5.1).

The second main argument is that progress towards equality is threatened by actions affecting the public services generally: these include the shift in the rationale for equality, organisational restructuring, the pressure on costs, contracting out and the use of performance pay.

Background, 1920–80

In the early decades of the century, discrimination against women in the public services was considered legitimate. Thus when the Sex Disqualification (Removal) Act 1919 was passed a proviso was inserted to allow restrictions to be placed on the mode of admission of women in the civil service and their conditions of service. Treasury regulations of 1921 required women civil servants to be single or widowed and it was lawful to reserve to men particular appointments in the civil service which were based abroad (Fredman and Morris 1989). In the early 1920s a few local authorities tried

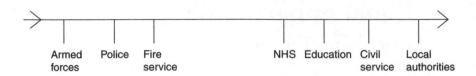

Figure 5.1 Action towards equal opportunities

to take a more progressive approach to their women employees, paying women the same as men for broadly similar work. However, in 1925 in *Roberts v. Hopwood,* a case centring on the London borough of Poplar, this policy was successfully challenged as *ultra vires.* It was held that Poplar's payment systems were unlawful as they were motivated by 'eccentric principles of socialistic philanthropy, or by a feminist ambition to secure the equality of the sexes'. Accordingly, it was not until after the Second World War that further significant progress was made. In 1955 the government introduced equal pay in the civil service, i.e. fifteen years before there was legislation on equal pay, as did local government, while teachers were given equal pay in 1962.

In 1970, i.e. five years before the Sex Discrimination Act, the civil service, concerned about the loss of experienced female civil servants, set up a committee, chaired by E. M. Kemp-Jones to make recommendations to enable women to combine a career in the civil service with their family responsibilities. Its recommendations, published the following year, were virtually unprecedented elsewhere in Britain. They included the provision of part time work, increased maternity leave and the establishment of a workplace nursery (Civil Service Department 1971). Some ten years later a joint management/union review group in the civil service, finding that only some of the Kemp-Jones recommendations had been implemented, produced a report (Management and Personnel Office 1982) which became the basis of a programme of action on women in 1984.

These developments owed much to legal imperatives: the Equal Pay Act 1970, the Sex Discrimination Act 1975, the Race Relations Act 1976 and equality legislation from Europe, not only the equal pay and equal treatment directives of 1975 and 1976 respectively but also progressive decisions from the European Court of Justice.

The developments also owed much to political imperatives. Until 1979 central government accepted that it had to be a good employer and set an example to other employers. After the Conservatives came to power in 1979, the government jettisoned what was a 'good employer' approach in many respects, such as consulting and bargaining with trade unions (Fredman and Morris 1989). Nevertheless, the Conservative government repeatedly emphasised its 'commitment to the civil service as a good employer, ensuring equality of opportunity' (Cm 2748 1995: 2). Yet, because of its *laissez-faire* ideology, it was against further regulation and rejected arguments for strengthening the discrimination laws, maintaining that voluntary action by employers was best. Thus it needed to show that it could make that approach work.

Meanwhile local government was proactive. Like central government, it was motivated by the good employer model. Furthermore, Labour-controlled local authorities paid increasing attention to the values of fairness and justice, with the result that equality was given a high priority, particularly by left wing Labour authorities such as the Greater London Council (GLC) (until its abolition in 1986) and London boroughs such as Lambeth and Camden. Another driving force was councillors' responses to local electorates in multi-racial areas in the context of local authorities' obligation under the Race Relations Act 1976 to eliminate racial discrimination and to promote racial equality in carrying out their functions.

In the 1980s over 200 local authorities adopted equal opportunities policies, while unions and management jointly revised pay structures for local authority manual grades in 1987 to take into account 'equal pay for work of equal value' principles (Coyle 1989). The GLC was at the forefront of the drive to equality, setting up a range of political and organisational structures to support its policies. In addition, it and its sister organisation, the Inner London Education Authority, copied the practice of contract compliance from the US federal government. In 1983 they made compliance with equal opportunity procedures and practices a condition of securing a contract to provide goods and services and established a contract compliance equal opportunities unit to review the practices of contractors seeking retention on an approved list. A study (Institute of Personnel Management 1987) found that the unit had some success, resulting in significant numbers of companies changing their employment practices and procedures and the GLC's approach being copied by nineteen other local authorities, but then the Conservative government implemented the Local Government Act 1988, which outlawed contract compliance with regard to sex and disability and circumscribed it in respect of race.

The present position

It is perhaps unsurprising that the public services have taken major initiatives on women. Altogether, 4.75 million people work in the public services (over 5 million in the public sector) nearly 3 million of whom are women, i.e. almost two-thirds. This compares with the proportion of economically active women of just under a half. But this overall figure conceals wide discrepancies. In 1996, 79 per cent of employees in the NHS were women but the equivalent figure for the armed forces was 7 per cent. Also just over half (52 per cent) of women employed in the public services worked part time, whereas very few men did (8 per cent).

According to the Labour Force Survey, the number of ethnic minorities in the public services as a whole in 1997 was in line with the proportion of ethnic minorities in Britain who were economically active. Yet there were wide variations. For instance, the proportion of ethnic minorities in the armed forces was 1.4 per cent, compared with 5.7 per cent in the civil service and 7 per cent in the NHS.

Just as there is considerable variation in the number of women and ethnic minorities employed in the public services, there is also wide variation in the extent of action on equality. Cockburn (1989) argues that organisations can be distinguished on the grounds of having an equal opportunities agenda of shorter or greater length. At its shortest, the agenda involves measures to minimise bias in recruitment and promotion procedures. At its longest, its most ambitious and progressive, it is a project of transformation.

The uniformed services

At one end of the continuum are the uniformed services, where there are well publicised cases of sexism and racism and the equal opportunities agenda is short. The justification for discrimination against women pivots on the argument that women do not possess the physical ability and strength to perform operational duties. To accept physically inferior women as colleagues undermines the notion of the danger of the work so crucial to the uniformed serviceman's occupational image and sense of masculinity. Moreover, the high female wastage rates and limited female promotion to higher ranks reinforce the notion that women are uneconomic to employ. Indeed, the armed forces were initially not covered by the Sex Discrimination Act, but servicewomen dismissed on grounds of pregnancy established the right to bring actions for compensation under the Equal Treatment Directive. After some high profile cases and sometimes high awards, the Act was amended in 1994 to include the armed forces but to permit discrimination 'for the purpose of ensuring the combat effectiveness of the armed forces'. Meanwhile the spate of sex discrimination cases has continued.

The rationale for discrimination against those who do not comply with the occupational norm of a white, heterosexual male also stems from the emphasis on teamwork and cohesiveness, especially in the armed forces and/or in times of danger, when reliance on colleagues may literally be a matter of life or death. There is an assumption that, for a team to be effective, it has to be homogenous (Office for Public Management 1996). This is epitomised by the fact that at the time of writing it is lawful to dismiss homosexuals from the armed services.

As to racism in the armed forces, a report by the Office for Public Management (OPM) found that it was 'pervasive, long-running and deeply entrenched . . . Many people, including some at senior levels, believe that there is no problem to address – it is simply a media construction . . . [They believe that], if there is a problem at all, it is confined to the occasional and unintentional mistreatment of an individual' (Office for Public Management 1996: 7). Indeed, equal opportunity policy statements were not issued until 1995 for the army and 1996 for the navy and the Royal Air Force (RAF) and formal policies do not necessarily change practice: the OPM found that racist name calling and racial taunts were general practice. It also found that some in positions of leadership were openly resistant to the prospect of increasing the proportion of ethnic minorities to the same level as their proportion in the population.

The OPM's findings are not inconsistent with those of the Commission for Racial Equality (CRE) (1996a). The CRE carried out a formal investigation into the Household Cavalry, which, it found, systematically failed to recruit blacks and Asians. But the CRE withheld a non-discrimination notice in 1996 when the MoD agreed to implement a wide-ranging equality action plan. A year later the CRE remained dissatisfied with the degree of progress (*Equal Opportunities Review* 1997). Indeed, it was not until October 1997 that service personnel were able to take claims of race discrimination to an employment tribunal and that the army introduced an equal opportunity action plan, a recruitment campaign targeted at ethnic minorities and a confidential telephone support line outside the chain of command for those complaining of sexual or racial harassment. In addition, ethnic minority recruiting targets were set by the minister for all the armed services (*Equal Opportunities Review* 1998). In response the CRE lifted its threat of a non-discrimination notice in March 1998.

As to the other uniformed services, although the police and fire services sought exemption from the Sex Discrimination Act, arguing that women could not/should not perform all the duties of an officer, they did not obtain it, unlike the armed forces. Nevertheless, the police are exempt in certain respects, including height requirements. The Metropolitan Police were the first force to issue a policy statement in 1987 and between 1984 and 1988 worked with the Equal Opportunities Commission to advance women's opportunities, while in 1989 the Home Office issued a circular urging all chief officers to eliminate discriminatory practices. Accordingly, there has been progress in the representation of women in all ranks of the service since 1990, and in 1995 they comprised 16 per cent of all police officers (Hansard Society 1996). Nevertheless, discrimination persists. The police culture is essentially hostile to women: there are still informal barriers, the virtual exclusion of women from some police specialisms and a lack of commitment amongst some chief officers (Little 1996). As the Hansard Society (1996: 17) said, 'it remains possible to identify a conflict of values between leaders and others within the service as a whole, which severely hinders women's opportunities'. Moreover, a Home Office study of ten forces found that four out of five policewomen said they had been sexually harassed (Millward 1993). Probably the best known case of discrimination in the police is that brought by Alison Halford against the Merseyside police force, alleging discrimination on grounds of non-promotion. It was settled out of court in 1991, though other cases have been the subject of awards. Even where the case has not succeeded, such as *Waters v. Commissioner of Police of the Metropolis* 1995, the police have attracted adverse publicity, avoiding liability on a technicality. Thus the commissioner was not held liable because the sexual assault of Waters by her male colleague in police accommodation took place when both parties were off duty.

However, police culture is hostile not only to women but also to ethnic minorities and, although some police forces have recently started a drive to encourage more people from ethnic minorities to become police officers, much remains to be done if a presence equivalent to the proportion in the labour force is to be achieved. According to the Police Complaints Authority (1997: 9):

> The number of allegations of sexual or racial harassment made by police officers against colleagues is a matter for concern. If the police are seen to treat their own colleagues in this way, how can they be relied upon to manage similar sensitive situations at the interface with the public?

In the fire services there is also severe under-representation of women, blacks and Asians relative to their presence in the labour force, and perhaps the worst case of discrimination concerned Tania Clayton, a female firefighter. An industrial tribunal found in her favour, as did the Employment Appeal Tribunal in 1996, and it was held that she had suffered numerous, often long running, acts of discrimination by colleagues and more senior officers. Against this background, progress, which had been slow, has started to be made. For instance, the height requirement for firefighters was abandoned in 1997. A distinguishing feature of the fire service, however, unlike the other uniformed services, is the proactive stance of the Fire Brigades Union, especially more recently. For instance, it financed the Clayton case even though some of its members had been involved in discrimination against her. It has established a national 'fairness at work' committee, appointed regional equality officers, set up a confidential telephone support line for members who are harassed and gives advice to representatives, including an education pack on negotiating a complaints procedure on workplace bullying (Fire Brigades Union undated). In contrast, in the armed forces there are no unions, while the Police Federation, which has a representational role but is not a union in law, has often been less than progressive.

National Health Service

Moving along the continuum, there is the National Health Service (NHS). Unlike the uniformed services, the majority of its employees are women, many of whom work part time, but women in general and part time women in particular are in a minority in senior positions. There have been a number of reports into women's employment in the NHS, identifying formal and informal barriers to women's promotion, including that by Davies (1990), Goss and Brown (1991) and the Equal Opportunities Commission (1991). In response the Department of Health, on behalf of the NHS in England, became a founder member of Opportunity 2000, a business-led, voluntary campaign to increase the quantity and quality of women's participation in the work force by the year 2000. It established a women's unit as part of the NHS Executive and set eight Opportunity 2000 goals to be achieved by 1994 as a milestone towards the year 2000 (NHS Management Executive undated). However, only one of the eight goals was met in full, although significant progress was made in respect of some, but not all, the others (*Personnel Today*, 1994).

The Department of Health has been faced with cases of speech therapists claiming equal pay for work of equal value (settling some claims out of court), but these cases have implications for pay in other female dominated professions in the NHS, such as nursing and physiotherapy.

As to racial equality in the NHS, a number of studies have identified formal and informal barriers to the recruitment and promotion of ethnic minority staff. These include work by Baxter (1988), the King's Fund (1990) and Beishon *et al.* (1995) in respect of nursing, and by the CRE (1996b) into consultants and senior registrars. In 1993 the NHS Executive issued a programme of action for ethnic minority staff and began annual ethnic monitoring (NHS Management Executive 1993). However, over a third of NHS employers (38 per cent) did not provide information on the ethnic origin of at least 90 per cent of their staff in 1996. Moreover, in the North Thames region and the West Midlands region, where there are high numbers of ethnic minorities in the population, non-compliance was 60 per cent and 57 per cent respectively (MSF 1997). Of those providing information, sixty respondents reported that they did not employ any blacks or Asians, including the West Yorkshire Ambulance Service, Leicestershire Mental Health Service Trust and Oldham Family Health Service Authority, all in areas of high concentrations of ethnic minorities. The statistics also show a significant drop in the proportion of younger Asian and black nursing, midwifery and health visiting staff: whereas 12 per cent aged forty-five and over were non-white in 1996, the comparable figure for those under thirty-five was 6 per cent (MSF 1997).

Accordingly, there are signs that much needs to be done, particularly in respect of racial equality, while equality for disabled people has barely reached the agenda. A 1994 survey found that trusts were 'giving considerably higher priority to setting numerical goals to address the under-representation of women than that of ethnic minorities or disabled people' (*Equal Opportunities Review* 1994).

Perhaps in recognition of this, the NHS women's unit was superseded by an equal opportunities unit in 1996. Its immediate tasks include developing training materials for board members of NHS trusts, commissioning a wide range of positive action programmes and improving the use and collection of ethnic monitoring data. If these initiatives are sustained, the NHS may move along the continuum. Moreover, especially since the 1997 general election, NHS managers have been making greater efforts to involve the unions (many of whom have long-standing progressive policies), realising that a joint approach is more likely to succeed than a purely managerial one.

Education

In the universities, too, equality for women has a higher profile than equality for ethnic minorities and disabled staff. Nevertheless, although over a quarter of academics are women, they are concentrated in the lower grades, comprising only 8 per cent of professors (Griffiths 1997). Moreover, although nearly all the universities and colleges of higher education had equality policies and issued guidelines on recruitment and selection procedures, only a minority had an action plan or trained *all* their staff involved in recruitment and selection, according to a recent survey. As to disabled people, only 41 per cent of respondent universities and 25 per cent of colleges had a policy on the employment of disabled people (Commission on University Career Opportunity 1997).

Higher education, with its diversity of pay structures covering groups such as academics, clerical and administrative workers, technicians and manual workers, is potentially vulnerable to claims of equal pay for work of equal value. Accordingly, the employers are developing a new job evaluation scheme which aims to compare all jobs from porter to professor. As Towers Perrin, the management consultants used by the employers, have found that women are consistently underpaid compared with their male counterparts, radical changes in pay structures seem likely.

As to primary and secondary education, most school and local education authorities have equal opportunities policies but they do not view equality issues as a 'high priority', according to research carried out for the Equal Opportunities Commission over the period 1984 to 1994 (Arnot *et al.* 1996). This has been exacerbated by local management of schools (LMS), which makes schools responsible for budgets (see chapter 1) and, as resources are scarce, has resulted in equal opportunities often being seen as a luxury.

The civil service

Moving along the continuum, the civil service has attempted to take action towards greater equality for women for several decades, with the 1984 programme of action being superseded in 1992 by a new programme. Statistics over the period 1984 to 1997 indicate that both the proportion and the number of female civil servants have grown even though overall there has been a fall in staff numbers. Moreover, there are now greater proportions of women in senior grades: for instance 15 per cent of posts in the senior civil service were filled by women in 1997, compared with 6 per cent in 1984. Perhaps the progress of women in the civil service owes much to the development of part time working at all levels: the number of part time staff grew from 15,774 in 1984 to 55,000 in 1997, with 12 per cent of women at Senior Civil Service level working part time. As to ethnic minorities, the first programme of action only dates back to 1990. Some progress has been made: 5.7 per cent of civil servants were of ethnic minority origin in 1997, compared with 4.2 per cent in 1989. However, although the number of ethnic minority staff has risen in the first management grade (executive officer), from 2.9 per cent in 1989 to 4.8 per cent in 1997, it has barely risen over the same period in the Senior Civil Service. Indeed, ethnic minority staff comprise 1.6 per cent of the Senior Civil Service (Government Statistical Service 1997).

Last but not least, in 1994 a programme of action for disabled people was introduced. Here again, there are disproportionately few disabled civil servants in the higher grades. In 1997, 3.8 per cent of all civil servants were self-declared disabled people but there were only 1.3 per cent in the Senior Civil Service (Government Statistical Service 1997).

The civil service, however, is alive to the need to make further progress. In 1998 a single, overarching programme for action to achieve equality of opportunity replaced three separate programmes for women, race and disability. In addition, it is seeking to improve the ethnic monitoring arrangements in departments and agencies, giving bursaries to disabled civil servants who have demonstrated outstanding potential and implementing the recommendations of the 1995 advisory panel to improve the representation of ethnic minorities and disabled staff in the Senior Civil Service, for example on posting policies, mentoring schemes and rehabilitation leave for those newly disabled (Cabinet Office 1998).

The official side of the civil service has a long tradition of involving the trade union side in equality issues, e.g. the joint review group on the employment of women in the civil service 1980–82 and joint efforts to promote ethnic monitoring in the civil service in the late 1980s. However, since Labour took office in 1997 there has been a deeper partnership on equality.

Local government

Local authorities, of all the public services, have been the most proactive on equality for the longest period of time. They have what Cockburn (1989) would call a fairly long equal opportunities agenda. However, it is important to note that, essentially, the main thrust has come from the large metropolitan authorities and that many small and more rural authorities have been slower to act. Overall, though, a multiplicity of initiatives have been taken, including target setting, measures to enable employees to combine work and parenthood, special women-only training for skilled manual jobs, mentoring, networking and fast track schemes for ethnic minority staff, secondments, sponsorship and bursary schemes for ethnic minority staff, job open days for disabled people, automatic shortlisting of disabled applicants and council sub-committees on equality and equality units. Most important, resources have been deployed and political will has been demonstrated at least in some councils.

In addition, local government has led other sectors nationally in addressing equality between full-timers and part timers, who are predominantly women. To this end, for instance, the sick pay schemes for manuals and non-manuals and the occupational pension scheme were changed in 1993 and the rules on holiday entitlement in 1994 (White 1997). Also at national level the Local Government Management Board (LGMB) has adopted various measures, such as a women's leadership programme to help women become chief executives and career development centres for black and ethnic minority managers. Yet progress still needs to be made. For instance, according to the LGMB (1996), in 1996 only 7.5 per cent of chief executives in local authorities in England and Wales were women and white managers in general were responsible for greater numbers of staff than black or ethnic minority managers.

The main union, Unison, has often very actively supported equality measures and together with the other unions concerned negotiated a new framework agreement on pay in 1997. The agreement, which covers 1.5 million local government workers, makes equal value a central principle. It provides for single status and a single pay spine for all below chief officer, and is based on a jointly developed job evaluation scheme. (See chapter 4.) Although the scheme is not mandatory, any authority which does not apply it runs the risk of legal challenge. Meanwhile, bonus payments, which are more common among male than among female manual local government employees (Local Government Management Board 1995), are being reviewed by a joint working group at the time of writing.

A public/private sector divide?

These initiatives, described above, are threatened by a number of recent developments which are discussed below. First, however, consideration is given to whether there is a public/private sector divide on equality, given that the public services range from the most progressive (local authorities) to the most backward (the armed forces). In the private sector, too, examples can be found of progressive companies and backward ones. Yet there are differences. The Opportunity 2000 campaign, which aims to improve the quantity and quality of women's jobs, reports that private sector member organisations appear to focus on career development and other enabling measures which help women to advance their careers and move up through the organisation. Public sector member organisations appear to focus on eliminating the barriers which impede women's progress by launching initiatives which help employees to strike a better balance between work and home, i.e. family friendly facilities (Opportunity 2000 1996). Moreover, a survey by the Department of Social Security (1997) found that women employed in the public sector were more likely to continue in paid work after the birth of a baby than women employed in the private sector (79 per cent, compared with 57 per cent in 1996), while an earlier survey found that the private sector lagged well behind the public sector in the levels of seniority at which it employed women and in the encouragement it gave mothers to continue working (Summers 1991). But although the public sector may lead the way on gender equality, it does not do so on racial equality. According to the 1992 survey of industrial tribunal applications, whereas 5 per cent of cases involved public sector employers overall, the figure rose to 38 per cent in respect of race discrimination (Tremlett and Banerji 1994). The reason for this is not clear: the proportion of ethnic minorities in the public sector is roughly in line with the proportion of economically active ethnic minorities.

The threats

Equal opportunity initiatives, as we have seen, are to be found in many areas of the public services, particularly central and local government. To some extent the socio-legal environment in which they are formulated is supportive: there is increasing awareness of equality issues, as the growth in the membership of Opportunity 2000 and the creation of a sister campaign to cover ethnic minority issues, Race for Opportunity, attest. Moreover, the spate of equality legislation continues, such as the European directive on parental leave and the government's review of the disability discrimination legislation. Yet, at organisational level, progress on equal opportunities in the public services is threatened. The main threats are the shift in emphasis from the social justice case to the business case as a rationale for equality initiatives, organisational restructuring, cost pressures and new contractual relations. In addition, performance pay in the civil service may be discriminatory.

The rationale for equality

Organisations' rationale for equal opportunities is being based increasingly on the business case. It is argued that equal opportunities can help organisations to compete in the labour market, attract the best people for the job and promote on the basis of merit, not stereotype. Moreover, it is argued that equal opportunities can enhance organisational effectiveness: organisations perform better if managers are diverse and have different perspectives and are better able to understand the organisation's customers. Although business case arguments are to be found throughout the public and private sectors, their prevalence in the public sector represents more of a break with the past. The private sector has always been profit oriented, while the social justice case resonated in the public services, where central and local government particularly were motivated by arguments of equity and fairness.

In theory, these business case arguments, based on self-interest, are likely to be persuasive and offer a way to get equality identified as a strategic issue and trigger action. But in practice the business case may threaten progress on equality. As Dickens (1994) points out, it is contingent and partial. Economic rationality in terms of cost benefit can point away from equal opportunities as well as towards it. An illustration of Dickens's point is provided by an NHS personnel manager who explained a lack of measures to improve the retention of female staff by the lack of turnover of qualified nurses (Corby 1995).

Organisational restructuring

Another threat to equality is organisational restructuring. As outlined in chapter 1, unified bureaucracies in the public sector have been broken up into semi-autonomous units, such as executive agencies in the civil service, hospital trusts in the NHS, grant maintained schools in education and direct service organisations in local authorities.

The effect on equality of these looser structures is detrimental. The centre is disempowered and can no longer drive policies forward. It can set a framework, issue codes and manuals on, for instance, recruitment and selection. It can also disseminate good practice and act as a forum for the exchange of information. Yet it cannot directly control. Thus the report by the Commission for Racial Equality (1996b: 5) on the appointment of NHS consultants and senior registrars said:

> The greatest concern today is that the structural changes which have taken place in the NHS mean that responsibility for recruitment to senior medical posts is now dispersed from regional health authorities to a large number of trusts, whose equal opportunity policies and practices are likely to be less well developed.

The looser structures also make monitoring more difficult. For instance, the civil service unions claimed that the delegation of pay and personnel management to departments and agencies prevented effective equality monitoring in the civil service (Institution of Professionals, Managers and Specialists 1997) and the Cabinet Office essentially confirmed this (1996: 13). More recently, however, the Cabinet Office (1998) has pointed out that against a background of delegation to departments and agencies of most human resource management responsibilities, including those for equal opportunities, progress has continued to be made.

Allied with this organisational restructuring is devolution to the line. It has been argued that line managers' enhanced powers in such traditional personnel management areas as recruitment and promotion are favourable to equality. As the report of the advisory panel on equal opportunities in the senior civil service put it, line managers traditionally considered 'personnel responsibilities in general and equal opportunities in particular to be someone else's problem. The new approach reinforces the responsibilities of line managers' (Cabinet Office 1995: 25). The research evidence, however, is less sanguine. For instance, a report on civil service promotion procedures, which looked at seven departments and agencies, found that many line managers were unaware of the potential for discrimination on grounds of gender, race and disability in staff appraisal reports and that there were departmental variations in the provision of training for line managers and in briefings for promotion board members and chairs (Stewart 1993). Updating this research, the author points out that most of the recent changes in promotion procedures have resulted in greater delegation to line managers, which will allow even greater variations (Stewart 1996).

In local government, research for the Equal Opportunities Commission (Escott and Whitfield 1995) found that managers of direct service organisations (DSOs), i.e. the semi-autonomous units within local authorities, appeared to have a poor understanding of equal opportunities.

Cost pressures

This devolution of responsibility to line managers is taking place at the same time as cost pressures on the public services increase. This has harmful effects on equality for four reasons. First, central equality resources are being cut back and so there is less support on equality issues for line managers. For instance, at Manchester City Council, separate equality units for race, gender and disability were first merged and then abolished. In 1996, according to the Council of Civil Service Unions, the equality unit in the Cabinet Office was reduced, with a loss of a third of its staff, while the equality unit in the Department of Transport was closed.

Second, cost reductions have led to lower staffing levels and organisational delayering. As women and ethnic minorities are concentrated at the base of organisations and at the lower levels in each occupational hierarchy, a reduction in promotion opportunities because of delayering means there is less likelihood of changing the organisation's gender and race profile. Furthermore, reduced staffing levels can lead to increased work loads, which may disproportionately impact on women. Coyle (1995) found in her study of five organisations (three in the public services) that excessively long working hours for managers had become the norm. Partly this is due to work intensification, because organisations have become flatter. Partly, long working hours have become an indicator of commitment. As a result, many women have 'to make a stark choice between their careers and their families' (Coyle 1995: 60).

Third, the severe funding restrictions throughout the public services inevitably impact on the resources available for equal opportunities. Oswick and Grant (1996), looking at fourteen public service organisations, found that among eight categories of personnel specialisms, cutbacks had affected equal opportunities and training most, while industrial relations and management services had fared best, experiencing only moderate reductions. Similarly, Coussey (1997), who looked at two civil service agencies and two local authorities, found that equality training was being sacrificed. In addition, in 1996 the Department of Social Security shelved for three years its ethnic origin follow-up survey in the department and its three agencies because there was no separate resource allocation for it (*Personnel Today* 1996).

Fourth, cost pressures across the public services are prodding organisations to economise on staff costs. For instance some local authorities, such as Islington and Camden, have cut maternity benefits and leave for the care of dependants (Incomes Data Services 1997). Also the number of casual staff and staff on fixed term contracts has risen and this has adversely impacted on women. For instance, according to the LGMB, in 1995 women comprised 69 per cent of permanent teachers but 85 per cent of non-permanent teachers According to the National Association of Teachers in Further and Higher Education (NATFHE) women were almost twice as likely to be employed on fixed term contracts in the new universities as men (Hart 1998). Furthermore, the use of casual staff can in practice obviate equal opportunities in recruitment. Thus in 1996 the Civil Service Commissioners said:

> In more than one case we found . . . that very large numbers of casual staff were being recruited, without fair and open competition, as the normal means of staffing a high proportion of continuing routine tasks. We also found instances of extensions to appointments made without fair and open competition being allowed as a matter of routine.
>
> (Civil Service Commissioners 1997: 19)

Contracting out

Another significant threat to equality in the public services is contracting out. The full details are given in chapter 7. Here the focus is on the adverse impact which tendering has had on equality. Research carried out for the Equal Opportunities Commission in Great Britain was based on thirty-nine local authorities and four services: cleaning and school catering, which have predominantly female work forces; refuse collection, which has a predominantly male work force, and sports and leisure management, which employs equal numbers of men and women. The research found that women, especially part time women, suffered a decline in hours and a decline in take home pay, unlike their male colleagues; and women were more likely than men to lose their jobs, while the number of disabled workers employed decreased (Escott and Whitfield 1995). Research by the Equal Opportunities Commission for Northern Ireland (1996) into health and education paints a similar picture, while Kelliher (1996), looking at NHS catering in England, found that concessions on hours and working practices were more often obtained from women, especially part timers, than men.

Since 1993 the Transfer of Undertakings (Protection of Employment) Regulations have applied to the public sector. The regulations aim to protect the terms and conditions of employees who are contracted out, but they do not apply to all contracting-out. Nor do they apply to public service employees who agree to modify their terms and conditions so that they are better placed for an in-house bid. So the gender impact of contracting looks set to continue. Moreover, although the move towards competitive tendering in the public services came from the Conservative government which held office until 1997, the Labour government seems set to retain tendering (see chapter 7).

Performance pay

Another threat to equality is the use of performance pay. Admittedly, performance pay is less prevalent in the public than in the private sector. It is found in the civil service for all grades, with some departments and agencies entirely basing an individual's pay progression on performance. But it is less significant elsewhere in the public services, where it mainly applies only to senior managers in the NHS and some local authorities (see chapter 4). There is some evidence that merit pay schemes discriminate against women and ethnic minorities. Cabinet Office figures (*Bulletin* 1991) indicate that as the grade rises the balance of performance markings changes, with more staff marked as performing significantly above the requirements of the grade at higher levels than at lower levels of the civil service. As there are fewer women than men and fewer ethnic minorities than whites at higher levels, there is a disproportionately adverse impact. Furthermore, a study by the Commission for Racial Equality, in which three departments participated, revealed that the performance ratings of ethnic minority staff in certain grades were significantly lower than those of white staff in the same grades (Cabinet Office 1993: 21). In addition, a Department of Transport study (Civil Service College 1995) found that in every grade ethnic minority staff received a significantly lower proportion of higher box markings than other staff. Nevertheless, performance pay looks set to continue in the civil service, as it provides managers with a way of rewarding the few while limiting the cost of the overall pay bill.

Conclusions

This chapter has shown that there is wide variation in the extent of initiatives in and progress towards equal opportunities in the public services, with some organisations having longer equality agendas than others. In the uniformed services there are numerous instances of overt sexism and racism, with the main emphasis being placed on measures to minimise bias in recruitment and promotion procedures. In many local authorities there is a record of positive action.

Just as one can describe a glass of water as half full or half empty, so one can view progress on equality from two perspectives. For instance, taking an optimistic stance, one can highlight the fact that the number of women in the first management grade of the civil service (executive officer) rose from 29 per cent in 1984 to 47 per cent in 1997. Alternatively, taking a pessimistic stance, one can highlight the fact that, although women comprise 51 per cent of all civil servants, they comprised only 15 per cent of senior civil servants in 1997 (Government Statistical Service 1998). Similarly, one can say optimistically that the percentage of ethnic minority civil servants is higher than the percentage of ethnic minorities in the economically active population. Alternatively, looking specifically at Asian representation in the civil service, one can say pessimistically that 'Britain remains an unequal and unfair society' (Vaz 1997: 28). Whatever one's perspective, the evidence suggests that much remains to be done, especially in respect of ethnic minorities and even in those organisations which have made a significant attempt to further equal opportunities.

Yet it remains doubtful whether much progress will be achieved. On the one hand, ministers are voicing concern about equal opportunities, including the Home Secretary in respect of the civil service and the Health Secretary in respect of the NHS, and the legal environment is supportive, e.g. the European Court of Justice has made a spate of progressive decisions. On the other hand, a number of developments in the public services threaten further progress. These include the organisational restructuring that has taken place, which has led to the breaking up of unified organisations into semi-autonomous units; delegation of personnel management to line managers who may be unaware of the equal opportunities dimension of their activities; pressure to cut costs, with equal opportunities providing a relatively easy target; and the continuation of tendering and outsourcing, which have had an adverse impact on part time women. Thus, ministers' warm words apart, the outlook for significant progress on equality in the public services remains at best uncertain.

References

Arnot, M., David, M. and Weiner, G. (1996) *Educational Reforms and Gender Equality in Schools*, Manchester: Equal Opportunities Commission.

Baxter, C. (1988) *The Black Nurse: an Endangered Species*, Cambridge: Training in Health and Race.

Beishon, S., Virdee, S. and Hagell, A. (1995) *Nursing in a Multi-ethnic NHS*, London: Policy Studies Institute.

Bulletin of the Council of Civil Service Unions (1991) 'Performance marking in the civil service', 11 (2): 24–6.

Cabinet Office (1993) *Equal Opportunities in the Civil Service for People of Ethnic Minority Origin: Third Progress Report 1992–93*, London: Cabinet Office.

Cabinet Office (1995) *Advisory Panel on Equal Opportunities in the Senior Civil Service*, London: Cabinet Office.

Cabinet Office (1996) *Equal Opportunities in the Civil Service 1993–95*, London: Cabinet Office.

Cabinet Office (1998) *Equal Opportunities in the Civil Service 1995–97*, London: Cabinet Office.

Civil Service College (1995) 'Evaluation of Staff Reporting Bias in Department of Transport', unpublished.

Civil Service Commissioners (1997) *Annual Report 1996–97* London: Office of the Civil Service Commissioners.

Civil Service Department (1971) *The Employment of Women in the Civil Service*, London: HMSO.

Cm 2748 (1995) *Taking forward Continuity and Change*, London: HMSO.

Cockburn, C. (1989) 'Equal opportunities: the short and long agenda', *Industrial Relations Journal* 20 (3): 213–25.

Commission for Racial Equality (1996a) *Ministry of Defence (Household Cavalry): Report of a Formal Investigation*, London: Commission for Racial Equality.

Commission for Racial Equality (1996b) *Appointing NHS Consultants and Senior Registrars: a Report of a Formal Investigation*, London: Commission for Racial Equality.

Commission on University Career Opportunity (1997) *A Report on Policies and Practices on Equal Opportunities in Employment in Universities and Colleges in Higher Education*, London: Committee of Vice-chancellors and Principals.

Corby, S. (1995) 'Opportunity 2000 in the NHS: a missed opportunity for women', *Employee Relations* 17 (2): 23–37.

Coussey, M. (1997) 'Public sector study' in *Decentralisation and Devolution: the Impact on Equal Opportunities*, Ware, Herts: Wainwright Trust.

Coyle, A. (1989) 'The limits of change: local government and equal opportunities for women', *Public Administration* 67 (1): 39–50.

Coyle, A. (1995) *Women and Organisational Change*, Manchester: Equal Opportunities Commission.

Davies, C. (1990) *The Collapse of the Conventional Career*, London: English National Board for Nursing, Midwifery and Health Visiting.

Department of Social Security (1997) *Maternity Rights and Benefits in Britain 1996*, Research Report 67, London: Department of Social Security.

Dickens, L. (1994) 'The business case for women's equality: is the carrot better than the stick?' *Employee Relations* 16 (8): 5–18.

Equal Opportunities Commission (1991) *Equality Management: Women's Employment in the NHS*, Manchester: Equal Opportunities Commission.

Equal Opportunities Commission for Northern Ireland (1996) *Competitive Tendering in Health and Education Services in Northern Ireland: Report of a Formal Investigation*, Belfast: Equal Opportunities Commission.

Equal Opportunities Review (1994) 'Equal opportunities in the health service: a survey of NHS trusts', 53 (January/February): 24–31.

Equal Opportunities Review (1997) 'Armed forces under attack', 73 (May/June): 8.

Equal Opportunities Review (1998) 'Ethnic minority goals set for armed forces', 78 (March/April): 7.

Escott, K. and Whitfield, D. (1995) *The Gender Impact of CCT in Local Government*, Manchester: Equal Opportunities Commission.

Fire Brigades Union (undated) *All Different, all Equal*, London: Fire Brigades Union.

Fredman, S. and Morris, G. (1989) *The State as Employer*, London: Mansell.

Goss, S. and Brown, H. (1991) *Equal Opportunities for Women in the NHS*, London: NHS Management Executive.

Government Statistical Service (1998) *Civil Service Statistics 1997*, London: Government Statistical Service.

Griffiths, S. (1997) 'The struggle for equality', *Times Higher Education Supplement*, 6 June, p. 19.

Hansard Society (1996) *Women at the Top: Progress Report after Five Years*, London: Hansard Society.

Hart, A. (1998) 'Casualisation grows – and hits women hardest', *Lecturer*, May, p. 2.

Incomes Data Services (1997) *Pay in the Public Services: Review of 1996, Prospects for 1997*, London: Incomes Data Services.

Institute of Personnel Management (1987) *Contract Compliance: the UK Experience*, London: Institute of Personnel Management.

Institution of Professionals, Managers and Specialists (1997) 'Equality pleas hit buffers', *IPMS Bulletin*, 7/97: 7.

Kelliher, C. (1996) 'Competitive tendering in NHS catering: a suitable policy?' *Employee Relations* 18 (3): 62–76.

King's Fund (1990) *Racial Equality: the Nursing Profession*, Equal Opportunities Task Force Occasional Paper 6, London: King's Fund.

Little, C. (1996) 'Gender discrimination in the police service', in J. Dine and B. Watts (eds) *Discrimination Law: Concepts, Limitations and Justifications*, Harlow: Addison Wesley Longman.

Local Government Management Board (1995) *Profit-related Pay/Surplus-Related Employee Share Schemes*, London: Local Government Management Board.

Local Government Management Board (1996) *Evening the Odds*, London: Local Government Management Board.

Management and Personnel Office (1982) *Equal Opportunities for Women in the Civil Service: a Report by the Joint Review Group on Employment Opportunities for Women in the Civil Service*, London: HMSO.

Millward, D. (1993) 'Sexual harassment claimed by 80 per cent of policewomen' *Daily Telegraph*, 22 January, p. 7.

MSF (1997) *The Tables are Bare*, London: MSF.

NHS Management Executive (undated) *Women in the NHS: an Implementation Guide to Opportunity 2000*, London: Department of Health.

NHS Management Executive (1993) *Ethnic Minority Staff in the NHS: a Programme of Action*, Leeds: NHS Management Executive.

Office for Public Management (1996) *Ministry of Defence: Review of Ethnic Minority Initiatives*, London: Office for Public Management.

Opportunity 2000 (1996) *Fifth Year Review*, London: Opportunity 2000.

Oswick, C. and Grant, D. (1996) 'Personnel management in the public sector: power, roles and relationships', *Personnel Review* 25: 4–18.

Personnel Today (1994) 'NHS flunks on targets for women', 22 November, p. 4.

Personnel Today, (1996) 'DSS cuts equality monitoring', 21 May, p. 1.

Police Complaints Authority (1997) *Annual Report 1996/97*, London: Stationery Office.

Stewart, M.(1993) 'Equal Opportunities and Promotion: a Report to the Cabinet Office', unpublished, London: Taylor-Stewart Associates.

Stewart, M. (1996) 'Equal Opportunities in Promotion Procedures: a Report to the Cabinet Office', unpublished, London: Taylor-Stewart Associates.

Summers, D. (1991) 'Mothers study finds job search shift', *Financial Times*, 8 April, p. 8.

Travis, A. (1997) 'Straw sets up race inquiry' *Guardian*, 25 July, p. 2.

Tremlett, N. and Banerji, N. (1994) 'The 1992 survey of industrial tribunal applications' *Employment Gazette*, January: 21–8.

Vaz, K. (1997) *The Glass Ceiling: Asian Representation in the Civil Service*, London: Vaz.

White, G. (1997) 'Employment flexibilities in local government', *Public Policy and Administration* 12 (4): 47–59.

6 Employment flexibility
Push or pull?

Ariane Hegewisch

Flexibility has been a central theme in government policy on employment and the management of public services in Britain for much of the last two decades. The European Commission (1997: 1) has identified the need to create 'more flexible organisations in public services' as one of the key challenges for creating employment growth and sustained competitive advantage for Europe. This concern with organisational flexibility is a reaction to the rapidly changing environment: a slowing down of economic growth, increased competitive pressures through globalisation, rapidly changing markets, the growing pace of technological innovation, and demographic pressure. The call for greater flexibility, which has emerged as a generic response to these challenges, is more easily defined by what it is not – rigidity, stability or predictability – than by what it is. The term can embrace anything from changing employment contracts to new organisation of work, from the management of diversity to organisational learning, delayering to the virtual organisation.

One way of trying to introduce greater clarity into the move towards flexibility has been differentiation between 'economic pull' factors and 'social push' factors. The first refers to employers' search for greater flexibility in labour use in response to competitive pressures, particularly in relation to costs. The second refers to employees' demands for greater flexibility and control over their working lives and the need to balance the requirements of paid and unpaid work.

In Britain the terms of the flexibility debate have been strongly influenced by one particular model, the model of the 'flexible firm', which provides one interpretation of the 'economic pull' factors. This chapter will begin by introducing the 'flexible firm' debate, followed by a brief review of employee-led pressures for greater flexibility. It will then review the empirical evidence for employment flexibility in public services along the lines suggested by the model: numerical flexibility, temporal or working time flexibility and functional flexibility. Evidence from the 1995 Cranet Survey allows us to examine trends in different parts of the public sector. The chapter will conclude by considering the implications of the move towards greater employment flexibility for management practices.

The debates on employment flexibility

During the last two decades the nature, extent and meaning of the shift towards flexible employment practices have been one of the central themes in British human resource management. The debate has centred on the model of the 'flexible firm', first proposed by Atkinson (1984, 1985). This identifies the search for cheaper and more cost effective use of labour as a key response to the changing competitive and technological environment:

> Employers are increasingly looking for a workforce which can respond quickly, easily and cheaply to changes . . .; such a workforce will be able to contract as readily as it expands to meet market requirements; such a workforce must not result in increased unit labour costs . . .; finally it must be capable of deployment over time to meet the needs of the job exactly through recourse to a range of working time options.
>
> (Atkinson 1985: 9)

The 'flexible firm' model suggests that employers are responding to these pressures by adopting a more strategic and diversified approach to their employees. The model distinguishes between 'core' employees – who are vital to the long term competitive advantage and survival of the organisation and who should be permanently employed – and 'peripheral' employees – whose jobs are less central to the company and whose skills can more easily be bought externally. The model introduces three different types of flexibility: numerical flexibility – the ability to adjust the total number of employees; temporal flexibility – the ability to change working hours in response to more varied demand patterns; and functional flexibility – employees' ability to perform a broad range of tasks and respond to new technological and environmental challenges. Added to this was a fourth component: financial or reward flexibility (see chapter 4). Functional flexibility is a key requirement for core employees, whereas the peripheral employment status is expressed by various forms of employment contracts, through to subcontracting and outsourcing, which allow the number employed to be adjusted in response to changes in demand. Working time flexibility applies to both groups, though arrangements such as annualised hours are generally more associated with core employees, whereas part time employment is included as one of the peripheral forms of employment.

The model itself was not intended to be prescriptive but rather presented the authors' interpretation of observed changes. Nevertheless, it was quickly taken up by management consultants and government as a 'good practice' guide (see, for example, NEDO 1986). Probably for this reason, the model was strongly criticised: for overestimating the actual level of change in the labour market; for suggesting that organisations were changing employment practices in a coherent and strategic manner when most evidence suggested that change was circumstantial and unplanned; for inconsistency in the allocation of core and peripheral status, particularly in relation to part time workers, and for promoting employment practices which resulted in greater inequality (see, for example, Pollert 1988, 1991; Hakim 1990; McGregor and Sproull 1992; Walsh 1990).

The message of the 'flexible firm' nevertheless found clear expression in government policy through a series of policies aimed at reducing regulation and employment protection in the labour market. The themes of the flexible firm are also clear in much of policy towards the reform of public services. Employment legislation on compulsory competitive tendering of ancillary services in health and local government imposed a distinction between core and peripheral employment, while market testing, the setting up of agencies and the greater emphasis on decentralised human resource management contribute to a flexibility framework for the civil service. The influence is both direct, for example through the criteria for monitoring and evaluation used by the Audit Commission (White 1997), and indirect, through promoting debate and discussion. A paper prepared by Trent Regional Health Authority in 1989, for example, which was widely circulated in the NHS in preparation for trust status (quoted in Corby and Mathieson 1997: 62), suggests that the distinction between core and peripheral staff 'may probably represent the biggest area of opportunity for achieving a successful enterprise, by reducing costs, improving flexibility, creating and rewarding incentive', claiming that such practices were already widely in place in private sector firms. There has thus been strong pressure on public services to adopt economic pull-type flexible employment practices.

At the same time pressures for social-push flexibility have also been strong. These are related to the stated policy commitment of public services to lead by example in the field of equality of opportunity. In the context of recruitment and retention difficulties in the late 1980s, and widespread discussion of the impact of demographic changes, employment flexibility increasingly came to mean the need to accommodate the demand for working patterns which deviated from 'standard' full time 'nine to five' working hours. Employers became much more open to the introduction of alternative working arrangements, such as job sharing or term time employment, in an attempt to attract and retain female employees with caring responsibilities. Public services have long led the way in this type of flexibility (Hegewisch and Mayne 1994; Horton 1996; Leighton and Syrett 1989). The increasing financial constraints of the 1990s and the easing of labour market pressures have made it harder to maintain the equal opportunity momentum in the public services; nevertheless bodies such as the Local Government Management Board (LGMB), the NHS Management Executive and the Cabinet Office continue to encourage new working patterns as part of broader equality goals (see chapter 5).

The debate has now moved on, acknowledging that much of the initial distinction between core and peripheral staff, and the allocation of different forms of flexibility to different forms of staff, was too simplistic. The original categories of flexibilisation nevertheless continue to be strong underlying themes in the British debates on flexibility. In the following sections we will therefore use them as signposts in reviewing how far employment practices have changed in different parts of public services. Trends are examined in relation to numerical or contract flexibility, temporal and functional flexibility. To review the evidence we draw on two sources of data: the Labour Force Survey,[1] a household based survey of employees conducted by the government; and the 1995 Cranet Survey,[2] based on information from personnel managers about employment practices in their organisations. These two sources of data allow us to provide a complementary picture of trends and to identify homogeneity and diversity of employment practices within and between sectors.

Numerical and contractual flexibility

Numerical flexibility refers to a range of measures which allow the organisation to adjust the level of labour input in response to changes in demand (Atkinson and Meager 1986). This includes non-permanent employment through fixed term contracts, casual work and temporary employment. Data from the Labour Force Survey show that workers in public services are persistently more likely to be on non-permanent contracts than other employees. In the spring of 1996, 10.4 per cent of employees in the public sector had non-permanent contracts, compared with 5.7 per cent in the private sector (Sly and Stillwell 1997: 351).

Fixed term contracts in particular are a public sector phenomenon: public sector employment accounts for 27 per cent of all employees, yet 53 per cent of all employees on fixed term contracts work in the public services. This is also confirmed by the organisation level data from the 1995 Cranet Survey: private sector employers are much less likely to use fixed term employment than public organisations (table 6.1) – a third of private sector organisations do not use fixed term contracts, more than double the level in the public sector. Public service organisations have higher existing levels of fixed term contracts and were more likely to have seen an increase in the use of fixed term employment in the three years preceding the survey.

Table 6.1 Fixed term employment: proportion of employees on fixed term contracts and the changing level of fixed term employment (% of organisations)

Proportion	Health (n = 133)	Higher education (n = 90)	Local government (n = 114)	Central government (n = 22)	Other UK employers (n = 930)
Over 20%	1	33	1	0	3
5% or less	67	30	78	85	58
Not used	2	0	14	14	33
Increase	71	77	70	57	41

Source: Cranet Survey 1995 (see note 2).

In the large majority of organisations, however, both private and public, fixed term employees are a small minority of all employees. It is the higher education sector which presents a stark exception: in a third of higher educa-tion establishments, according to the Cranet Survey, at least 20 per cent of employees have such contracts (table 6.1), 16 per cent of all employees in education (including primary and secondary schools), according to the Labour Force Survey.

The public sector share of temporary employment is, at 38 per cent of all temporary employees in the economy, also considerably higher than in the private sector (Sly and Stillwell 1997: 351). Only the employment of agency temps is less likely than in the private sector. Given tight budget constraints in the public sector, this is not surprising, with the exception of the health service. Many NHS hospitals have relied heavily on the use of agency staff in recent year (see, for example, Corfield Wright 1997: 43); however, the published Labour Force Survey data do not differentiate between health and other public services. The Cranet Survey finds higher education again most likely to have a high share of temporary workers, though the differences are not quite as marked as with fixed term contracts (table 6.2).

Unlike most other European countries British employment legislation does not clearly distinguish between temporary and fixed term employment, and the definition is essentially left to each employer. Fixed term employment is more likely for professional jobs, pilot projects or fixed term tasks; tempo-rary employment is more likely for short term replacements. In practice, however, the differences are fluid, and a person who in one public authority would be on a fixed term contract might be on a temporary contract fifty miles down the road. The same lack of clarity applies to casual workers. Some employers have a cut-off point of thirteen weeks; previously the period all employees must have received written terms and conditions by. Others may have a limit of one month. In some cases casual workers may have worked on and off for the same employer for years – raising issues over their employment status (and hence entitlement to longer term benefits such as sick pay). Public sector organisations tend to be more formal in their approach to employment contracts – part of the 'good employer' tradition

Table 6.2 Temporary employment: proportion of employees on temporary contracts and the changing level of temporary employment (% of organisations)

	Health	*Higher education*	*Local government*	*Central government*	*Other UK employers*
Proportion	*(n = 133)*	*(n = 90)*	*(n = 114)*	*(n = 22)*	*(n = 930)*
Over 20%	3	15	4	0	4
5% or less	59	62	64	71	69
Not used	3	0	0	10	5
Increase	74	71	77	62	57

Source: Cranet Survey 1995 (see note 2).

and probably also reflecting the influence of trade unions, which are concerned to prevent the casualisation of employment. This has been offered as an explanation for the higher level of non-permanent employment in the public sector: not a reflection of greater uncertainty in employment than in the private sector, but a greater tendency to 'codify' the employment relationship (Rubery 1989). However, it probably also demonstrates that public sector employers continue to have less control over their budgets, and are more likely to be subject to constraints on the overall level of growth in staff complements.

Public sector organisations, across all sectors, are considerably more likely to have increased their reliance on temporary and fixed term employment in the recent past (tables 6.1–2). In the private sector temporary employment usually increases when there is an economic upturn. Temporary employment is also clearly seasonal, with strong variations during the year. Temporary employment in health services, education and public administration is much more stable – there are fewer signs of seasonal changes in demand (Casey *et al.* 1997: 28–9), evidence perhaps of a more structural shift in employment towards temporary contracts. There are, however, differences within the public services: the employment services, for example, change the level of casual employment in response to fluctuations in unemployment (see also chapter 5).

The reasons given by personnel managers for the increase in temporary and fixed term contracts do not differ systematically between private and public sector organisations, but there are illuminating differences within the public sector (table 6.3). Central government organisations, for example, are much more likely to use non-permanent contracts as a result of 'recruitment freezes', an explanation for temporary employment which has long been associated with all the public sector but in practice is not so common elsewhere. Cost reduction also figures more strongly as a reason in central government, and to some extent in local government. This reason is least likely to be found in the health service – not surprisingly, given that hospitals

Table 6.3 Main reasons for the increase in temporary or fixed term contracts (% of organisations)

Proportion	Health	Higher education	Local government	Central government	Other UK employers
Recruitment freeze	20	7	20	46	15
Fixed time projects	36	48	31	8	35
Reducing staff costs	15	20	26	31	25
Other	29	26	23	15	25

Source: Cranet Survey 1995 (see note 2).

often have to hire expensive agency staff to deal with staff shortages and high turnover. In one London NHS trust the turnover of nurses was over 40 per cent per year; and without agency nurses the hospital would have been unable to continue its operations (Corfield Wright 1997: 43). Turnover is high for a mixture of reasons, including the intensification of work, shift patterns and, not least, low basic wages. The need to employ more expensive agency staff further reduces resources and makes it harder for hospitals to address the more fundamental reasons for staff shortages.

Universities and institutions of higher education are most likely to cite fixed term contracts as a reason for non-permanent employment. The advertisement of permanent contracts, particularly for research projects and junior lecturers, has become a rarity. The Association of University Teachers (AUT) has become seriously concerned about the level of fixed term contracts, which in their view has reached endemic proportions, and has conducted research into the career prospects and terms and conditions of temporary employees.

In local government, non-permanent employment increased significantly during the Local Government Review – the uncertainty over the outcome of reorganisation pushed many authorities to stop all permanent recruitment until the end of the review (Hegewisch forthcoming). Compulsory competitive tendering is another reason for the systematic increase in temporary contracts. Job security has fallen particularly in the provider areas (see chapter 7). Annual purchaser–provider contracts in the health services have similarly led to an increase in fixed term contracts. The new Labour government has promised to replace annual contracts with longer term agreements; if implemented this may lead to a reduction in fixed term contracts.

A review of high users of flexible contracts in local government (Hegewisch forthcoming) showed that personnel departments often no longer have an overview over the extent of temporary employment. Many computerised personnel information systems have not yet been adjusted to the surge in temporary employment and cannot distinguish between types of contracts. A more important reason is the devolution of staff budgets to departmental heads and line managers. In many authorities, as long as broad 'good practice' guidelines are followed, decisions about the type of contract for new staff have been delegated to departmental managers. Central personnel departments were often unable to provide details on the actual levels of temporary employment. In one large metropolitan authority it was only when unions pushed for a systematic audit of contracts that the level of temporary employment was found to be in excess of 30 per cent of the work force – to the considerable surprise and disbelief of many line managers. The unions had pushed for the review because of growing concern about the erosion of permanent employment. They were especially concerned that the use of temporary employment would inadvertently undermine the authority's commitment to equality of opportunity in recruitment and selection. While the personnel department shared that concern, it was also worried that a considerable number of people on temporary contracts were in fact entitled to permanent status; with consecutive renewals of temporary contracts their length of employment had exceeded two years, and hence was over the threshold of protection against unfair dismissal. Interestingly, though, on the whole this particular local authority was not particularly concerned about the overall level of non-permanent employment as long as basic procedures were being followed. This attitude is not shared by all local government employers. The personnel director of the social service department in a county council said: 'You get a trade-off in terms of the level of competence and motivation with people who do not feel part of the organisation.' Uncertainty over the Local Government Review at the time meant that in principle all new employment was non-permanent. But the authority felt that as a result of this policy it was attracting less well qualified applicants in its care departments and therefore amended the policy to allow permanent appointments for front line staff.

A rather different reason for the use of temporary work is the growing number of women who take maternity leave; and of course reasons such as cover for holidays, sickness and other absences also continue to figure strongly (Casey *et al.* 1997; IDS 1995). After several years of budget constraints there now is less scope to cover such absences by a temporary reorganisation of work.

Non-permanent employment, then, is a practice particularly associated with public services; European comparisons show that the UK is no exception in this (Bruegel and Hegewisch 1994; Marshall 1989). A number of recent legislative initiatives, at UK and European level, concerned with the increase in insecure employment are likely to have an impact. The proposal to lower the qualifying period for unfair dismissal from two years to one (Department of Trade and Industry 1998a), for example, is likely to have an effect on the repeated renewal of temporary contracts in public services; currently the two year period tends to serve as a cut-off point where temporary contracts are monitored. The introduction of a statutory right to minimum holidays as part of European legislation requires a revision of pro-rata benefits for casual workers.

Given the commitment of the Labour government to move away from strict competitive tendering requirements in local government and review the use of purchaser provider contracts in the NHS, the institutional factors pushing public services towards the use of temporary and fixed term contracts are likely to diminish. Other factors, however, such as budget constraints, are unlikely to disappear. The evidence suggests that a systematic evaluation of the costs and benefits of non-permanent employment is not taking place in the majority of public service employers, and that this might have an impact on the effectiveness of public services in the longer run.

Part time employment

The status of part time employment has been much debated in the flexibility literature. Within the original 'flexible firm' model part time work is one of the peripheral forms of work which provide numerical as well as temporal flexibility. Many studies since have argued that in many organisations, not least in the public sector, part timers are part of the long term and essential core of the organisation. Moreover, the chance to work part time has been an important element of many equal opportunity policies, explicitly targeted at the recruitment of core staff. International comparisons of the employment of part time workers show that British employers are much more likely to use part time employment as part of a cost saving strategy, but that other reasons such as retention are also very important (Bielenski *et al.* 1992). Other UK studies suggest that there is a growing division in the terms and conditions of part timers, with some enjoying good employment conditions, others being pushed into a clearly peripheral and almost casual status (Neathey and Hurstfield 1995).

Part time employment is certainly not a new phenomenon in the public sector. Health and social services, catering and cleaning services have relied heavily on part time employment for a long time. Other parts of the public sector, particularly public administration, have relied less on such employment.

This is confirmed by the results of the 1995 Cranet Survey. In the health service two-thirds of organisations employ at least a fifth of their staff part time. None of the surveyed central government organisations has similarly high levels (table 6.4). The survey also reminds us not to generalise about part time employment in local government. The majority of female local government staff are now part time, and 39 per cent of all local government employees (Mortimer 1997, cited in White 1997). This mainly reflects the large authorities with responsibility for education and social services; part time employment is much less common in the many smaller local authorities. The Labour Force Survey, which distinguishes between employees in public administration and education (and in other words categorises people across organisational boundaries), confirms that part time employment in public administration is, at 14.5 per cent, below the national average of a quarter of all employees, whereas education has the highest level of part time employment at 37 per cent (Casey *et al.* 1997: 15).

Table 6.4 Part time employment: proportion of employees on part time contracts and the changing level of part time employment, 1992–95 (% of organisations)

Proportion	Health (n = 133)	Higher education (n = 90)	Local government (n = 114)	Central government (n = 22)	Other UK employers (n = 930)
Over 20%	65	38	38	0	11
6–20%	26	54	41	38	17
5% or less	9	8	21	57	66
Not used	0	0	0	0	8
Increase	64	64	73	52	46

Source: Cranet Survey 1995 (see note 2).

Once again public sector organisations are considerably more likely to have increased part time employment than private sector employers (table 6.4). A contributing factor has been the contracting out of ancillary services in health and local government, which has often led to an increase in part time work as part of strategies aimed at decreasing direct labour costs and increasing efficiency. Much of the shift towards this type of part time employment took place in the late 1980s when organisations were first forced to competitively tender these services but part time employment continues to expand into new areas. Within the health service, for example, part time employment has increased particularly among maintenance staff, albeit from a low base (Corby and Mathieson 1997: 65).

There also has been a persistent increase in part time employment among non-manual staff. In local government, the number of non-manual part time staff increased by 43 per cent between 1985 and 1995 (Mortimer 1997); this is perhaps more an indication of the low starting point than of overall high levels of part time employment in these grades. Part time employment is also quite a recent phenomenon in the civil service, and here it is very clearly linked with equal opportunities objectives. The number of part time employees in the civil service tripled to 48,000 between 1984 and 1994 (Horton 1996: 113). There is active encouragement of the part time option as a way of combining family and career commitments, including in higher grades. This, the voluntary changing to part time employment of female staff after maternity leave, was also a major reason for the increase in part time employment in local government (Hegewisch forthcoming). Within the health service part time employment in senior grades has been much more limited, in spite of a high level of commitment to making managerial jobs more accessible to employees not able to work full time. Part timers continue to be concentrated in the bottom grades (Corby 1995: 34) (see also chapter 5).

The clearest way to put part time employment at the service of equal opportunities is job sharing. Job share policies are now a standard component of HR policies in most public sector organisations, much more so than in the private sector (table 6.5). Proportionately twice as many employees job share in the public as in the private sector, although in the early 1990s this did not amount to more than 2 per cent of staff in public services, according to the Labour Force Survey. There is some indication of a 'snowball' effect, and that at least in some central and local government organisations job sharers have moved beyond being a rarity towards a position where they are a common means of responding to changing demands by employees. Personnel managers in local authorities mentioned that it was now much less common for them to be involved in the setting up of job share contracts or even to have to enforce the rights to job share because most line managers could turn to colleagues who already had experience with the use of job share contracts when faced with a request for job sharing by one of their employees (Hegewisch forthcoming).

Table 6.5 Organisations with job share policies/employment of job sharers, by sector (%)

Health	Higher education	Local government	Central government	Other UK employers
(n = 133)	(n = 90)	(n = 114)	(n = 22)	(n = 930)
93	85	94	95	41.5

Source: Cranet Survey 1995 (see note 2).

Temporal or working time flexibility

Part time employment and job sharing are the most obvious ways of making working hours respond to fluctuations in demand (whether from employees or from clients and customers). There are a growing number of working patterns which do not conform to a standard 'nine to five' working day, Monday to Friday week. Term time employment, where employment patterns are matched to the school year, making it possible for women to look after their children during holiday time, have been long established, especially in education. Flexible working hours ('flexitime'), where employees can vary their starting and finishing times around a core period when everyone has to be present, are one of the most established forms of working time flexibility (Brewster *et al.* 1997: 167–8). Flexitime mainly responds to employee demands for greater flexibility, although employers can also benefit by, for example, being able to keep offices open for longer. In the case of a national library, core hours are no more than two hours, 10.00–12.00 in the morning, giving employees a very wide choice of working hours (LRD, quoted in TUC 1998: 9). However, flexitime can be quite bureaucratic and time consuming to administer. Attendance recording systems are not common for non-manual employees in the public sector, which means that employees first have to spend time filling in attendance forms manually, someone has to evaluate the forms, and the co-ordination of time in and time out takes additional managerial time.

A more recent, and probably more employer–focused, innovation in working time is the use of annualised hours. Annualised hour contracts have as their reference point the annual working time, and variations in weekly working hours are possible in response to peaks and troughs in demand during the year. There is no standard way of setting up annualised hours contracts, but usually arrangements include a period over which hours need to be averaged – often quarterly – and a minimum notice period at which weekly hours may be changed. A major reason for introducing annualised hours contracts is to reduce the need for overtime payments and the use of casual or temporary employment at times of high demand.

Data from the 1995 Cranet Survey show that there are a substantial number of employers who have some annualised hours schemes, even though the actual number of employees on such contracts remains small. It also

Table 6.6 Annualised hours contracts: proportion of employees on annualised hours contracts and the proportion of organisations with increased level of annualised hours contracts (% of organisations)

	Health	Higher education	Local government	Central government	Other UK employers
Proportion	*(n = 133)*	*(n = 90)*	*(n = 114)*	*(n = 22)*	*(n = 930)*
Over 20%	1	17	3	11	8
5% or less	25	20	41	26	9
Not used	75	57	55	63	80
Increase	19	37	27	11	11

Source: Cranet Survey 1995 (see note 2).

shows that again public sector organisations are more likely to have introduced this arrangement than other UK employers. Annualised hours contracts are particularly common in higher education, and indeed also apply to many teaching staff who are employed by local authorities. According to the Labour Force Survey 19 per cent of all employees in education are on annualised hours contracts; in the economy overall only 6 per cent of employees have such contracts (Casey *et al.* 1997: 15). The pressures on resources and the need to compete in the CCT process have also pushed many local authorities to explore annualised hours for their parks and maintenance staff.

One such example is provided by Redditch Council, where annualised hours contracts were introduced for thirty-five male gardeners (TUC 1998). The gardeners now work a four day week in winter and longer hours in summer; substantial savings have been made through cutting the use of external contractors during the busy period and have been redistributed to create new jobs and to provide new opportunities for training for the gardeners. The employees, though not their union, were initially quite suspicious of the scheme but are now fully in favour, not least because it allows them to become more involved with their children during the winter months. Key to the success of this scheme has been the active involvement of the union in the design of the scheme, and a policy of sharing the benefits. This is not always the case, and in some circumstances the absence of consultation has led to considerable resistance.

The most common form of flexible working patterns, however, is one that is generally overlooked – variable working hours or unpaid overtime. According to the Labour Force Survey, 43 per cent of all employees say that they work full time, and that in practice their working time varies from week to week and from day to day. Only 28 per cent of adults now work full time with fixed weekly and daily hours (Casey *et al.* 1997: 15). This is particularly common among managers and professional workers. A study by the civil service unions IPMS, FDA and NUCPS, conducted in 1994 among people on senior grades in the civil service, found that three-quarters of respondents worked in excess of three to ten hours' per week unpaid overtime (Pillinger 1997: 61). Delayering and staff reductions have been a common occurrence in recent years for these groups, and people react by putting in longer hours to cope with higher personal work loads. This trend is not necessarily positive for employers – stress and higher levels of illness are often a complementary result; another victim is equal opportunity policies, because job share policies are easily undermined when in practice everyone is expected to work into the evening (see chapter 5). The Local Government Management Board is becoming increasingly concerned about the 'long hours' culture and is looking for ways to keep working hours at least in recognisable proximity to the formally agreed contractual hours. Similarly negotiations have begun in the Department for Education and Employment to reduce excessively long working time (Pillinger 1997: 61).

The European Working Time Directive is one reason for the current attention to long hours; it is likely to be introduced into British law by October 1998 and at the time of writing is subject to consultation (Department of Trade and Industry 1998b). The directive, broadly, contains the following stipulations (Haggart ed 1997: 6–22):

- Maximum working week of forty-eight hours (on average, over a four month period).
- A daily rest period of eleven hours and a weekly continuous rest period of twenty-four hours.
- Night shifts (defined to cover the hours between midnight and 5.00 a.m.) should on average not exceed eight hours' duration.
- Night workers must be covered by the same health and safety protection as other workers.
- In the case of regular night work, the local health and safety executive needs to be informed.

There are a number of derogations and exemptions. Chief executive officers and their deputies regularly have to work in excess of forty-eight hours; the directive exempts people who have autonomous control over their working time. However, the unions representing people at this level are arguing that nevertheless they should be covered. Many people in residential social care, the health service, the fire service and customs and excise regularly work twelve hour night shifts; such working arrangements will be illegal under the directive unless they are agreed with the trade unions. Other occupational groups which have suggested that they may not be guaranteed the right to a rest period of eleven hours are environmental health officers, housing wardens, officers servicing committees in local government or workers in municipal theatres who work late but may have to be at work again in the morning during normal office hours. Unison, the largest trade union covering workers in health and local government, has already concluded agreements in some areas of the health service leading to the introduction of eight hour night shifts with eleven hour rest periods in one NHS trust. The new arrangement is reported to have reduced stress levels, improved the ability of employees to plan their social lives and assisted management to improve staff planning (Unison 1997). Another group regularly working in excess of forty-eight hours per week is teachers, although annualised hours schemes, with longer holiday periods, are intended to compensate for this. The directive raises complex issues of work organisation, particularly in terms of arranging shift patterns. It is likely to take a couple of years after the introduction of the new legislation to work out the implications, through negotiations and case law. It is already clear that the issue of working time will be a key item on the bargaining agenda of public service trade unions during the next few years (Pillinger 1997: 62).

Tele- and home working

Tele- and home working are clearly not directly related to working time flexibility. Nevertheless they share many common features by giving employees more choice over the place, and often the time, of their work. It also, like flexi-time for example, helps employees to cut out unproductive travelling time. Tele- and home-based working has been widely discussed for a number of years. Common to the discussion are predictions that in the very near future a large proportion of the work force will work under such distance arrangements, and that in any case the practice will see explosive growth. For just as many years the actual evidence on the ground has been thin. Tele-working in particular remains unused by the vast majority of employers, and few employers have made recent attempts to build up tele-working (table 6.7). However, there are a number of innovative examples such as the one of Surrey County Council, where tele-centres have been introduced as a means of reducing commuting times (White 1997).

Home-based work, whether it is permanent or involves the possibility of choosing to work at home occasionally, is a little more common (table 6.8). Central government organisations in particular have started to use it, in recognition of the fact that it is often more productive for professional employees to have some quiet time out of the office to carry out certain

Table 6.7 Tele-working: proportion of employees doing tele-work and organisations increasing the level of tele-working (% of organisations)

	Health	Higher education	Local government	Central government	Other UK employers
Proportion	*(n = 133)*	*(n = 90)*	*(n = 114)*	*(n = 22)*	*(n = 930)*
Up to 5%	4	12	14	0	10
Not used	94	88	86	100	88
Increased	1	9	7	0	6

Source: Cranet Survey 1995 (see note 2).

Table 6.8 Home based working: proportion of home based employees and organisations increasing the level of home working (% of organisations)

Proportion	Health (n = 133)	Higher education (n = 90)	Local government (n = 114)	Central government (n = 22)	Other UK employers (n = 930)
Up to 5%	13	18	27	40	22
Not used	84	80	72	60	75
Increased	11	9	17	35	12

Source: Cranet Survey 1995 (see note 2).

duties. There are also a number of local authorities which have begun to explore the possibilities of less stringent rules about presence in the office. The policy approaches are not narrowly concerned with tele- or home working, but more broadly with 'working away from the office'. One local authority, for example, defines everyone as a 'home worker' who spends at least 50 per cent of their working time out of the office (Hegewisch forthcoming). This might include as broad a range of occupations as highway wardens, peripatetic music teachers or finance officers travelling between schools. Whatever the reason for not being office based, similar issues are raised in relation to communication, insurance and the use of office equipment, and links with support staff who remain office based. The need to find cost effective and comprehensive ways of dealing with personal liability insurance and health and safety is another requirement for an effective home-based work policy, and one where solutions are not always easy or straightforward. However, there are a growing number of employers piloting such working space flexibility, and hence there is a growing body of practical experience newcomers can draw upon.

Functional flexibility

Functional flexibility implies that employees are able, through their knowledge, skills and working arrangements, to respond flexibly and quickly to new challenges in the external environment. It is at the centre of discussions about the new organisation of work in the European Union (European Commission 1997) and is at the core of the flexible firm model. Functional flexibility, however, is less easy to define than working time or working place flexibility, and hence less easy to survey. It can be a redefining of jobs, the introduction of new work processes and team working, or the reskilling and training of employees to perform a wider range of tasks. One way of trying to estimate the extent of change towards functional flexibility is the widening, or narrowing, of job content. According to the 1995 Cranet Survey there has been a considerable move to widen job roles, in the public sector as elsewhere (table 6.9). The trend affects most groups, although it is less pronounced for manual workers. From the survey itself it is not clear whether

Table 6.9 The widening and narrowing of job content, by broad employee group
(% of organisations)

Employee group	Health (n = 133)	Higher education (n = 90)	Local government (n = 114)	Central government (n = 22)	Other UK employers (n = 930)
Management	68	54	52	45	57
Professional/ technical	46	50	41	27	48
Clerical	46	48	40	36	53
Manual	43	39	34	9	44

Source: Cranet Survey 1995 (see note 2).

this widening involves a genuine redesign of work or whether it is a recognition of the intensification of work that has taken place in many organisations as a result of delayering and cost cutting.

Looking at sector differences, it is not surprising that health service employers are most likely to say that managerial roles have widened, given the recent emphasis on more managerial approaches in the NHS. There are also a number of examples of the reorganisation of ancillary work, although, as Corby and Mathieson (1997: 63) indicate, ancillary workers are less than one in ten of the health service work force. Progress on change in key medical care areas is more mixed. Nine out of ten nurses in a recent Unison survey said that they were carrying out a broader range of tasks than a few years ago (Unison 1996, cited in Corby and Mathieson 1997), corresponding to the findings of the 1995 Cranet Survey. On the other hand there is little evidence of systematic attempts to redraw the lines between the responsibilities of doctors and nurses. The attempts that are being made to redefine the jobs of nurses as often include a narrowing of tasks and the introduction of new hierarchies between different levels of nursing as widening of job roles. Control of wage costs and recruitment difficulties appear to be the major motive for these initiatives.

The Cranet Survey also suggests considerable change among local authority employers. However, the recent case study survey of flexibility in local government by the LGMB discovered hardly any concrete examples of functional flexibility. Personnel managers were much more concerned with contract flexibility than work organisation (Hegewisch forthcoming).

Interestingly, according to the Cranet Survey, the trend towards wider job roles is least strong among central government employers – in fact, for each of the employee categories, a higher proportion of central government employers say that job content has narrowed rather than broadened. The setting up of agency status and development of agencies' own staffing structures, at least in some organisations, has resulted in tighter controls over jobs, which have reduced the scope for wider job roles.

Another attempt to estimate the level of functional flexibility has been made in the 1996 EPOC (Employee Participation in Organisational Change) survey by the European Foundation; this defines functional flexibility broadly as team delegation over decisions concerning teams' work (European Foundation 1997). Such a definition of functional flexibility has its origins in the move towards quality circles and new team-based work organisation in manufacturing, particularly in the car industry. Nevertheless, an analysis of the public sector sample from this survey shows that public service organisations are just as likely as private sector employers to have delegated work to teams. This is particularly so in education and health and social welfare, but much less developed in public administration (Hegewisch *et al.* 1998). This is not surprising, considering the professional traditions in many of these services. Much of social welfare work, for example, involves team approaches; but it is an important reminder that much professional work in the public sector by its very nature means that employees have to work independently across a broad range of circumstances. However, more common than team work is individual delegation of responsibilities to employees. The tradition of individual professional autonomy over aspects of work can be a major barrier to the introduction of greater team work, particularly across professional borders. This resistance has been criticised by the Audit Commission (1997, cited in White 1997: 52).

Implications for management

The increasing diversity of working patterns presents clear challenges to human resource management. Standardised or informal patterns of communication, training, career development and assessment are no longer adequate and are likely to miss, if not alienate, workers on flexible employment contracts.

One of the key challenges is communication. When everyone is in the office broadly at the same time, it is likely that they can relatively easily update themselves on new developments and keep their colleagues informed about progress in their own work. When some people work part time or work outside the office for part of the time, communication, between managers and employees and between colleagues, has to become much more organised and explicit. This requires additional time and effort from both manager and employees, ranging from having to make additional efforts to ensure that team meetings can be attended by everyone to taking time to briefing employees about developments since they were last in the office.

Training is traditionally offered on a full-time basis. Policies which focus on providing equal access for part timers to training opportunities are unlikely to be adequate, given that most training courses are provided on a full-time basis and hence are less accessible to people who work part time because of domestic commitments. Unless there are a significant number of part time workers, it may not be easy to offer it on a part time basis. However, over time many organisations have managed to come up with new solutions in this area. A more serious current problem is the implications for the stock of skills of the work force of the move towards non-permanent contracts. There is growing concern over skill shortages and a decline in training as a result of the increase in temporary work. Employers are traditionally the major training provider once people leave formal education. Short term contracts clearly provide a disincentive for employers to invest in training the benefits of which they may not be able to reap. They can also lead to a reduction in the provision of initial vocational training. The BBC, for example, after increasing the share of external providers in its production department, is now coming up against skill shortages (Corfield Wright 1997). In some skill areas, such as clerical work, temporary agencies have started to fill some of the gap by offering training free of charge. However, the training tends to be concerned with basic skills, such as the introduction of new word processing packages. It does not provide a solution in more professional work areas.

Even where employers have made considerable efforts to deal with the formal issues raised by the diversity in working patterns there often remains an implicit problem with attitudes and the assessment of those who do not work the 'standard' working patterns. This is particularly so in relation to part time and home workers, who can suffer from attitudes which judge lack of presence in the office as lower commitment or who may find it harder to build up the range of experience required for consideration for promotion. While, at least in the public sector, it is now frowned upon to say that part time workers are less motivated, clearly in practice the assumption continues to be present. Given the growing importance of individual performance assessment in the public services, not least because of the introduction of performance-related pay (see chapter 4), it has become doubly important to try and openly address such prejudices and increase the awareness of managers doing the assessment.

Then there is the issue of attitudes and motivation. In relation to people on longer fixed term contracts, particularly in research and policy development, it is often just when the end of the contract is in sight, and hence attention focuses on finding a new job, that the employee, as a result of the work done so far, will be able to contribute most to the organisation. The uncertainty and lack of motivation at that stage can reduce the benefit to the employer. Temporary employees often face resentment from permanent employees, not least because permanent employees have to spend time to induct new staff. But temporary employees can also be seen as a symbol of cuts and employment reduction in the organisation and hence may be the victims of general dissatisfaction in the workplace. Employee attitude surveys offer one means of assessing the impact of high levels of temporary work on satisfaction at work, among both permanent and temporary employees.

The growing diversity of working and contractual patterns challenges tradition ways of managing and motivating staff in most areas of human resource management. Particularly where new working arrangements are introduced for the first time the ground needs to be prepared carefully with existing employees and their union representatives. Overall the shift towards new working patterns requires a more explicit style of management which takes account of the diversity of requirements within the work force and includes means of monitoring whether the intended results of effectiveness and efficiency are being achieved in practice.

Conclusion

The preceding review of employment practices demonstrates the variety of employment contracts and working time arrangements in public services. Compared with the private sector, public service organisations are more likely to have introduced contract flexibility, to employ more part time workers, to be more proactive in policies such as job sharing and are more likely to have annualised hours schemes. Even in fields such as home-based working, public services are ahead of the private sector in piloting new schemes. Public organisations have not only been at the forefront of pressure for cost-led flexibility but have been more ready to respond to employee-led pressure for greater control over working time and location. Evidence on functional flexibility, however, is less clear, perhaps an indication that concern with external flexibility tends to detract from internal functional flexibility.

While the prescriptive value of the 'flexible firm' model for the public sector, and indeed employment in general, has been strongly criticised, direct and indirect pressure from government through policy and financial targets appears to have made a contribution to the changing nature of the work force. The 1997 change of government is likely to remove or at least reduce some of the external constraints on permanent employment such as compulsory competitive tendering and annual purchaser–provider contracts in the health service. Legislative changes are also likely to limit the scope for basic cost savings from the use of part time and temporary contracts. This includes the introduction of the EU Working Time Directive, of minimum paid leave for all employees and of the national hourly minimum wage in 1999. Nevertheless, in so far as budget cuts and more general uncertainty over financial resources have been a driver towards non-permanent contracts, it is unlikely that the change in government will lead to a sudden reduction in levels of non-permanent employment.

It is equally likely that the push for employee-centred flexibility will continue. Public services have gone a considerable way towards responding to demands for more flexible working patterns. This ability to accommodate greater diversity in employment patterns is likely to present an advantage to public service employers in attracting and retaining good staff, and in realising further improvements in service quality and delivery. However, the realisation of such advantages depends on the adjustment of management practices, particularly in the areas of communication, training and performance management.

Finally, there is the broader issue of the changing nature of work. The move to less secure and less homogeneous working patterns affects public sector organisations not only as employers but also as providers of services. The move towards greater contract flexibility in particular involves a redrawing of the line of responsibility between the employer, the individual and the state (Brewster *et al.* 1997), and shifts this responsibility from the organisation to the state and the individual. The closer tailoring of labour costs to changes in demand implies that the costs of the economic downturn, when employment levels are released, now have to be carried either by individual workers or, through benefits, by the state. Similar arguments apply to training. Thus, while contract flexibility may reduce the direct wage costs of public services, at the same time it contributes to a general increase in the demand for public services, and hence requires increased expenditure, because public organisations have to provide support for citizens when they are between jobs. Working practices have changed, but new social institutions – in terms of insurance, training and education, financial services and mortgages, for example have been slow to evolve to deal with the greater contractual flexibility. This flexibility paradox is likely to be one of the great social policy challenges of the new century.

Notes

1 The Labour Force Survey is conducted quarterly on behalf of the government among 80,000 UK households; respondents are asked questions about their employment status, hours of work and place of employment. It thus reflects the point of view of employees, not the employer. The Labour Force Survey is the main statistical basis in the UK for estimating the extent of different contractual forms of employment. Basic results and more in-depth analysis are regularly published in *Labour Market Trends*. Each EU member state is committed to carry out a Labour Force Survey on at least an annual basis.
2 The Cranet Survey of International Strategic Human Resource Management is conducted by a network of twenty-two European universities, co-ordinated by Cranfield School of Management; the survey started in 1990 and is now repeated at three to four yearly intervals. Data are collected by means of a postal questionnaire which is sent to personnel managers in private and public sector organisations with at least 200 employees. In 1995 the survey was conducted in twelve countries. In the UK 1,289 organisations responded, including 133 trusts/hospitals, 114 local authorities, ninety universities and higher education institutions, and twenty-two central government organisations. Primary and secondary education is included under local government.

References

Atkinson, J. (1984) 'Manpower strategies for flexible organisations', *Personnel Management*, August: 32–5.
Atkinson, J. (1985) *Flexibility, Uncertainty and Manpower Management*, IMS Report 89, Brighton: Institute of Manpower Studies.
Atkinson, J. and Meager, N. (1986) *New Forms of Work Organisation*, IMS Report 121, Brighton: Institute of Manpower Studies.

Audit Commission (1997) *The Melody Lingers on: a Review of the Audits of People, Pay and Performance*, Abingdon: Audit Commission Publications.

Bielenski, H., Alaluf, M., Atkinson, J., Bellini, R., Castillo, J. J., Donati, P., Graverson, G., Huygen, F. and Wickham, J. (1992) *New Forms of Work and Activity*, survey conducted for the European Foundation, Dublin: European Foundation.

Brewster, C., Tregaskis, O., Hegewisch, A. and Mayne, L. (1996) 'Comparative research in human resource management: a review and an example', *International Journal for Human Resource Management* 7 (3): 550–604.

Brewster, C., Mayne, L., Tregaskis, O., Parsons, D., Atterbury, S., Soler, C., Aparicio Valverde, M., Picq, T., Weber, W., Kabst, R., Wåglund, M. and Lindström, K. (1997) 'Working time and flexibility in the EU: main report'; report prepared for the Commission of the EU (DGV), Cranfield: Cranfield University Publications.

Bruegel, I. and Hegewisch, A. (1994) 'Flexibilisation and part-time work in Europe' in P. Brown and R. Crompton (eds) *Economic Restructuring and Social Exclusion*, London: UCL Press.

Casey, B., Metcalf, H. and Millward, N. (1997) *Employers' Use of Flexible Labour*, London: Policy Studies Institute.

Confederation of British Industries (1988) *Workforce 2000: an Agenda for Action*, London: CBI.

Corby, S. (1995) 'Opportunity 2000 in the NHS: a missed opportunity for women', *Employee Relations* 17 (2): 23–37.

Corby, S. and Mathieson, H. (1997) 'The National Health Service and the limits to flexibility', *Public Policy and Administration*, special issue, 12 (4): 60–72.

Corfield Wright (1997) *Flexible Working Means Business*, London: Corfield Wright.

Department of Trade and Industry (1998a) *Fairness at Work*, Cm 3968, London: Stationery Office.

Department of Trade and Industry (1998b) *Measures to Implement the Provisions of the EC Directive on the Organisation of Working Time* (Working Time Directive), White Paper URN 98/645.

European Commission (1995) *Employment in Europe*, Luxembourg: Office for Official Publications of the EU.

European Commission (1997) *Partnership for a New Organisation of Work*, Green Paper, Communication (97) 128.

European Foundation for the Improvement of Living and Working Conditions (1997) *New Forms of Work Organisation: can Europe Realise its Potential?* Dublin: European Foundation.

Haggart, G. (1997) *Flexible Working Practices*, Kingston: Croner Publications.

Hakim, C. (1990) 'Core and periphery workers in employers' workforce strategies: evidence from the 1987 ELUS survey', *Work, Employment, Society* 4 (2): 157–88.

Hegewisch, A. (forthcoming) *Flexible Working Patterns in Local Government*, report for the Local Government Management Board, London: LGMB.

Hegewisch, A. and Mayne, L. (1994) 'Equal opportunities policies in Europe' in C. Brewster and A. Hegewisch (eds) *Policy and Practice of European Human Resource Management: the Price Waterhouse Cranfield Survey*, London: Routledge.

Hegewisch, A., Kessler, I., Ommeren, J. V. and Brewster, C. (forthcoming) *Direct Participation in Social Public Services*, Dublin: European Foundation.

Horrell, S. and Rubery, J. (1989) 'Gender and working time: an analysis of employers working time policies', *Cambridge Journal of Economics* 15: 373–91.

Horton, S. (1996) 'The civil services' in D. Farnham and S. Horton (eds) *Managing People in the Public Services*, London: Macmillan.

Horton, S. (1997) 'Editorial: Employment flexibility in the public services: concepts, contexts and practices', *Public Policy and Administration*, special issue, 12 (4): 1–13.

Hunter, L. and McInnes, J. (1992) 'Employers and labour flexibility: the evidence from case studies', *Employment Gazette*, June: 307–15.

Hutchinson, S. and Brewster, C. (1994) *Flexibility at Work in Europe*, London: Institute of Personnel and Development.

Incomes Data Services (1995) *Temporary Workers*, IDS Study 579, London: IDS.

Kessler, I. (1990) 'Personnel management in local government: the new agenda', *Personnel Management*, November: 40–4.

Leighton, P. and Syrett, M. (1989) *New Patterns of Work: Putting Policy into Practice*, London: Pitman.

Marshall, A. (1989) 'The sequel of unemployment: the changing role of part-time and temporary work in Western Europe' in G. and J. Rogers (eds) *Precarious Work*, Geneva: ILO.

Mayne, L., Tregaskis, O. and Brewster, C. (1996) 'A comparative analysis of the link between flexibility and HRM strategy', *Employee Relations* 18 (3): 5–24.

McGregor, A. and Sproull, A. (1992) 'Employers and the flexible workforce', *Employment Gazette*, May: 225–34.

Mortimer, G. (1997) 'The future of work', *Local Government Management* 1 (20): 13.

Neathey, F. and Hurstfield, J. (1995) *Flexibility in Practice: Women's Employment and Pay in Retail and Finance*, London: Industrial Relations Services.

National Economic Development Office (1986) *Changing Work Patterns: a Report by the IMS*, London: HMSO.

Pillinger, J. (1997) *Working time in Europe: towards a European Social Dialogue in the Public Services*, report prepared for the European Federation of Public Sector Unions: Brussels: EFPSU.

Pollert, A. (1988) 'The "flexible firm": fixation or fact?' *Work, Employment, Society* 2 (3): 281–316.

Pollert, A. (ed.) (1991) *Farewell to Flexibility*, Oxford: Blackwell.

Rubery, J. (1989) 'Precarious forms of work in the UK' in G. and J. Rogers (eds) *Precarious Work*, Geneva, ILO.

Sly, F. and Stillwell, D. (1997) 'Temporary workers in Great Britain', *Labour Market Trends*, September: 347–54.

Trade Union Congress (1998) *The Time of our Lives: a TUC Report on Working Hours and Flexibility*, London: Trades Union Congress.

Unison (1997) *Working Time Directive: the A&E department Northwick Park and St Mark's Trust working with Unison*, London: Unison.

Walsh, T. (1990) 'Flexible labour utilisation in the private services', *Work, Employment and Society* 4 (4): 517–30.

White, G. (1997) Employment flexibilities in local government, *Public Policy and Administration*, special issue, 12 (4): 47–59.

7 Tendering and outsourcing

Working in the contract state?

Trevor Colling

Contracting has emerged as a powerful instrument in central government attempts to reform public management. Through the late 1970s, during the Conservative Party's years in opposition, leading intellectuals and 'think-tanks' on the right developed radical critiques of the state and of public services (Graham and Clarke 1986). Derived in varying degrees from the work of Hayek and Friedman, these cohered around a marked preference for market mechanisms over public administration. Benefits, it was said, lay in the superior distribution of information, the opportunity to 'choose' between providers, and the accountability ensured by customer sovereignty in competitive markets. A contrasting critique of the welfare state emerged in which service providers were captured easily by pressure groups and vested interests to the point where the needs of 'customers' were obscured. With such distorted incentives, public service administrators were incapable of efficient management and tended instead to build 'empires' which secured their interests and those of their employees.

Policies developed subsequently in government have ensured that market relations are enshrined throughout the public sector. This chapter focuses upon competitive tendering or market testing, that is, competition among a range of organisations for the opportunity to provide public services. Its impact on organisations and their work forces is assessed and it is argued that contracting provides a vivid illustration of 'centralised decentralisation' (Hoggett 1993). Focusing upon the performance and costs of specified services has required greater local decision-making over service levels and delivery mechanisms. A variety of contractual arrangements have emerged, with variation apparent within and between sectors. Local management preferences for direct provision by in-house employees have been marked and sustained. Yet reform has taken place within tightening parameters. Policy choices over competition and private sector provision have been shaped by direct ministerial sponsorship (the civil service) and extremely prescriptive regulations (local government). In the context of intensifying financial restrictions, the shift to contracting has been characterised by quests for cost savings. In contrast to the variety of organisational responses, these common pressures have fostered generally hardened approaches to the management of labour in contracted services.

Four substantive sections provide the structure for this argument. First, the detail of reform by contracting is discussed, establishing both common threads and their configuration in different service contexts. Given the central objective of reforming public service management, the next section discusses organisational and managerial responses to reform. Consequences for employees are examined in the third section, focusing upon manual groups, for which the largest body of evidence is available. Common trends are picked out relating to employee representation, pay and benefits, and the reorganisation of work. The penultimate section assesses contending pressures for reform and the prospects for the further development of contracting, including its further extension to white-collar and professional work.

Contracting and changing public management

Public authorities have always procured some goods and services from private sector providers but the series of reforms enacted through the 1980s marked a step change. Radical extension of contracting programmes transformed large public bureaucracies into networks of inter- and intra-organisational relationships. Changing the values and style of public management has been a central objective of reform.

The most comprehensive contracting regimes have been imposed upon local authorities. Competitive tendering, where private contractors are invited to compete with in-house work forces for the right to provide specified services, was established first for highways and building maintenance functions by the Local Government Planning and Land Act 1980. A second round of legislation, the Local Government Act 1988, covered practically all ancillary services (e.g. building cleaning, grounds maintenance, refuse collection) and required authorities to expose them to competition regularly, hence the acronym CCT (compulsory competitive tendering). Professional and technical services (including finance, legal and personnel functions) were incorporated into the local government legislation in 1992.

Local government's constitutional position required reform to be introduced through primary legislation, and its mandatory and prescriptive nature differentiated local government from other public service contracting environments. Tendering is governed by the legislation itself, statutory instruments (SIs) issued subsequently, and 'guidance' from ministers and bodies such as the Audit Commission. Interpretation of these rules is policed by District Auditors and by private companies competing for contracts, which are able to complain to the Secretary of State or embark upon independent legal action.

Reform in health and the civil service established similar principles but relied upon ministerial pressure and directives. In health, catering, cleaning and laundry services were opened to competition in 1983 and arrangements akin to these were instituted within the civil service (Whitbread and Hooper 1993). Other services were added on an *ad hoc* basis throughout the 1980s.

Civil service functions subject to tendering during this period included fisheries, aerial surveillance, messenger services and radio communications (Walsh 1995: 120). As in local government, tendering was extended formally to white collar and professional services. Under 'Competing for Quality' policies introduced in the civil service in 1991 the value of services subject to competition increased from £44 million to £1,072 million (Cabinet Office 1996: 4). Services involved included scientific, technical and research functions, facilities management and information technology support.

Contracting regimes in health and the civil service permitted a greater degree of local management discretion but its significance should not be overstated. For example, in contrast to local government, 'Competing for Quality' policies did not require contracting *per se*. Civil service managers were placed under a general duty to improve the efficiency of government but decisions were left to them as to which services were to be reviewed and how they were to be overhauled. Permissible options included closure of the service, privatisation (via trade sale), market testing (in which in-house providers compete against private sector bidders), strategic contracting-out (in which private sector companies compete but there is no in-house bid) or internal restructuring. But government preferences for maximising competition were reiterated through management procedures. Though ostensibly carrying equal weight, it was understood widely that these 'prior options' were arranged in order of preference. Those opting for internal restructuring had to be certain they could deliver savings on a similar scale to those promised by competition. Plans drawn up by departments were scrutinised initially by ministers, many of whom supported competition, and then by the Prime Minister's efficiency adviser. Where the options selected were at variance with evidence from other departments, managers could be 'put on challenge' or, in more informal parlance, 'beaten up by Peter Levene' (Richards *et al.* 1996: 26). Within departments and larger executive agencies, Market Testing Units were established, often in powerful finance divisions, to co-ordinate their own programmes and those of other bodies for which they had a sponsoring role (Massey 1994: 1).

Despite contextual differences, the attempt to introduce commercial models of management through contracting was common across all sectors. This has had three distinct elements: the insertion of new personnel from the private sector, the creation of entrepreneurial pressures, and encouragement to focus on customers rather than employees.

Straightforward transfer of functions to the private sector was seen widely as the most effective mechanism through which to reform management practice. Central government preferences on this point were expressed pointedly. For example, the Cabinet Office envisaged quite specific outcomes in its early commitment to extend contracting in the civil service. 'We believe the process of buying public services from private contractors is still only in its infancy. We propose to move the process decisively forward' (quoted in Richards *et al.* 1996: 20).

Contracting guidance and regulations have remained formally neutral, in the sense that no preference is stated in favour of either public or private sector provision. But many measures have had the effect of weighting tendering procedures towards private sector bids. For example, clause 7(7) of the Local Government Act 1988 stipulates that authorities shall not 'act in a manner having the effect, or intended or likely to have the effect, of restricting, distorting or preventing competition'. Duties to encourage private sector competition have been emphasised subsequently. Contract packaging may be 'anti-competitive', within the terms of the Act, where it is judged to have the effect of discouraging private sector interest. Authorities are now advised that good faith should be demonstrated by consulting potential bidders prior to constructing the contract (Steel and Liddle 1996: 6).

Irrespective of whether work is awarded internally or externally, management restructuring required by tendering creates potentially entrepreneurial pressures within public organisations. Services managed through hierarchical structures are replaced by market relations requiring boundaries between purchasers and providers. In-house service providers are encouraged to operate as if they were independent contractors, maintaining their own accounts, generating a return on their assets, and providing or purchasing their own support services (finance, payroll, personnel, etc.).

Finally, at the heart of the tendering regulations lies an attempt to reorder public management priorities away from employment and the work force, towards customers and service users. Those responsible for the early development of contracting programmes were unambiguous about their objectives. 'The root cause of rotten local services lies in the grip which local government unions have over those services in many parts of the country . . . Our competitive tendering provisions will smash that grip once and for all' (Nicholas Ridley, quoted in Painter 1991: 193). Provisions prevent authorities taking account of 'non-commercial' matters, including employment policy. Attempts to ensure consistent employment rights and standards across organisations (and through the course of transfers) have been thus discouraged and undermined.

It is necessary to mention at this point potential counter-pressures to this project emanating from the Transfer of Undertakings (Protection of Employment) Regulations 1981, commonly referred to as TUPE. These implement the European Acquired Rights Directive (ARD) 1977 and have the effect of protecting the terms and conditions of employment (including rights to consultation and representation by a trade union) of staff transferring from one employer to another. Downplayed for much of the 1980s, particularly by government ministers, case law has increasingly emphasised that such protection is available to public sector employees affected by contracting. TUPE's impact has been marginal to date, however, partly because of the complexity of the judgements involved and partly because of loopholes in the regulations. In the absence of clear guidelines, TUPE was applied in only a minority of cases during the first round of CCT

(Colling 1995a; Escott and Whitfield 1995: Hardy *et al.* 1997). Even where TUPE applies, employers may introduce changes to collective agreements following transfer. Though most civil service transfers have been subject to TUPE, at least a third of those staff affected have reported changes in their terms and conditions of employment following market testing (Cabinet Office 1996: 51). Though important symbolically and in some specific cases, TUPE has not altered to date the course or dynamics of reform by contracting.

Management and organisational change

Organisational responses have been complex, with variation apparent between services and over time. General trends can be characterised as increased resignation, diverse patterns of restructuring and continuing resistance to key principles.

Resignation

Initial management opposition to contracting has been significant across all sectors. Anticipation of resistance in the NHS led the Department of Health and Social Security to deny initially that it planned to introduce contracting for ancillary services. When the circular appeared the following year, ministers' expectations were met in full.

> A blind prejudice against the health unions and a somewhat ill-defined desire to increase managerial efficiency are the motivating forces behind this piece of lunacy. At a time when the health services are already stretched to the limit, it is unreasonable to expect health managers to receive with equanimity the gross burden which this circular confers.
>
> (*Health and Social Services Journal*, quoted in Ascher 1987: 30)

The introduction of contracting has frequently been grudging, to say the least. Health authorities were permitted at first to determine their own timetables provided these were completed by September 1986. Yet one-third of hospitals had still to tender any of their catering, laundry or domestic services nine years after this deadline (Butler 1997; Milne 1997). Similarly, in the first eighteen months of 'Competing for Quality', only four of twenty-one civil service departments had completed their market-testing programmes and the exercises which did take place involved relatively small groups of staff. When measured by value, 77 per cent of services in total were tested to schedule, but this slipped to 57 per cent when measured by number of employees (Hassell 1994: 41).

As contracting programmes have taken hold, however, reservations have turned to resignation. Acceptance of the inevitable explains the change to some degree, particularly in local government, where compulsion left few doubts about central government intentions. But contracting has not been developed in a vacuum and other pressures have also been at play. Budgetary restrictions, discussed in chapter 2, have coincided with increases in the level and diversity of demand for public services. Squaring such circles has persuaded many managers to focus scarce resources on 'core' services. Further impetus has been provided by reformed accounting practices following marketisation. Trusts developed within the internal market for health services, for example, are required to behave as commercial entities, submitting business plans and accounts, paying capital charges to the Exchequer and making a return on their assets. New financial management systems developed subsequently have decentralised budgets within hospitals and identified the costs of support and technical functions. Quests for internal savings have intensified as a result, and a broader range of services have become subject to market testing and contracting out (Bach 1992: 3). Financial considerations and the need for flexibility are among the most common reasons offered by NHS managers for contracting out (Decker 1995).

Restructuring

Organisations and management structures have been transformed by contracting. In contrast to the singular models of contractual arrangements envisaged initially, a variety of relations have emerged across and within sectors (Colling 1993, 1995b).

Policy advisers responsible for shaping contracting initiatives tended to assume a simple binary divide between hierarchy and contract. Hierarchical relations were inevitably rendered self-serving and inefficient in the absence of competition. For this reason 'the administrative model ... should give way to the contract model' (Mather 1991: 15). Characteristics of this model include clear division between clients and contractors, with service provision regulated by reference to a legally enforceable contract. Contracts should specify in detail the nature and level of services required and provide remedial mechanisms for poor performance, culminating in financial penalties (Mather 1991: 15).

Such a 'classical' contract relationship is conjured through the regulations governing CCT in local government. Divisions between client and contractor functions tended to be stark, particularly in the early days. Contracts and specifications assumed biblical importance in that they were consulted frequently, were generously proportioned, and they aspired to answer any question that might possibly arise about the subject at hand. One example, discussed by Vincent-Jones (1994: 222), evokes the possible extent of this formality.

The building cleaning contract comprises twenty-nine sections (sixty-two pages) and eight schedules including provision for termination, rectification, variation, performance bonds and guarantees, British

Standards, payment deductions, random sampling, inspections and computer monitoring. The building cleaning specification [comprises] twenty sections and fifty-four pages, with seventeen appendices (seventy-two pages) and a Schedule of Tasks and Frequencies (approximately ninety pages). Eight surface categories are distinguished: vinyl/linoleum, rubber, carpet, woodblock, terrazzo/marble/ceramic, quarry tile, stone and asphalt, with further differentiation of fittings such as venetian blinds, soft and hard furniture, carpets, and light attachments. Separate cleaning tasks (washing, scrubbing, polishing, dusting, vacuuming, mopping, sealing, shampooing) are specified for each in exhaustive detail.

Such contract-driven arrangements do not meet the needs of many public organisations. The limited supply of some specialist services, coupled with changing political and budgetary pressures, makes it difficult to enshrine purchasing commitments in contracts. It is not always easy to monitor contract performance. Deducing whether household refuse has been collected is relatively straightforward but establishing that the refuse truck really needed a new clutch, and that one has been fitted, are rather more complex tasks. As Deakin notes (1994: 7), 'the purchaser is often dependent on the contractor for knowledge of what has been done or even . . . what should be done'.

These differing circumstances require contractual arrangements with greater sensitivity to variations in the distribution of knowledge and trust between purchasers and providers. In addition to the 'classical' model, three other kinds of contractual relationship have been observed in public sector contexts (Bennett and Ferlie 1996).

Relational contracting recognises that reliance upon formal rights provides scant protection unless reinforced by social relations based on trust and obligation. Regulated contracts are those in which elements are subject to third party control or influence. These are particularly relevant in public sector organisations, which are subject to intervention by government (ministerial/political pressure), the law (statutory regulation of breadth and quality of services) and a peculiarly high concentration of professional bodies (e.g. the General Medical Council). Finally, pseudo-contracts retain extant professional and administrative hierarchies but relabel them in market terms. Though few sectors are as immune to competitive pressure as this model may suggest, it describes aptly organisations retaining strong corporate controls on their contractors.

Resistance

Though public service managers may have been persuaded of the value of contracting in some circumstances, the notion that in-house provision is innately inferior continues to prove unconvincing. Private sector involvement in providing contracted services has developed slowly overall and hardly at all in some areas.

Up to 1986 contractors won only 18 per cent by value of contracts awarded in the NHS (Whitbread and Hooper 1993: 72). Growing pressure on trusts in the wake of the NHS reforms has produced some private sector gains but nearly 80 per cent of 'hotel' services are still delivered by directly employed staff. Kelliher's sample of 129 large NHS catering contracts were all retained in-house (1995).

Despite pressure to privatise or contract out civil service functions, nearly half the contracts awarded in the first tranche of market testing went to in-house teams. Of the 389 market tests completed, 147 were awarded in house after competition, thirteen were withdrawn from testing to make changes internally, and six were restructured without any competition. Of the remainder, 113 were outsourced with no competition and a further eighty-two were awarded externally after a tendering procedure (Massey 1994: 3).

In local government, the strictest contracting regime, direct service organisations have retained nearly three-quarters (72 per cent) of contracts when measured by value (*Municipal Journal*, 6 March 1998, p. 27). Being the most comprehensive, these figures also reveal marked geographical differences in private sector market penetration. Contractors remain confined largely to their strongholds in London, the south and south-east and nearly 100 authorities have yet to award a contract to the private sector (ibid.).

Often born initially from a philosophical preference that public services should be planned and delivered by public organisations, motives for retaining direct provision may now be pragmatic, driven by financial and operational concerns. In uncertain policy environments, contracting enables public authorities to retain cost flexibility within a regulatory framework which nevertheless imposes performance disciplines on the contractor. Though often greatest where private contractors are employed (Walsh and Davis 1993: Whitbread and Hooper 1993) cost reductions from in-house providers come with additional benefits (Painter 1991). The ambiguous legal status of contracts between public bodies (e.g. between a local authority and its direct service organisation) permits purchasers to vary annual budgets for their in-house providers, and disregard prices agreed at the time of the contract, without fear of legal challenge. Indeed, services which are income generating can be required to contribute profits to broader organisational budgets (Nichols and Taylor 1995). Such is the context in which employee relations matters are considered, and it is to these that we now turn.

Contracting and employee relations

Such common pressures have ensured that diverging patterns of contractual relationships have been accompanied by similar trends in the management of labour (Colling 1993, 1995a). Though variations are apparent, public service managers have seized market forces eagerly and used them as 'a convenient method for justifying the dissolution of existing relationships' (Bennett and Ferlie 1996: 62). Where consistent employment standards have been retained at all, they have been redefined and offered on management's terms. The following sections highlight common developments focusing on manual workers, the group with the longest experience of contracting to date.

Recognition and representation

Relations between managers and public sector unions have been placed on a substantially different footing. Though unions have retained a role greater than envisaged initially, decentralisation and the disaggregation of membership interests have mounted substantial challenges to union organisation and weakened unions' capacity to defend their members' interests.

Derecognition has not been widespread, principally because contracts have been awarded to non-union firms in only a small minority of cases. Even where transfers to the private sector have occurred, contractors acknowledging the emerging importance of TUPE have become tolerant of union recognition. Companies like Capita, Mitie, Serco and Onyx UK now feature regularly in surveys of new recognition deals (LRD 1997: 5). But procedural agreements have tended to be narrower and more qualified than those still extant in the public sector (Colling 1997; Foster and Taylor 1994). Where negotiating rights are ceded at all (as opposed to the right to represent members), bargaining units may be defined restrictively and the negotiating structures and terms of reference are left open to local discretion.

Public sector managements have also taken the opportunity to reconstruct their collective employment relations. Confining trade union influence to local operational matters has been a key consequence of reform and sometimes an explicit objective. National agreements remain important, particularly in health and local government, but they have been implemented with increasing selectivity and eventually revised. Changes have also been made to procedures at organisational levels. Comprehensive local redundancy agreements in local government and the NHS were early casualties and grievance and disciplinary procedures have been foreshortened, leaving the final and appeal stages to contract managers rather than the senior echelons of the host organisation.

Trade union organisation has been disorientated along two key axes. First, centralised union structures, developed by public sector unions to resource predominantly national bargaining, have been strained by the radical devolution of management activity. Demand at local level for bargaining expertise, legal advice and background information has increased substantially. Second, union memberships and their interests have been fragmented horizontally. By defining certain services separately and exposing them to varying operational and competitive pressures, contracting potentially resurrects divisions within what have always been extremely diverse work forces. Where members transfer to employers spread over the private sector, the potential for sectionalism is increased further.

These pressures have been configured differently by sector and by union. Decentralising pressures emanating from the relatively large and high profile contracts in the civil service have been mild when compared with the arrangements thrown up by over 400 local government employers. On the other hand, unions have responded from different starting points. Those with predominantly private sector memberships have faced the comparatively simple task of developing further already devolved structures. They have also been prepared (organisationally and ideologically) to develop relations with private sector contractors from a relatively early stage. Unions which have traditionally served exclusively public sector work forces have had to restructure their organisations and their *modus operandi* to a greater degree. In 1997 the newly merged Public Services, Tax and Commerce Union (PTC, since merged again) rationalised senior national structures, increased the corps of negotiating officers and expanded the research department (IRS 1997a: 13).

Remuneration and benefits

Analysis of New Earnings Survey data suggests real earnings growth for most manual groups covered by contracting (Elliott and Duffus 1996: 59). Local government groups appear to have done well, registering increased earnings of between 1.1 per cent and 5.3 per cent each year between 1985 and 1992. That most public sector contractors have continued to comply with national agreements and to implement agreed pay increases explains this to some degree. But careful scrutiny highlights important variations and changes in pay composition and differentials.

First, significant differences between public and private sector providers are apparent in the NES data. Private sector earnings growth lagged behind that of most public sector comparators for the latter half of the 1980s and collapsed altogether in the recessionary early 1990s (Elliott and Duffus 1996: 59). Second, there is variation between sectors. Hospital porters, cooks, cleaners and kitchen helpers received real pay cuts between 1980 and 1985. Earnings growth thereafter was modest and significantly below even private sector groups until the early 1990s. Third, aggregate data underestimate the extent of change because they offer few indications of adjustments required in the pay–effort bargain to attain the earnings levels recorded. Earnings growth is attributable in some cases to the buying out or consolidation of additional payments in the context of job cuts and dramatically increased productivity (James 1998: 5). Finally, the data confine analysis to those in full-time employment and consequently underestimate the growth in earnings inequality. In services characterised by part time employment, changes in hours and reduced access to bonus and premium payments has had significant ramifications for women, who comprise the majority within such work forces (Escott and Whitfield 1995). Up to 90 per cent experienced cuts in pay following contracting, and the cuts have been proportionally greater (between 16 per cent and 25 per cent) than cuts affecting male employees (Dickens 1997: 178; Escott and Whitfield 1995). Consequent increases in the number and success rates of equal value cases in manual areas are an effective index of the extent to which payment systems have been disordered by contracting and competition.

Reorganisation and work loads

Closer attention to employment costs and the allocation of work has been the principal consequence of contracting. In contrast to much of the post-war period, where public policy required employment maximisation, contracting requires detailed scrutiny of employment levels, productivity and job design.

Employment levels

Figure 7.1 illustrates employment trends for selected services in local government and the civil service. To draw the focus down to those areas most affected by contracting, services including the armed forces, education, social services and the police have been excluded. In both cases, slight increases in employment coinciding with the introduction of contracting have been recouped subsequently in significant job cuts. Downward trends in civil service employment are particularly marked in the period following the introduction of 'Competing for Quality' in 1992.

These trends are suggestive only and need to be interpreted with care. It should be borne in mind that they include the effects of other employment changes, both positive and negative, and that some employment reductions are more properly regarded as employment transfers (because proportions of work groups lost to public bodies will be re-employed by the private sector).

But the contribution to work force reductions made by contracting should not be understimated. Net reductions in local government have been attributable almost entirely to contracting. Between 1988 and 1993 the work force was reduced by 29,207 (3.7 per cent), with CCT responsible for 99.6 per

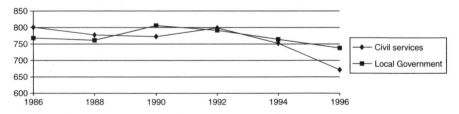

Figure 7.1 Employment trends in local government and the civil service 1986–96.
Source: Office of National Statistics (1997)

cent of the trend (LGMB 1993: 7–8). Moreover, real cuts in employment following transfer have been common among private and public sector contractors. Over half of all local government direct service organisations (DSOs) have reduced employment to some degree (Walsh and Davis 1993) and case study evidence highlights reductions of up to two-thirds in some instances (McIntosh and Broderick 1996; Escott and Whitfield 1995).

Productivity

Work force reductions have been accompanied by attempts to increase productivity. A variety of methods have emerged according to differences in the type of service, their degree of mechanisation and the composition of the work force. Innovative forms of work design have been rare, however. Increased monitoring or supervision of effort levels, job role expansion and work intensification have been more common elements.

Organisational targets set by contracts and internal performance reviews have prompted closer controls over employee discretion and monitoring and surveillance has increased. Reductions in the number of middle managers have been accompanied by role expansion for team leaders, who have taken primary responsibility for quality assurance and for changing working methods. Surveillance within contracting organisations has been replicated by client/purchasing managers. In local government, the proportion of work inspected formally increased in every service subject to CCT, more than doubling in some instances (Walsh and Davis 1993: 99).

Changed working methods have led to adjustments in the skill requirements for a wide range of manual jobs. Though leading potentially to multi-skilling or up-skilling, change has more usually been associated with the simple expansion of job roles. Building functions, for example, have sought often to extend the stock of skills held by the remaining employees but new skill acquisition has been partial only. Plumbers fitting new bathroom suites have been asked to plaster and tile the surrounding area, for example. Only rarely have employees been retrained to industry standard in an entirely new trade. Indeed, formal training and apprenticeships have been early casualties in many skilled areas affected by contracting (Walker 1993: 69).

Finally, increasing the pace at which work tasks are performed and reducing the opportunities for informal breaks have been common outcomes of changed working practices. Union surveys of manual staff affected by contracting have highlighted as the most common sources of stress not having enough time for work tasks; lack of control over the scheduling of work; and decreasing opportunities for breaks in the working day (McAnea 1996). Part time staff (usually women) appear to be particularly vulnerable. Home helps and school meal workers were found to be doing an average of two hours a week unpaid overtime in order to maintain service levels (McAnea 1996). But male employees working full time have not been immune.

McIntosh and Broderick detail changes in a refuse collection service where the average number of houses on an urban route increased nearly three-fold, from 850 to 2,219. Improved technical capacity, including the use of 'wheelie bins' and larger trucks, delivered some performance improvements but loaders were expected to service 555 properties a day, an increase of 96 per cent on previous levels (1996: 419).

Flexibility

Quests for economies of scale and internal efficiency savings have begun to produce multi-functional contractors and some limited quests for functional flexibility. Larger private contractors now offer a range of services rather than specialising in one area. Public sector contractors have tended to develop in similar fashion. 'Super-DSOs', which combine a number of services subject to tendering, have become common in local government and the bundling of ancillary functions into single contracts for 'hotel services' has had a similar affect in the NHS. Employees in these contexts are required to move between specified services as contract circumstances demand.

Working hours have been reconfigured, particularly in those areas with direct customer interfaces (leisure services, for example) or where seasonal variations are strong (grounds maintenance) (Walsh and Davis 1993). Weekly, monthly or even annualised hours agreements have been developed, offering managers greater control over the timing of work and overtime and un-social hours payments.

Part time working, which has long been an integral feature of public service employment, has increased further but the impact of contracting has been complex. Pressure to reduce support service overheads has contributed to increases in part time working for non-manual staff. Among manual staff, however, part time employees have taken the brunt of adjustments in employ-ment and their numbers have actually declined. In four local government services analysed by Escott and Whitfield (1995) part time employment fell by 22 per cent, double the decline among full time staff and more than the 15 per cent reduction for the sector as a whole (White 1997: 50).

Strong trends towards temporary and fixed term working are attributable partly to the growth of contracting. Over half of all staff on fixed term contracts work in public administration, education and health (IRS 1997b: 4) and one in eight local government workers is now on a temporary contract (*Municipal Journal*, 23 January 1998, p. 7). Temporary contracts have become particularly common in contracted services characterised by women's employment (Escott and Whitfield 1995). The explanation appears to lie in the opportunity to reduce work forces radically without recourse to cumber-some redundancy and/or TUPE procedures. Contracting occasioned an 8 per cent increase in the number of NHS catering units employing tem-porary staff and a slight increase in the number of staff employed but they were the first to be laid off following tendering procedures (Kelliher 1995).

Future prospects

Contracting practice is developing at a rapid rate and the key trends reported thus far are bound to be affected. Three sets of pressures will be influential in the near future. White-collar contracting will become increasingly important and will have a different set of dynamics from those discussed here (Walsh 1995). Reform of the expectations and regulations governing public sector contracts and the rights of employees under them also seem likely following the election of a Labour government in 1997.

White-collar contracting

Regulations and guidance covering white-collar contracting differ in important respects from those for manual work. Cost savings are not expected to the same degree, the focus on quality is commensurably greater, and tendering and contract procedures are more sophisticated. In local government, for example, a proportion of professional services can be protected from competition; *de minimis* levels exempt further small functions where tendering costs outweigh potential savings; and credits are permitted for work already contracted out (Shaw *et al.* 1996; Steel and Liddle 1996; Watt 1996).

The implications for employees and their management may be distinct for these and other reasons. Professional and technical staff transferring to the private sector may realistically expect improved pay and career prospects (Kessler and Coyle-Shapiro 1997). Indeed, it is claimed often that strategic contracting out has been driven by the desire to improve pay levels for staff and reduce labour turnover (Oughton 1994). As a minimum, TUPE is more likely to be applied in tendering exercises affecting white-collar functions.

Yet the differences are easily overstated. Budgetary constraints within commissioning organisations remain intense and savings from white-collar functions will be as welcome as those from other sources. Moreover, white-collar work in the public services includes many functions which bear few of the hallmarks of professional power and expertise associated with the stereotype. In data processing and financial services, for example, there is evidence of rationalisation already where individual contracts have been merged and sourced from regional centres. Since winning a major contract with the Inland Revenue, Electronic Data Systems has merged thirteen data centres into three (Olins 1997: 24). Though still emerging, patterns of workplace restructuring appear to be following familiar trends even if the scale and pace of change are relatively muted. Between 1992 and 1995 market testing reduced the number of civil servants by 20,200 (40 per cent of all job reductions during the period) and resulted in the internal transfer of a further 14,500 (GSS 1996: 8; Cabinet Office 1996: 46). More than half (52 per cent) of civil servants working in in-house teams reported that their job had worsened following market testing and the figure was higher still (63 per cent) among staff transferred to the private sector (Cabinet Office

1996: 47). Among both in-house and transferred staff the most common causes of declining job satisfaction were increased work loads, inadequate resources, and increasing stress and insecurity.

Reform of contracting practice

Commitments to reform contracting practice were established quickly after the election of the Labour government. A new regime based on achieving 'best value' is to replace CCT in local government (DETR 1998) and parallel developments are likely in other services. Reviews of current market testing policies are being conducted by the NHS Executive and the Cabinet Office is revising its guidance to civil service departments in line with twelve new guiding principles (Butler 1997; Cabinet Office 1997).

Definitions of 'best value' remain unclear at the time of writing. Detailed guidelines for local government are to be drawn up following studies in thirty-six pilot areas and further consultation. Processes and procedures seem set to converge around a revised model of 'prior options' as practised in the civil service. 'Best value' reviews will make use of the 'four Cs': they will challenge the need for a particular service; compare its performance, taking account of the views of service users and providers; consult local taxpayers, service users and the wider business community in setting performance targets; and compete in the sense of demonstrating that the preferred means of delivering services is the most effective available (Calpin 1998: 29). Competition will continue as 'an important management tool' but will not in itself demonstrate best value. Value for money criteria will be supplemented by benchmarked measures of effectiveness and service quality.

To the extent that reform along these lines relaxes the more prescriptive regimes, it brings the potential for a greater range of processes and outcomes. But competition and contracting will remain central features of public service management. Pending reform, further rounds of manual and white-collar tendering will proceed in England and Wales, and five authorities have been excluded from the moratorium on CCT in Scotland (*Municipal Journal*, 20 February 1998, p. 9). Tendering exercises here are bound to provide an influential legacy for the first wave of 'best value' arrangements. In the longer term, the theme of encouraging private sector involvement in the delivery of services seems set to endure. Indeed, a commitment to 'work in partnership with the private sector, *extending* the circle of those involved in public service' is the second of twelve new guiding principles for civil service market testing (Cabinet Office 1997: 2, emphasis added). Even if the tenor of reform has become more pluralistic, the determination of central government to propel it remains undiminished. Reserve powers proposed currently would compel local authorities unable to demonstrate best value to use competitive tendering or, in extreme cases, surrender the management of services in question to another authority or a business consortium (*Local Government Chronicle*, 6 March 1998, p. 1). Finally, and significantly, the financial environment in which reforms are developed will remain tight. Domestic and European policy commitments continue to limit increases in public spending and there appears to be reluctance to exploit even the available room for manoeuvre. Revision of funding levels and mechanisms in local government, for example, has been made conditional upon the successful implementation of best value (Travers 1998). Benchmarking in these circumstances will be no soft option for service providers and may still be used to generate savings.

Review of employment rights

Employees' experience of these revised arrangements will depend centrally upon the extent to which their employment rights are strengthened. General labour market reforms have considerable relevance to contracting regimes. A new individual right to be represented by a trade union may offer a toehold in non-union contracting organisations and a further stepping stone to formal recognition for bargaining purposes. Competitive strategies based on crude reductions in labour costs, particularly in manual services deemed semi- or 'unskilled', will be undermined by the national minimum wage.

More direct reform seems likely, though details are unclear as yet. A review of those sections of the Local Government Act prohibiting the consideration of non-commercial factors has generated expectations that contract compliance will be possible once again (that is, the ability of public organisations to require from their suppliers particular employment and management standards) (James 1997). Pressure to clarify and extend TUPE protections has also been building. Unions have long sought the clear application of TUPE to all public sector transfers; the inclusion of pension rights; and the strengthening of provisions on continuity of employee representation. Parts of this agenda are currently being advocated jointly with public and private sector employers but the omens have been been mixed, to say the least. The need to ensure that 'best value' regulations reflect properly the Acquired Rights Directive featured prominently in early discussions between employers, unions and shadow ministers (*Financial Times*, 1995, p. 9), and consultation on revisions of TUPE was launched in the first year of the Labour government (Department of Trade and Industry 1997). In the meantime, however, the existing framework was thrown into disarray by increasingly restrictive interpretations of the Acquired Rights Directive in the European Court of Justice. In particular, the judgement in the case of *Süzen v. Zehnacker Gebaudereinigung GmbH Krankenhausservice* appeared to limit significantly the circumstances in which the directive applied to public sector contracts (IRS 1997c: 10). Subsequent attempts in local government and the civil service to proceed with transfers without TUPE protections underlined the need for reform. At the time of writing, however, consensus amongst the EU member states on reform of the directive is not readily apparent and no plans to revise TUPE independently have been announced.[1]

Conclusions

The argument presented here is that increased managerial control over the labour process has been the principal consequence of contracting in the public sector. Hogget's notion of 'centralised decentralisation' is relevant here. Managers have used their autonomy in ways not anticipated or intended when the legislation was introduced. In particular, in-house services have been retained in the majority of cases and to that degree, work forces have been protected from the vagaries of the market place. Yet management concern to maintain control of public services, be they delivered by private or public sector providers, has extended often into a desire to extend control over the allocation, performance and reward of work tasks. Though the consequences have been uneven between organisations and services, it has been argued here that destabilised collective employment relations, disordered payment systems and increased work intensification have been significant general trends.

Having matured rapidly, these substantial service markets are to be subject to further change and reform. White-collar contracting will have distinct dynamics and may offer potentially positive outcomes for employees. Some of the underlying pressures, however, are identical, and, in areas where the skill or professional requirements are low, outcomes similar to those in manual areas might be expected. Much depends upon reform of the policy frameworks governing contracting and employment rights. These will permit a greater range of methods of market testing and may foster sophisticated approaches to contracting as a consequence. But the competitive evaluation of jobs and performance will remain a central tenet of public service management. Whether employees will continue to pay the price of the organisational flexibility delivered by contracting is an open question.

Note

Revisions to the directive were subsequently pushed through at the close of the UK's presidency of the European Union in June 1998. Reflect compromises between the member states, their precise implications for public sector workers were unclear. Transfers arising from contracting-out were included specifically and reference was made to definitions of a transfer (adopted from the Suzen case) which might permit a transfer to proceed without protections. Much depends now on clarification from the UK government and independent revisions to TUPE.

References

Ascher, K. (1987) *The Politics of Privatisation: Contracting Out Public Services*, London: Macmillan.

Bach, S. (1992) 'Competitive Tendering in the NHS: Prospects for the Future', unpublished, Coventry University of Warwick.

Bennett, C. and Ferlie, E. (1996) 'Contracting in theory and practice: some evidence from the NHS', *Public Administration* 74 (1): 49–66.

Butler, P. (1997) 'Private investigations', *Health Service Journal*, 12 June, p. 20.

Cabinet Office (1996) *Competing for Quality Policy Review: an Efficiency Unit Scrutiny*, London: HMSO.

Cabinet Office (1997) *Government's Twelve Guiding Principles for Market Testing and Contracting Out*, news release, CAB 114/97, 4 November.

Calpin, D. (1998) 'Getting better all the time', *Municipal Journal*, 6 March 1998.

Colling, T. (1993) Contracting public services: the management of compulsory competitive tendering in two county councils', *Human Resource Management Journal* 3 (4): 1–16.

Colling, T. (1995a) 'Renewal or rigor mortis? Union responses to contracting in local government', *Industrial Relations Journal* 26 (2): 134–45.

Colling, T. (1995b) *From Hierarchy to Contract? Subcontracting and Employment in the Service Economy*, Warwick Papers in Industrial Relations 52, Coventry: Industrial Relations Research Unit.

Colling, T. (1997) 'Organising in the Disorganised State: the Prospects for Public Service Unionism in Outsourced Environments', Employment Research Unit annual conference 'The Insecure Workforce', Cardiff Business School, September.

Deakin, N. (1994) 'The Enabling State: the Role of Markets and Contracts', paper to the Employment Research Unit annual conference 'The Contract State: the Future of Public Management', Cardiff Business School, September.

Decker, D. (1995) 'Market testing: does it bring home the bacon?' *Health Service Journal*, 19 January, pp. 26–7.

Department of the Environment, Transport and the Regions (1998) *Modernising Local Government: Improvising Services through Best Value*, London: Stationery Office.

Department of Trade and Industry (1997) *European Acquired Rights Directive and Transfer of Undertakings (Protection of Employment) Regulations 1981: Public Consultation*, London: Employment Rights Directorate.

Dickens, L. (1997) 'Public sector competitive tendering: the missing equality dimension', *Industrial Law Journal* 26: 177–81.

Elliott, R. and Duffus, K. (1996) 'What has been happening to pay in the public service sector of the economy? Developments over the period 1970–1992', *British Journal of Industrial Relations* 34 (1): 51–85.

Escott, K. and D. Whitfield (1995) *The Gender Impact of CCT in Local Government*, London: HMSO.

Financial Times (1995) 'Contractors and unions join forces', 20 February, p. 9.

Foster, D. and Taylor, G. (1994) 'Reinventing the Wheel: Privatisation and the Crisis of Public Service Trade Unionism', Employment Research Unit annual conference 'The Contract State: the Future of Public Management', Cardiff Business School, September.

Government Statistical Service (1996): *Civil Service Statistics* 1996, London: HMSO.

Graham, D. and Clarke, P. (1986) *The New Enlightenment: the Rebirth of Liberalism*, Basingstoke: Macmillan.

Hardy, S., Adnett, N., and Painter, R. (1997) *TUPE and CCT Business Transfers: UK Labour Market Views*, Survey Report 1, Stoke on Trent: Staffordshire University Law School.

Hassell, N. (1994): 'Testing market testing', *Management Today*, May: 38–44.

Hoggett, P. (1993) 'New Modes of Control in the Public Service', paper to the Employment Research Unit annual conference 'The Contract State: the Future of Public Management', Cardiff Business School, September.

Industrial Relations Services (1997a) 'Creating a new union: the birth of the PTC', *Employment Trends* 631: 13–16.

Industrial Relations Services (1997b) 'Majority of employees on fixed term contracts work in the public services', *Employment Trends* 642: 4.

Industrial Relations Services (1997c) 'Change in contractor not a business transfer', *Industrial Relations Law Bulletin* 566: 10–12.

James, M. (1997) 'Armstrong unveils plans to bolster employees' rights', *Local Government Chronicle*, 24 October, p. 4.

James, M. (1998) 'Biased bonus lacks productivity link', *Local Government Chronicle*, 30 January, p. 5.

Kelliher, C. (1995) 'The dog that didn't bark in the night? Competitive tendering and industrial relations in the NHS', *Industrial Relations Journal* 26 (4): 306–19.

Kessler, I. and Coyle-Shapiro, J. (1997) 'Employee perceptions: overlooked in outsourcing?' Annual conference of the British Universities Industrial Relations Association, University of Bath, July.

Labour Research Department (1997) 'Unions see rise in recognition deals', *Labour Research*, April, p. 5.

Local Government Management Board (1993) *Survey of the Employment Effects of Central Government Initiatives, March 1991–March 1992*, London: LGMB.

Massey, A. (1994) 'Market testing: some preliminary remarks', *Public Policy and Administration* 9 (2): 1–9.

Mather, G. (1991) 'Government by contract', *Inquiry* 25, London: Institute of Economic Affairs.

McAnea, C. (1996) 'A heavy load', *Municipal Journal*, 1 November, pp. 18–19.

McIntosh, I. and Broderick, J. (1996) 'Neither one thing nor the other: compulsory competitive tendering and Southburgh cleansing services', *Work, Employment and Society* 10 (3): 413–30.

Milne, R. (1997) 'Market type mechanisms, market testing, and market making: a longitudinal analysis of contractor interest in tendering', *Urban Studies* 34 (4): 543–9.

Nichols, G. and Taylor, P. (1995) 'The impact of local authority leisure provision of CCT, financial cuts and changing attitudes', *Local Government Studies* 21 (4): 607–22.

Office for National Statistics (1997) *Economic Trends: Annual Supplement* 23, London: Stationery Office.

Olins, R. (1997) 'Reinventing government', *Sunday Times* Business Focus, 20 April, pp. 24–7.

Oughton, J. (1994) 'Market testing: the future of the civil service', *Public Policy and Administration* 9 (2): 11–20.

Painter, J. (1991) 'Compulsory competitive tendering in local government: the first round', *Public Administration* 69 (1): 191–210.

Richards, S., Smith, P. and Newman, J. (1996) 'Shaping and reshaping market testing policy', *Public Policy and Administration* 11 (2): 19–34.

Shaw, K., Snape, S. and Hinde, K. (1996) 'Protecting the "core business": local authority responses to compulsory competitive tendering for financial services', *Local Government Policy Making* 22 (5): 22–9.

Steel, G. and Liddle, J. (1996) 'Emergent or deliberate strategies? Is CCT making local authorities hot around their white collars?' *Local Government Policy Making* 23 (3): 3–14.

Travers, T. (1998) 'Freedom at a price', *Guardian*, 29 April, p. 7.

Vincent-Jones, P. (1994) 'The limits of near-contractual governance: local authority internal trading under CCT', *Journal of Law and Society* 21 (2): 214–37.

Walker, B. (1993) *Competing for Building Maintenance: Direct Labour Organisations and Compulsory Competitive Tendering*, London: HMSO.

Walsh, K. (1995) *Public Services and Market Mechanisms: Competition, Contracting and the New Public Management*, Basingstoke: Macmillan.

Walsh, K. and Davis, H. (1993) *Competition and Service: the Impact of the Local Government Act 198*, London: HMSO.

Watt, P. A. (1996) 'Compulsory competitive tendering for the finance service in local government', *Local Government Policy Making* 23 (3): 15–20.

Whitbread, C. and Hooper, N. (1993). 'NHS ancillary services' in A. Harrison (ed.) *From Hierarchy to Contract*, Oxford: Transaction Books.

White, G. (1997) 'Employment flexibilities in local government', *Public Policy and Administration* 12 (4): 47–59.

8 Quality management

A new form of control?

Miguel Martinez Lucio
and Robert MacKenzie

The question of quality management has emerged as a significant issue within the employee relations of the public services. Both ideologically and organisationally it has been a central feature of the ongoing process of commercialisation. It appears, furthermore, unlikely that the broad trajectory of public service commercialisation and marketisation developed under the Conservative government since the 1980s will alter fundamentally following the election of a Labour government in 1997. However, the development of quality management in the public sector continues to be influenced by contextual factors: political regulation, bureaucratic and political intervention, and extensive trade union influence (Jenkins *et al.* 1995).

This chapter examines the development of quality management systems in the public services and their relationship with the employee relations process. The first section outlines the background to the shift towards these new types of management practices, explaining the logic behind their use in the public sector. Second, the chapter considers two features of management strategy that are relevant to the development of public sector employee relations: the customer and performance measurement. The chapter illustrates how reference to the customer's demands and performance measures has been used as part of an attempt to develop a greater degree of managerial control over the employee within the public sector. As a result, work has become intensified through these new management practices. The chapter argues that such developments within the public sector have contributed to changes in the basic trust relations that have historically underpinned relations between employees, unions and management whilst also contributing to some ironic outcomes in the nature of public sector industrial relations. The chapter therefore assesses the actual impact of these changes. Third, the chapter focuses on the way these changes have led to new problems and conflicts in the sphere of public service industrial relations and at the way trade unions have responded to such developments. It argues that public sector industrial relations have become 'politicised' as a consequence of such management practices (Fairbrother 1994). The chapter indicates how the new language and practice of management evolved and how counter-references to quality also emerged in the form of union strategies.

The increasing use of quality management techniques raises a range of new and significant issues in terms of public sector industrial relations. First of all there is the question of performance measurement and the ongoing attempts to evaluate the performance of public service organisations and their employees. This has contributed to an ongoing interest in employee evaluation, surveillance and, according to some, control (Reed 1995). Second, the evolution of quality management techniques has led to management referring to 'customer interests' in their relations with employees. In this respect, the relevance of quality management in the public sector is that it is both a technique for controlling the behaviour of employees and a means of prioritising consumer interests over those of producers (Du Gay and Salaman 1992). Therefore, whilst the institutions of joint regulation appear to have remained largely intact within public sector industrial relations – even after eighteen years of Conservative government – the reality is that the engagement with managerial projects, such as Total Quality Management, among others, has contributed to a shift in the nature of ideological relations and employment processes which have rarely been systematically observed by academics working in the area.

The advent of quality techniques in the public sector must therefore be seen as part of the process by which management tries to develop 'a relatively limited repertoire of justificatory principles' to transform workplace relations and their role within them (Armstrong *et al.* 1981: 16). Management is constantly trying to seek compliance through negotiations and references to ideological principles. These principles become resources in steering and transforming organisations. Quality management, in the form of performance measurement and customer interests, constitutes a new way of legitimating organisational change. As demonstrated by the introductory chapter, the area of public services is wide, so in this chapter we can only outline some of the main issues and outcomes. The chapter draws on debates about the civil service, education, health and social work but the conclusions drawn are valid in most areas of non-commercial public services.

The emergence of 'quality' in the public services

It is a commonly held belief that organisational interest in the development of management systems to improve quality is fundamentally driven by a desire to enhance the quality of public service (Citizen's Charter, HMSO 1991). The engagement with private sector management techniques, especially Total Quality Management (TQM), became attractive to the Conservative government, for various reasons. From its 'origins' TQM developed from its initial focus on quality circles in the Japanese model of the 1970s to the use of quality control as part of a system of externalisation and subcontracting in particular (Tuckman 1994), and later to an interest in the issue of customer care (Wilkinson *et al.* 1998). Given the context of increasing externalisation in the form of subcontracting, there was a need to guarantee production and service delivery processes within the private sector and, more recently, the public sector. It was pursued through performance measurement systems, managerial commitment and leadership, the exerting of external customer rights, the construction of internal markets and internal customers (whereby employees viewed their fellow employees as customers in their own right) and the implementation of compulsory competitive tendering (see Kirkpatrick and Martinez Lucio 1995a).

The public services developed distinct performance measurement techniques and customer involvement in a range of ways, and sometimes such moves to managerialism were quite uneven (Ackroyd *et al.* 1989). In 1991, however, the government decided to organise and co-ordinate these developments under one overall project called the Citizen's Charter, which would bring together the main quality control systems of all the public services and communicate relevant data to the public. It represented an attempt to bring together the range of performance measurement systems, plus the 'voice' mechanisms provided to customers, the 'exit' mechanisms (i.e. the right not to use a public service) available, and the general 'rights' public service recipients held regarding service delivery (Kirkpatrick and Martinez Lucio 1995b). Not without its critics,[1] the Citizen's Charter – which in many respects remains public policy at the time of writing – was an attempt to market the move towards a quality based culture within the public sector, and empower individuals *vis-à-vis* the suppliers of their services (Heery 1993). In many respects it attempted to develop a culture of 'blame', whereby public service employees were held responsible for failures in service delivery, which diverted attention away from the broader issues of social service provision and the political-economic context. In some cases, such as social work and education, this stigmatising of the profession was supported by focusing on the employment activity of the individual employee, as opposed to examining the broader structure and context of the service.

The main thrust of the government argument is that the nature of the relationship between the provider and the consumer of a service needs to be clarified, within a context that has become characterised by constant flux and change: thereby maintaining, and improving, the quality of public services. This is debatable. There are various reasons why quality is increasingly considered to be a central issue for management intervention. First, it is seen as an essential ingredient of public service commercialisation and marketisation. The use of private sector management techniques has been increasingly adopted in the public sector as part of the process of commercialising its objectives and orientation. These techniques were seen as providing the public sector with a language that was regarded as central to the supposed efficiencies achieved in private sector organisations. Such management techniques were also seen as contributing to the adjustment of employee behaviour, i.e. the replacement of a public sector ethos of service with a more cost-conscious market orientation (Wilkinson *et al.* 1998). These techniques provide a new language of public sector employment, whereby the priorities of the consumer would become paramount, thus allowing for the reformulation of what were considered to be restrictive workplace practices. Both government officials and management have sought to invoke the needs of the customer to provide legitimacy for their actions and a source of power in their relations with unions and employees when seeking to change working practices.

Second, quality contributes to organisational control. The main emphasis from the mid-1970s to the late 1980s was on controlling the input dimension of public service provision – the costs – and not the output dimension, i.e. the quality of the service and the interface with the customer (Kirkpatrick and Martinez Lucio 1995b). However, since the mid-1980s, the ongoing constraints and control of input factors, in the face of growing public demand for state services, meant that the deterioration of public services increasingly became a reality. This necessitated new types of organisational control at the level of the customer, to ensure standards, and supposedly quality (Kirkpatrick and Martinez Lucio 1995a). In this respect, the adoption of quality management techniques was seen as central to a new form of public governance (Reed 1995). Quality management through performance measurement would also allow a framework of organisational control to emerge, in a context where central and local government were externalising a range of services through subcontracting and internal market mechanisms (Hoggett 1996). Job intensification would be possible within such a context, and would allow more effective use of limited resources. Non-professional work was, initially, far more likely to be the subject of contracting-out to private tender than was the case with professional work (see below). Furthermore, the historical employment practices associated with such activities as housing services and refuse collection could be transformed by more focused and explicit performance measures (Fitzgerald *et al.* 1996). This question of eroding the traditional autonomy of employment practices explains why, from the late 1980s onwards, the Conservative government began to engage with the discourse and practice of performance measurement and customer interests.

Third, in terms of industrial relations, the adoption of quality techniques was seen as allowing the prioritising of consumer interests over producer/ employer interests – keeping in mind that the latter had been central to the traditions of union–management relations in the public sector. Post-war industrial relations in the public sector evolved without much reference to external questions of organisational and employee performance, public service impact and cost efficiencies. Pay was fundamentally based on broad comparative criteria or, from the 1970s onwards, general drives for cost containment driven by macro-level government concerns (Winchester 1983; Winchester and Bach 1995; White 1996). Therefore, engagement with the issue of quality was central to the attempted reorientation of the context of industrial relations practices on pay negotiation and employment activity generally. As Heery pointed out, moves towards a discourse of customer rights within the public sector were dealing with the desire

to specify and tighten the obligations of service providers, [and] represents a significant shift in the guiding assumptions of public service
government. Largely gone is the traditional concern to act as a 'good
employer', while in its place a new obligation has assumed priority, to
act as a 'good provider' to the customer. The government has sought
to shift the balance of advantage in the producer-consumer relation
towards the (individual) consumer.

(Heery 1993: 286)

Fourth, the introduction of quality techniques in the public sector has
contributed to control over the labour process, which was seen to be relatively more autonomous from management than was often the case in the
private sector. Strong professional groups have been renowned for maintaining effective control over their work (Johnson 1973). In the case of
academics, schoolteachers, key parts of the medical profession, and even
librarians, the government confronted collectives which exerted control over
their method of work and had low levels of public accountability (Davies
and Kirkpatrick 1995a, b). Such professionals worked on the basis that
they best understood the interests of their patients or students, and that they
could serve those interests with minimal managerial interference (Johnson
1973). According to Clarke and Newman:

> markets were constructed as an alternative to the flawed processes of pro-
> fessional representation of need in social welfare . . . Professional power
> rested on an argument that needs were not transparent but required the
> application of expert knowledge in order to identify them accurately and
> to respond to them appropriately. The marketised model of social welfare
> represented a direct challenge to such professional paternalism.
>
> (1997: 114)

The increasing economic constraints upon the state, coupled with the
burgeoning demands and the effective organisation of the recipients of public
services,[2] fuelled government support for the enhancement of managerial
authority through such mechanisms of quality management as performance
measurement and customer 'rights'. The weakness of management structures
and prerogative constituted a major historical characteristic of the public
sector. The desire, therefore, for the erosion of the autonomy of public sector
professionals has been one of main imperatives for the development of quality
oriented management in the public sector. Within this new model, management attempted to become a major arbiter and mediator of consumer
interests *vis-à-vis* professionals within the public sector, in certain circumstances using quite symbolic representations of customers to challenge
professional autonomy (Pollitt 1993; Ackroyd and Soothill 1994).

In their work on the literature of quality management in the private sector
Rosenthal *et al.* (1997) argue that control and intensification of employment

practices are portrayed as being central to management objectives in introducing quality techniques. They suggest, in opposition to Ogbonna (1992) and Delbridge *et al.* (1991), that this question of control is overstated. There has been a history of public organisations being interested in the question of quality as a genuine province of consumer involvement, especially in the area of local government (Miller 1996). However, we argue that government interest in quality management in the public services was driven at least as much by the four issues outlined above as by an interest in broad consumer rights and 'employee empowerment'.[3]

The impact on employees: customers' rights and performance management

Hoggett (1996) has argued that the plethora of new management techniques in the public sector can be described as a new form of organisational control. Fundamentally he points to three elements of this 'strategy' that together provide a significant dimension of public sector management, within a context of organisational 'decentralisation'. First, there is centralisation of control over policy and strategy, with operational decisions being the main focus of local level public organisations and their managers. Second, the role of competition is emphasised as a way of controlling local organisations; third, there is increasing use of performance measurement as a means to ensure operational outcomes.[4] In this respect Hoggett is right to assert that it is the combination of these factors – along with, presumably, the overall impact of restructuring and economic considerations – that provides public organisations with a more constrained set of choices. This begins to place increasing pressure on management at the level of service delivery to find cost savings and quality improvements within the work force itself. This section therefore looks at two key elements of this new form of control that are relevant in the context of public services – customer rights and performance measurement. It notes some of the repercussions of these developments on public sector employment, and the issues that are emerging in workplace politics. It also outlines the way these issues are likely to develop under a Labour government.

Customer rights

The use of customer care and customer involvement has been central to the way in which producer interests have been replaced by market interests. In the case of the health services, the patient has been redefined as a customer seeking quality services from health workers and their managers. Discussing local government, Wilkinson *et al.* (1998) argue, through examples in local government and social services, that the political mediation and development of TQM vary considerably and that there is no one uniform model. In some cases the training of employees in customer care has heightened the sense of responsibility and involvement that employees feel towards their customers, and their service. However, Wilkinson *et al.* (1998) acknowledge that resistance and the political interpretation of rights are more complex in the public sector, and that quality has been fundamentally more politicised as a consequence. Shaw (1995) maintains that the nature of customer relations within social services, where customers tend to demonstrate greater dependence and vulnerability, limits the potential of market type interactions, contrary to the assumptions of some of the reformers of such services. In some areas the 'market' has instead emerged in terms of contractual relations between units of social service provision and 'purchasing' authorities, and not in terms of customer empowerment. The emphasis on contractual relations to govern their activities seems to militate against the high trust relations between providers (social workers) and recipients of services that are assumed by those with an interest in quality management (Charlesworth *et al.* 1996).

In the civil service – for example, in the Benefits Agency and the Inland Revenue – Total Quality Management has been an integral part of the development of decentralisation and commercialisation (Fairbrother 1994).

> As part of the quest to engender a service or enterprise ethos, senior management have looked to various forms of human resource management and specifically TQM. Central to these initiatives is an attempt by management to recast employment relations in terms of the individual rather than the collective, as reflected through trade unionism. To realise this objective it is common for line managers to be given an enhanced role in dealing with their workforce, particularly in relation to promotion procedures, merit payments and the like. This has involved the development of such practices as team briefings, quality circles, and TQM procedures.
>
> (Fairbrother 1994: 66)

The involvement of employees and their reward became increasingly tied to the question of innovation and effort with respect to the needs of the customer, as manifested in a range of performance measures and operational targets. The customer becomes, in theory, the point of reference within employment relations at the expense of the work force as a collective.

In terms of the use of the individual customer within employment relations, the relabelling of the consumer of public services may have serious repercussions in various circumstances (Thompson 1995). Rights have been defined narrowly in terms of the nature of the delivery of public services, as opposed to the actual scope of service and the broader issues affecting provision. The aim has been to focus customer interest on the way in which the service is provided and on the role of the public service employee, hence leaving broader distributional, resource allocation and organisational control issues to one side. Attempts to involve local and national interest groups in the decision making forums of health authorities have been made, but the process has been uneven in development and limited. In health, for instance, the language of quality has focused on matters of either cost and time or rates of delivery, not of satisfaction with service delivery, although there is increasing use of customer satisfaction surveys. In terms of employment relations, this has meant that the focus has been on accelerating throughput and emphasising cost factors. The process of 'relabelling' patients as customers is significant in that it transforms the nature of the rights that patients possess (Thompson 1995). To do more with the same, or even less, has become a feature of health service delivery. And for many employees of the National Health Service this has come to represent a move from 'working in a church', with its socially ethical framework, to 'working in a garage', with its emphasis on turnover (Nottingham and O'Neill 1998).

The case of health is complex, owing to the range of services and the distinct nature of the actors whom patients have to interact with, from general practitioners to consultants, among others. Yet the empowerment of individual consumers in terms of service delivery rights has tended to accentuate the question of throughput. The emphasis on throughput may be inefficient, as it leads to earlier discharge, which may in certain cases result in the readmission of the patient and even long term problems of illness. In organisational drives for functional flexibility and increasing levels of job loading, managers cite the perceived needs of the customer as a reason for change. The point of contact, the immediate moment of gratification and interaction, is furthermore emphasised over more ongoing relations and types of interaction. This has major repercussions in terms of work loads and levels of stress, and even raises safety issues such as violent behaviour against staff. The latter arises partly from the resourcing of health services and changing sociological circumstances. However, the use of quality indicators, such as time frames and attendance patterns, exacerbates these problems. Appraisal systems and developments in individual reward systems have tended to revolve around issues of service delivery, although these human resource management techniques are not exactly noted for their consistency within the sector. Nevertheless, their introduction is legitimated by reference to the 'needs of the customer'.

These contradictory developments are compounded by the fact that the 'customer' is on occasions organised. Thus, in the case of health, the customer has often been the purchasing authority or general practitioner acting on behalf of the individual. Crucially the mediation process in which such purchasing bodies engage is not solely financial in form.[5] Plus there are organisations which represent certain health interests and constituencies of patients (Klein 1989). In defining the customer there are therefore the final recipients of service provision plus a host of intermediaries and proxies; add to all this the ambiguous position of the 'internal customer' as a reference point for performance. The concept of the customer thus covers a heterogeneous collection of agents with varied interests, who may differ in their propensity or opportunity to organise or agitate in the representation of those interests. Furthermore, in the passage from production to consumption, the process of service provision may engage several agents, each of which may be conceptualised as a customer, before reaching the point of consumption by the service recipient. This renders problematic the synonymity of customer interests and consumer interests. In the light of these disparities and ambiguities, the question of customer involvement and customer rights becomes far more complex and much more political in its nature. The use of the image and language of the customer as a management 'instrument' of control in such areas as health, education and social services therefore tends to be characterised by contradictions.

Obsession with measurement

Whilst the representation of customer interests is highly contested and uneven, given the politicised nature of the public sector consumer, the question of performance measurement has emerged as a key factor within public services management. This is one area where continuity between Conservative and Labour governments is most visible.

In the civil service the use of targets and performance indicators has underpinned the emergence of merit pay systems and bonuses. Quantitative measures have allowed for relatively unsophisticated merit pay systems to emerge. Targets in the Benefits Agency, for example, are linked with the number of cases an employee handles. The targets in turn are used in the appraisal of staff and in the development of a crude and direct system of work measurement (Fairbrother 1994: 88). In the area of probationary officers, case targets are allocated a certain amount of time (in certain types of work this means four hours per visit/peripheral case). This places pressure on part time probationary officers in particular. Part time staff cannot use organisational resources and do not have constant access to networks of professional colleagues. In both these cases the increased monitoring of work routines is used to focus on certain employees who are seen to 'fail the customer'.

In the case of education this question of performance measurement has become an important feature of management control. Quality assessments of teaching practice and administration, along with the use of the output measures in terms of exam results, have now become a common part of school education. Schoolteachers are faced with externally derived measures of performance, which have contributed to a decreasing level of trust between head teachers and their staff, owing to the impact these measures have upon recruitment, promotion and working conditions. Declining resources and standardised teaching processes have been reinforced and managed through an increase in the use of performance measures which identify weak 'producers', regardless of their geographical or social context (Ironside and Seifert 1995). The idea of facilitating greater consumer choice – or parental choice – is, in formal terms, central to such performance measurement processes. However, the use of performance measurement techniques allows the onus of adaptation and service delivery to be placed upon the employee – in this case the teacher. Research shows that the outcome has been increasing work load levels, uncertainty and demoralisation, leading to increasing turnover levels (Sinclair *et al.* 1996). The culture of quality has given rise to a culture of blame, exemplified in the way 'bad teachers' became scapegoated within the system.

In the case of further education, the issue of performance control is aimed not solely at minimising the damage of decreasing resources but also at maintaining standards within a context of rising student–staff ratios. In this area, quality indicators have been driven less by notions of excellence than by that other side of TQM discourse 'conformance to standards' (Randle and Brady 1997). That is to say, the establishment of a minimum level, below which the delivery of a service cannot be allowed, itself becomes a benchmark of quality. Quality indicators and controls can measure input and output factors only in a quantitative manner, driving the content of teaching to an increasingly lower academic standard. This has linked the quality debate with overall concern about deskilling in the lecturing profession, similar developments being witnessed in further and higher education. The greater emphasis on throughput has raised the issues of work loads and the increasing experience of 'Taylorisation' (Miller 1996; Dearlove 1997). Furthermore, in higher education the increasing interest in quality indicators of academic research has meant that rewards and career development have been undermined by the way teaching and administration have been made secondary to research activity. In many respects it is in higher education that the plethora of performance measures has led to increasing fragmentation of the work force and the use of casual labour for the main functions of teaching and administration. The move was driven by the government's attempt to reproduce the dominant features of industry within the norms and processes of academia (Ryan 1998). In terms of employee relations and the labour process generally it has contributed to a debate on the 'proletarianisation' of academic labour (Dearlove 1997).

All this means that employment in the public services appears to be increasingly routine and controlled, with the execution of work separate from its conception.[6] For some observers the nature of the mass service delivery, standardisation and increasing supervisory control which has emerged in the public services since the 1980s is evidence of arrival at the Fordist stage of capitalist development (Murray 1989), but the heterogeneous nature of the public sector, and of the experience of employment within it, means that the generalisation of such a framework is problematic.[7] In the case of the health service, Seifert (1992) argues that these developments, such as 'Taylorisation', have contributed to an emergence of traditional conflict-based industrial relations, replacing the consensual pattern of the Whitley tradition. Competition between staff may undermine patterns of dialogue and consensus.

The 'Taylorisation' argument is interesting, although it ignores the greater fragmentation of the work force and the way new elites are emerging within it who may exploit performance measures for personal gain. It also understates the politics of quality, in terms of how performance measures may be mobilised by employees in their individual relations with managers (Rosenthal *et al.* 1997) and also in their collective relations (see the following section). Much depends on the position of employees within the organisation in question. This raises gender issues and compositional factors within the work force.

One thing is certain: the culture of blame, the interest in performance monitoring and the use of indicators to increase work-related effort levels have been assimilated into the Labour government's public sector policies and discourse. Whilst the tendency to privatise and develop market relations within the state – through compulsory competitive tendering and public organisations competing with each other in internal markets – has not been accelerated, the government has exhibited a political fascination with the whole question of performance measurement and the concept of 'failure'. Therefore the area of performance measurement is one where management strategies appear consistent, although somewhat problematic, given that they seem less about facilitating choice than about intensifying the pressure upon public employees.

The trade union response

In response to these new management techniques, new union strategies and responses have emerged which call into question any simple reading of the undermining effect of new management initiatives on public sector employee relations. Given the regulated nature of public sector employment, the role of unions in mediating such developments has moved to centre stage in recent years. It is clear that a range of issues have emerged within the public sector, with regard to increasing work loads, the apparent process of 'Taylorisation' and the move away from collegiate and supportive workplace relations. It must be recognised, nevertheless, that these processes have been uneven in their development. The increasing amount of multi-tasking in the public sector has been supported by the use of 'customer' rights and performance measurement. Furthermore, management has increasingly used these rights, and the transparency that measurement presumably gives rise to, to legitimise the commercialisation of public services. These issues have impacted on key elements of the employee relations framework, and the contradictory nature of their impact has given rise to a range of conflicts.

The first impact is on pay. It is difficult to assess the impact of quality management on pay because this has often been the subject of contradictory developments within the public sector, in terms of uneven and sometimes non-existent decentralisation, the role of pay review bodies and the continued role of centralised relations (Bailey 1996; White 1996). Yet whilst it could be argued that pay disputes in the public sector tend to be more transparent because of the declining rate of conflict in the private sector, there are indirect links between questions of quality and pay-related conflict. Much of this could be due to the covert and latent conflict that is created by constant references to efficiency indicators and performance measures, on the one hand, and the lack of corresponding pay increases on the other. The increasing managerial use of performance measures provides a reference point for the way in which pay disputes are handled strategically.[8] Similar developments are apparent in the way in which the customer has become a player within key disputes on pay. The ambulance service dispute of 1989 was a classic case where the needs of the customer were incorporated into the public relations strategy of the unions (Terry 1991; Blyton and Turnbull 1994). In 1996 the issue of declining standards in higher education and deteriorating conditions in terms of class sizes and resources were tied rhetorically by those unions involved to the whole question of deteriorating working conditions in higher education. The calling into play of the customer's rights by management as a source of legitimacy (Armstrong *et al.* 1981) and as a source of authority for change has led to counter-references and meanings of the customer which evoke more progressive, less market-oriented understandings of quality and social rights. It has been argued that, with an increasingly shopfloor and branch-based tradition, public sector unions could exploit the issues of 'quality' and decentralised public management in a range of unexpected ways (Fitzgerald *et al.* 1996). For example, quality issues can arouse union concern and interest in resourcing issues. In terms of pay issues it is therefore to be expected that governments will continue to 'shield' matters of pay through pay review boards and the ongoing intervention of central government (White 1996). Therefore government may desire to limit the location of decision making on pay within new management discourses of quality and performance – apart from uneven developments in performance-related pay – as they may trigger a range of conflicts and pay disputes which are influenced in their form and content by the impact of performance measures and the question of customer rights.

The question of increasing work loads has become another central theme within public sector industrial relations and trade union responses, in terms of hours worked, related issues of the quality of the working environment and the impact of more interventionist management systems. The juxtaposition of this with performance indicators which may illustrate increases in performance levels influences the question of pay and the way in which reward is visualised by public sector employees. This has also impacted upon public sector managers, who, according to a major survey (Mansfield and Poole 1991), experienced an increase in working hours from 1981 to 1991 equivalent to an average of almost twenty extra hours per week. It has been suggested that one of the outcomes in terms of the labour process in the public sector has been the increasing level of 'contractualisation'.[9] That is to say, the use of performance measurement, coupled with the need to conform to some type of minimum standard in terms of interaction with customers, has meant that rules and regulations have been increasingly invoked by employees in their relations with managers. The establishment of more systematic work load systems, the development of more detailed job content, and the orienting of career development in terms of perfor- mance measures, point to an increasing amount of '*de facto* juridification' of employment processes. This is noticeable at every level within education and in the areas of social work, where increasingly individuals are working within bureaucratically negotiated frameworks which are not based on the same levels of trust and autonomy as in previous years (Dearlove 1997).

It is for this reason that in the case of unions such as Unison and the Civil and Public Services Association (now part of the Public and Commercial Services Union) commentators have spoken in terms of renewal and politici- sation of union activity and structures based on the effects of decentralisation, assertive management behaviour and the performance and work load issues discussed above (Fairbrother 1994). What is more, the ongoing characteristics of public service, social rights and political contingencies which constitute service delivery within the sector (Batstone *et al.* 1984; Jenkins *et al.* 1995) will provide unions with a range of counter-resources within the workplace. Yet the question of the trade unions' response is always complex, owing to the nature of union traditions and identities (Martinez Lucio and Weston 1992). With regard to the question of increasing 'politicisation' of public sector indus- trial relations, various developments in terms of trade union strategy have emerged, in part owing to the use of quality management techniques.

First, contractual relations between the state, levels of management, employees and the customer may push the nature of public service and their employment relations toward a commercialised system, wherein a more instrumental and low trust approach to issues is central.[10] The move to a 'Taylorised' public sector is seen to necessitate an instrumental ethos on behalf of employees in terms of hours, customer commitment within the realities of the resources provided and willingness to use conflict strategies when necessary.

Second, there are trade union activists who are using the language of performance measurement, and in particular customer rights, in quite inno- vative ways. Albeit they are limited in scope, potential 'alliances' between public sector workers and consumers have emerged at key moments on the basis of defending public services. The intervention of local communities in debates over the closure of schools, fire stations, postal sorting offices and hospitals provides high profile examples of such alliances. In the case of the fire services the closure of stations in 1997 and 1998 was countered by quite organised alliances between public organisations, local communities and the trade unions around the issue of maintaining quality services. Furthermore, the agenda-shaping impact of public opposition to the privatisation of the Post Office in the mid-1990s represented an effective alliance of consumer interests and union policy (Martinez Lucio 1995). Where industrial conflict can harm the public, as in the ambulance service, the disputes in 1989 developed with a high media profile and strategic use of conflict so that citizens were not affected in any detrimental manner. These developments are premised upon alternative readings of the meaning of consumer rights and questions of performance. The question of consumption rights and the matter of quality can have various meanings, and can be developed through distinct trade union and community projects in a variety of ways (Pffefer and Coote 1991). The complexity and political nature of the definition of the customer have repercussions for the way trade unions intervene in the debate on service delivery and employment processes. Alliances between interests in 'production' and 'consumption' therefore seem to be increasingly common in public sector industrial relations, as witnessed in the way that unions have highlighted the relation between deteriorating public services and declining employment conditions. Unions have not always organised at these levels in an effective manner. They have not always articulated the employment issues emerging from the new managerialism beyond the limits of a purely employee relations framework (Miller 1996). However, the changing boundaries between the workplace and consumption – which has seen the increased use of consumption issues within the workplace – have begun to challenge and unsettle the employee relations processes of the public sector, which has been 'insulated', ironically, in the past from political and social issues (Martinez Lucio and Stewart 1997). This has shaken the traditional tendency to view employment issues such as pay and conditions in a narrowly defined and isolated manner.

These two union strategies – 'contractualisation' and 'social alliances' – need not be in opposition to one another, but they do represent distinct ways in which the question of quality management can politicise industrial relations. The boundaries of the employment relation within the public sector are therefore being challenged by (1) the use of performance measurements and the reference to consumption issues by management and (2) the subsequent counter-strategies elaborated by unions and their members. Hence the process of politicisation is complex.

Tensions between these two strategies, however, do emerge, and politicisation within public sector industrial relations may be limited. In the first instance, as Miller (1996) has argued, in the case of local government the negative local reaction of unions such as Unison to the urban left's dual strategy – of resistance to central government and the elaboration of alternative welfare strategies in alliance with consumer groups in the 1980s – arose because public sector unions increasingly modelled their behaviour on the 'private sector, blue-collar' model. According to Miller, that model was inappropriate, owing to its failure to accommodate questions of public ethos and social alliances. This is a case where innovative alliances around quality issues were undermined by 'traditional' – private sector-type – union identities. Second, social alliances through innovative forms of industrial conflict may clash with the growth of 'new market unionism', which has become dominant in a significant part of the trade union movement. Heery (1993) pointed out perceptively that the emergence of the discourse of the customer and the market was creating a social and ideological basis for a new style of market unionism, although this may also mean the marginalisation by the unions of activists seeking more radical solutions. This may act as a constraint upon the way contradictions within performance measurement and customer rights are exploited, elaborated and used by unions. The reason is that broad agreements or understandings between government, various levels of managers and trade unionists may be sought on employment issues that limit debate on employee control and working conditions. For example, the desire to find some kind of stability in employment and to limit numerical flexibility may be sought through a compromise on questions of functional flexibility, job loading and working conditions which are elaborated and legitimated by the use of systems of quality management in quite determinate ways. In this respect, questions of performance measurement and customer rights may prove to be a continuing political dilemma in public sector employee relations.

Conclusion

The development of performance measurement and customer rights have had a complex but important impact on public sector employee relations. There are many reasons why employment relations in the public sector have changed. The role of more systematic forms of performance controls, nevertheless, coupled with the constant reassertion of a managerial prerogative based on emphasising the 'needs' of the customer more than those of the producer, has contributed to a greater degree of organisational control and demoralisation amongst public sector employees. There is concern – granted, it is not universally shared – that the processes of work in the public sector are becoming increasingly similar to those of low trust, private sector manufacturing environments. With the advent of a Labour government – and its interest in 'discipline' and control within employment and work – such developments are not being reversed.

The move to copy key private sector practices, however, in what continues to be still a relatively regulated and bureaucratic context, has led to a new set of issues within what remains a highly unionised environment. There are weaknesses and even contradictions in the development of the 'new management practices'. There are those who argue that such organisational developments are primarily rhetorical in nature and that they are not strategically developed and supported in any systematic manner (Chandler 1996). What is more significant is the argument that, whether consistent or not, public sector workers are experiencing new work pressures which are contributing to a new awareness of the nature of their employment relationship and the subsequent need for more radical responses to change. Performance measurement and customer rights are seen to be changing the consensual rules that once underpinned public sector industrial relations. How unions respond, however, is unclear. The strategic choices facing them, as mentioned above, are complicated by the confusion over their role within a Labour administration and within public sector decision making structures. However, the politicisation of the public sector's employee relations since the 1970s has continued and, coupled with the new forms of managerial behaviour within the workplace, may form the basis of new types of industrial conflict. The move to the market is more intriguing than anybody could have imagined.

Acknowledgement

We are grateful to Ian Kirkpatrick for discussions regarding the chapter, and for being a constantly engaging friend.

Notes

1 There is a range of critical literature on the subject of the Citizen's Charter (see Kirkpatrick and Martinez Lucio 1995a).
2 The rise of the student movement since the 1960s coupled with the greater impact of social movements in such areas as health services meant that professionals in the public sector were increasingly being challenged over their decision-making processes (Parkin 1968; Klein 1989). Although it should therefore not be forgotten that many of the initial challenges to professional power within the welfare state emerged from consumer groups, social movements and interest groups, the emerging New Right of the 1970s and 1980s attempted to mirror and refract some of these demands through an individualistic, consumerist discourse that would undermine professional power within the state (see Kirkpatrick and Martinez Lucio 1995a). The New Right's ability to manipulate such interests and demands on the welfare services was in part based on the failure of the left to respond to them (Hall 1988).
3 This lack of interest in the question of management intentions is a problem with Rosenthal *et al.*'s argument. Management is complex, and at times differentiated in its interests, but one should not deny the role of long term objectives and intentions, no matter how contradictory or unclear.
4 For an interesting and similar approach to this question of the articulation of distinct elements of control within the private sector, see Garrahan and Stewart's (1992) argument concerning the new regime of subordination.
5 There may be proxy customers acting on behalf of others (parents in school education, for example).
6 In other sectors the nature of change has been seen as much more contradictory, having varying effects on the skills and identity of the work force (Noon and Blyton 1997).
7 Indeed, it has been suggested by some observers that there are sections of the public sector which are in fact organised on a post-Fordist basis, which holds wholly different implications for industrial relations within these areas (Hoggett 1996).
8 See Stewart (1997) for an interesting discussion of the issue of performance and conflict in the private sector.
9 This outcome may not even be the desired objective of management constituencies. It may represent a more immediate, tangible form of control for managers

when compared with the broader set of human resource management and organisational change initiatives being imposed on management from above (Colling 1997).

10 See Deakin and Walsh (1996) for a broader discussion of this contracts issue in terms of public services.

References

Ackroyd, S., Hughes, J. and Soothill, K. (1989) 'Public sector services and their management', *Journal of Management Studies* 26 (6): 903–19.

Ackroyd, S. and Soothill, S. (1994) 'The New Management and the Professional', paper presented to the Employment Research Unit conference, 'The Contract State and the Future of Public Management', Cardiff: Cardiff Business School.

Armstrong, P., Goodman, J. and Hyman, J. D. (1981) *Ideology and Shopfloor Industrial Relations* London: Croom Helm.

Bailey, R. (1996) 'Public sector industrial relations' in I. J. Beardwell (ed.) *Contemporary Industrial Relations*, Oxford: Oxford University Press.

Batstone, E., Terry, M. and Ferner, A. (1984) *Consent and Efficiency*, Oxford: Blackwell.

Blyton, P. and Turnbull, P. (1994) *The Dynamics of Employee Relations*, London: Macmillan.

Chandler, J. (1996) *The Citizen's Charter*, Aldershot: Dartmouth.

Charlesworth, J., Clarke, J. and Cochrane, A. (1996) 'Tangled webs? Managing local mixed economies of care', *Public Administration* 74 (1): 67–88.

Clarke, J. and Newman, J. (1997) *The Managerial State*, London: Sage.

Colling, T. (1997) 'Managing human resources in the public sector' in I. Beardwell and L. Holden (eds) *Human Resource Management: a Contemporary Perspective*, London: Pitman.

Davies, A. and Kirkpatrick, I. (1995a) 'Face to face with the "sovereign consumer": service quality and the changing role of professional academic librarians', *Sociological Review* 43 (4): 782–807.

Davies, A. and Kirkpatrick, I. (1995b) 'Performance indicators, bureaucratic control and the decline of professional autonomy: the case of academic librarians' in I. Kirkpatrick and M. Martinez Lucio (eds) *The Politics of Quality in the Public Sector*, London: Routledge.

Deakin, N. and Walsh, K. (1996) 'The enabling state: the role of markets and contracts', *Public Administration* 74 (1): 33–49.

Dearlove, J. (1997) 'The academic labour process: from collegiality and professionalism to managerialism and proletarianisation?' *Higher Education Review* 30 (1): 56–75.

Delbridge, R., Turnbull, P. and Wilkinson, B. (1992) 'Pushing back the frontiers: management control and work intensification under JIT/TQM factory regimes', *New Technology, Work and Employment* 7 (2): 97–106.

Du Gay, P. and Salaman, G. (1992) 'The cult(ure) of the customer', *Journal of Management Studies* 29 (5): 615–33.

Fairbrother, P. (1994) *Politics and the State as Employer*, London: Mansell.

Fitzgerald, I., Rainnie, A. and Stirling, J. (1996) 'Coming to terms with quality: Unison and the restructuring of local government', *Capital and Class* 59: 103–34.

Garrahan, P. and Stewart, P. (1992) *The Nissan Enigma*, London: Cassell.

Hall, S. (1988) *The Hard Road to Renewal*, London: Verso.

Heery, E. (1993) 'Industrial relations and the customer', *Industrial Relations Journal* 24 (4): 341–59.

Heery, E. (1997) 'A return to contract? Performance-related pay in a public service', *Work, Employment and Society* 11 (3): 73–95.

HMSO (1991) *The Citizen's Charter: Raising the Standard*, Cmnd 1599, London: HMSO.

Hoggett, P. (1996) 'New modes of control in the public services', *Public Administration* 74 (1): 9–32.

Ironside, M. and Seifert, R. (1995) *Industrial Relations in Schools*, London: Routledge.

Jenkins, S., Noon, M. and Martinez Lucio, M. (1995) 'Negotiating quality: the case of TQM in the Royal Mail', *Employee Relations* 17 (3): 87–98.

Johnson, T. (1973) *Profession and Power*, London: Macmillan.

Kirkpatrick, I. and Martinez Lucio, M. (1995a) 'The uses of "quality" in the British government's reform of the public sector' in I. Kirkpatrick and M. Martinez Lucio (eds) *The Politics of Quality in the Public Sector*, London: Routledge.

Kirkpatrick, I. and Martinez Lucio, M. (1995b) 'The politics of quality in the public sector' in I. Kirkpatrick and M. Martinez Lucio (eds) *The Politics of Quality in the Public Sector*, London: Routledge.

Klein, R. (1989) *The Politics of the NHS*, London: Longman.

Lovering, J. (1994) 'Restructuring and the sex-typing of jobs' in R. Penn, M. Rose and J. Rubery (eds) *Skill and Occupational Change*, London: Routledge.

Mansfield, R. and Poole, M. (1991) *British Management in the Thatcher Years*, Corby: British Institute of Management.

Martinez Lucio, M. and Weston, S. (1992) 'Trade union responses to Human Resource Management: bringing the politics of the workplace back into debate' in P. Blyton and P. Turnbull (eds) *Reassessing Human Resource Management*, London: Sage.

Martinez Lucio, M. (1995) 'Quality and "new industrial relations": the case of the Royal Mail' in I. Kirkpatrick and M. Martinez Lucio (eds) *The Politics of Quality in the Public Sector*, London: Routledge.

Martinez Lucio, M. and Stewart, P. (1997) 'The paradox of contemporary labour process theory: the rediscovery of labour and the disappearance of collectivism', *Capital and Class* 62: 69–78.

Miller, C. (1996) *Public Service Trade Unionism and Radical Politics*, Aldershot: Dartmouth.

Murray, R. (1991) 'The state after Henry', *Marxism Today*, May: 22–7.

Newman, J. (1995) 'Making connections: frameworks for change' in C. Itzin and J. Newman (eds) *Gender, Culture and Organisational Change*, London: Routledge.

Noon, M. and Blyton, P. (1997) *The Realities of Work*, London: Macmillan.

Nottingham, C. and O'Neill, F. (1998) 'Out of the church and into Quick Fit: nurses and the secularisation of health policy' in A. Dobson and J. Stanyer (eds) *Contemporary Political Studies*, Nottingham: Political Studies Association.

Ogbonna, E. (1992) 'Managing organisational culture: fantasy or reality?' *Human Resource Management Journal* 3 (2): 42–54.

Parkin, M. (1968) *Middle Class Radicalism*, Manchester: MUP.

Pffefer, N. and Coote, A. (1991) *Is Quality Good for You?* London: Institute of Public Policy Research.

Pollitt, C. (1993) *Managerialism and the Public Services*, Oxford: Blackwell.

Randle, K. and Brady, N. (1997) 'Further education and the new managerialism', *Journal of Further and Higher Education* 21 (2): 229–39.

Reed, M. (1995) 'Managing quality and organisational politics: TQM as a governmental technology' in I. Kirkpatrick and M. Martinez Lucio (eds) *The Politics of Quality in the Public Sector*, London: Routledge.

Rosenthal, P., Hill S. and Peccei, R. (1997) 'Checking out service: evaluating excellence, human resource management and Total Quality Management', *Work, Employment and Society* 11 (3): 481–583.

Ryan, D. (1998) 'The Thatcher government's attack on higher education in historical perspective', *New Left Review* 227: 3–32.

Seifert, R. (1992) *Industrial Relations in the NHS*, London: Chapman & Hall.

Shaw, I. (1995) 'The quality of mercy: the management of quality in the personal social services' in I. Kirkpatrick and M. Martinez Lucio (eds) *The Politics of Quality in the Public Sector*, London: Routledge.

Sinclair, J., Ironside, M. and Seifert, R. (1996) 'Classroom struggle? Market-oriented education reforms and their impact on the teacher labour process', *Work, Employment and Society* 10 (4): 641–61.

Stewart, P. (1997) 'Striking smarter and harder at Vauxhall', *Capital and Class* 61: Spring.

Terry, M. (1991) Annual review article 1990, *British Journal of Industrial Relations* 29 (1): 97–112.

Thompson, A. (1995) 'Customising the public for health care: what's in a label?' in I. Kirkpatrick and M. Martinez Lucio (eds) *The Politics of Quality in the Public Sector*, London: Routledge.

Tuckman, A. (1994) 'The yellow brick road: Total Quality Management and the restructuring of organisational culture', *Organisational Studies* 15 (5): 727–51.

White, G. (1996) 'Public sector pay bargaining: comparability, decentralisation and control', *Public Administration* 74 (1): 113–28.

Wilkinson, A., Redman, T., Snape, E. and Marchington, M. (1998) *Managing with Total Quality Management*, London: Macmillan.

Winchester, D. (1983) 'Industrial relations in the public sector' in G. Bain (ed.) *Industrial Relations in Britain*, Oxford: Blackwell.

Winchester, D. and Bach, S. (1995) 'The state: the public sector' in P. Edwards (ed.) *Industrial Relations: Theory and Practice in Britain*, Oxford: Blackwell.

Part IV
Players

9 Personnel managers

Managing to change?

Stephen Bach

The continuous process of public service reform that characterised the Conservative governments of 1979–97 reshaped the organisation and management of public services. The establishment of a variety of market regimes, coupled with a commitment to devolve authority to managers for operational performance, had major implications for the personnel function. These developments coincided with a substantial debate about the ideology and practice of human resource management, which in the public services were also influenced by theories relating to the new public management. Although there has been much confusion and disagreement surrounding the significance of these developments, by the mid-1990s there was a degree of consensus that, despite strict financial controls and the political sensitivity of public services, managers had been granted an unprecedented degree of discretion to shape the way they recruited, rewarded and deployed their staff and that they were using those freedoms to alter organisational values, enhance work force flexibility and enforce stricter performance standards. Whether these developments were to be celebrated as representing the successful transplantation of best personnel practice from the private sector or condemned as eroding the public sector ethos was widely debated (Colling 1997; Ferlie *et al.* 1996; Winchester and Bach 1995).

In the realm of policy prescriptions discussion of personnel practice has increasingly resembled the models of human resource management advocated in the private sector. No trust annual report or executive agency business plan would be complete without the mantra that 'people are our most important asset'. As in the private sector there has been similar emphasis on developing a strategic approach towards the management of people, devolving responsibility to line managers and demonstrating that personnel specialists add value to their organisations. This is a far cry from the preoccupations of the personnel function in much of the post-war period, when it was highly centralised and oriented to the implementation of standardised procedures which were relatively undifferentiated across the public services (Farnham and Horton 1996).

This chapter begins with a consideration of the different models of the personnel function before examining its historical development in the public services. It is suggested that distinctive features of the public sector context inhibited the development of the personnel function and encouraged an essentially administrative role with limited influence. The market-style reforms of successive Conservative governments had major implications for personnel specialists, and a central question has been the degree to which these reforms have encouraged a more strategic approach to personnel management. It is suggested that there have been concerted attempts to devolve personnel practice to individual employer units and, within them, to line managers, although these developments have been uneven. It is argued, however, that the reforms have failed to foster a more strategic approach to personnel management, partly because of the short-term contract culture that has prevailed across the public services, coupled with budgetary restrictions and the centralising tendencies apparent within the public services. Finally, the discussion considers whether the prospects for the personnel function, and a more purposeful approach to personnel management, have been enhanced by the election of a Labour government.

Evolution and organisation of the personnel function

The development of the personnel function in the UK has been shaped by the context in which personnel practice is conducted. Historical accounts suggest that from its origins in welfare work personnel specialists have acquired a range of activities linked with changing economic and legal circumstances and shifting managerial priorities (Torrington 1989). More recently analysis has shifted to an examination of the internal organisation of companies and the relationship between structure, strategy and ownership in shaping the role and organisation of the personnel function (Marginson *et al.* 1995; Purcell 1995).

There have been many attempts to classify personnel roles and although different labels have been attached to them there are considerable similarities in approach (see Legge 1995). Storey (1992), drawing on case studies in fifteen public and private sector companies, identified four types of personnel specialist based on two different dimensions. The first dimension considers the extent to which personnel specialists are interventionary or non-interventionary; the second dimension considers whether the type of intervention is strategic or tactical. 'Handmaidens' are reactive and non-interventionary, providing routine services at the behest of line managers. 'Advisers' are also non-interventionary but act as internal consultants, concentrating on more strategic activities in supporting line managers. 'Regulators' are more interventionary and are custodians of the personnel rules within the organisation and act as 'managers of discontent', maintaining a stable industrial relations climate. Finally, 'changemakers' are highly interventionary and strategic, seeking to orientate employment relations to the changing needs of the organisation.

The scope for personnel specialists to adopt particular roles is influenced by the organisation of the personnel function, in which the traditional department is only one possibility. Adams (1991) identifies four main variants with increasing levels of externalisation. They range from the 'in-house' agency in which some activities are charged to other departments to 'internal consultancy' and a 'business within a business' model in which the personnel function becomes a trading company servicing its own and other organisations. The fourth variant is 'external consultancy', in which no internal personnel capacity is retained. All these approaches require some form of contract or service level agreement and within the public services there has been increasing interest in these different patterns of delivery (for example, Audit Commission 1994).

A common feature of the analysis of the roles and organisation of the personnel function is that they share a contingency approach in which the distinctive characteristics of the organisation and the priorities of managers condition the role played by personnel specialists. In a context in which it is widely believed that the distinctive features of public service management and organisation have been eroded, it could be anticipated that a different model of personnel management would have emerged in recent years. Before examining this issue, the distinctive features of traditional personnel management practice are examined.

The historical legacy

In the aftermath of the Second World War some of the distinctive characteristics of public service employment relations were consolidated during a period of continuous growth in the size and scope of the sector. Although there were important variations within the public services, a number of common features shaped management practice. These resulted in a relatively undeveloped personnel role which could be characterised as in the 'handmaidens' tradition in the 1950s and 1960s with some evolution into the 'regulators' role as industrial relations became more turbulent and conflictual during the 1970s. This arose from certain key features of public service management.

The first comprised a distinct set of management values. Public services developed as a coalition of separate professional hierarchies, each with its own set of values shaped by a lengthy training process and separate regulatory requirements. Distinct occupational identities have been reinforced by their labour market position, with professional staff, such as doctors, teachers, social workers and academics, being served by a national labour market in which their primary loyalty is to their profession rather than to a specific employer (Pratchett and Wingfield 1996). These features of public service management stifled the development of the personnel function because professional staff were 'managed' by their colleagues and the purpose of public service organisations was equated with the actions of professional service providers, limiting the personnel role to servicing the needs of professional staff (Winchester 1983). Moreover, in contrast to their private sector counterparts, managers were frequently trade union members, which signified that they retained many of the same values as the staff they managed.

Second, within the public services there has been a tradition that the state should be a 'model employer', although the approach has not always been consistently applied. Central to this tradition was a willingness to recognise trade unions and to institutionalise their position through the establishment of national joint industrial councils. These negotiated detailed terms and conditions of employment. Integral to public service values was the requirement to act with probity and treat citizens equally through the application of uniform criteria. To support this ethos, standardised employment procedures were devised which assigned an essentially routine and administrative role to the personnel function, not least because there was little scope for local interpretation of national agreements.

Even at national level the role of the personnel function was severely circumscribed because collective bargaining arrangements were dominated by civil servants and Treasury officials (Winchester and Bach 1995). In addition to the Treasury's concern to maintain tight control over the public service pay bill, the centralised character of public service employment relations arose from the political sensitivity of public service provision, particularly in health and education (see Bach and Winchester 1994). This ensured that policy decisions were made in the higher echelons of central government by ministers and top civil servants, who frequently ignored the personnel consequences of their decisions.

By the early 1970s the limitations of these patterns of management organisation were becoming apparent. There was concern that the emphasis on separate functional departments was a recipe for poor co-ordination and implementation of policy (Winchester 1983: 161). A unifying thread of the critical reports on management practice in the public services was to note the absence of, and the requirement for, a more developed personnel function to ensure more coherent personnel practices. Within the civil service the Fulton report (1968) proposed a higher status for personnel work to remedy inadequate career planning and to ensure a greater focus on the motivation and rewards of individuals. This was to be achieved by the establishment of a Civil Service Department (Farnham and Horton 1996: 75). In local government a similar stimulus was provided by the Bains report (1972), which envisaged a major role for the personnel function within a reformed, corporate-style management structure. Bains advocated personnel representation at top management level and suggested that the personnel function could encourage a stronger management ethos by stimulating training linked with managerial rather than with solely professional requirements (White and Hutchinson 1996: 194). The first official recognition of the need for a separate personnel function in the NHS arose during the 1974 reorganisation, when the new health authorities were required to appoint personnel officers, although the conception of the personnel function was narrow, concentrating on routine staffing issues (McCarthy 1983).

This period proved to be the first of many false dawns for the personnel function, as can be illustrated by the experience of the NHS. McCarthy (1983) suggested that even the modest aspirations established for the personnel function proved difficult to achieve. Personnel officers remained subservient to administrators who, in their struggle for influence with professional staff, invariably wished to retain control over personnel matters. In addition, a shortage of suitable personnel officers was exacerbated by reluctance to fund the new function which undermined its development. These limitations remained partially hidden by the centralised character of collective bargaining, which assigned an essentially 'handmaiden'-style role to personnel practitioners at workplace level.

Public service restructuring

Successive Conservative governments, in office continuously for almost two decades from 1979, were committed to radical changes. Whilst the most visible features of their policies concerned their attack on trade union power and uncontrolled public spending, they developed a strong critique of public sector management values and policies. It was argued that managers had been too submissive in their dealings with trade unions and professional groups; the interests of 'producers' had prevailed over those of the 'consumers' of services, and the absence of market criteria and performance indicators had allowed lax management practice to prevail. The emphasis was on shifting from a predominantly administrative personnel function to one modelled on private sector best practice, with a strategic and business orientation (Farnham and Horton 1996: 316).

This transformation had three main components: reforming the management of public services, introducing compulsory competitive tendering (CCT) and establishing systems of internal markets (Winchester and Bach 1995). First, drawing on organisational forms prevalent in the private sector, the government invoked the model of the multi-divisional organisation to reshape the management and organisation of public services (Bach 1995; Kessler and Purcell 1996). Alongside a squeeze on financial resources and strong central control of expenditure, individual public services were fragmented into their constituent business units – executive agencies, direct service organisations, NHS trusts, grant maintained schools and the 'new' incorporated universities and colleges. These organisational units were frequently further subdivided into cost centres, requiring the devolution of personnel management responsibility. The government actively encouraged managers from the private sector to apply for senior management posts as a signal of the value they attached to private sector 'best practice'. Senior public service managers, who remained the majority, harboured few illusions about the role they were expected to play in changing the culture of a restructured public service sector.

This opened up the spectre of a radically reformed and more diverse role for the personnel function. It was anticipated that personnel would play a more strategic role, particularly within the corporate centre, with detailed consideration of the link between business and personnel strategy and ensuring that personnel policies were internally consistent. With the loosening of prescriptive central government regulation personnel specialists would have greater scope to exercise a degree of strategic choice in establishing the personnel policy most suited to their organisational requirements. New skills would have to be acquired to cope with issues delegated from central government, such as local pay bargaining, and to equip managers with expertise, such as marketing skills, which used to be the province of the private sector.

Second, the introduction of compulsory competitive tendering in the NHS and local government and of market testing in the civil service emphasised the way in which competition and contractual arrangements would be expected to reinforce these managerial reforms (see chapter 7). Even prior to personnel services being subject to CCT, personnel specialists were ambivalent about its value (Bach 1989). When services were contracted out they lost control of a major component of their work force, thus diminishing their influence. In the health service contracting services out has hindered the personnel function's capacity to develop innovative forms of cross-functional working because of the mixture of in-house and contracted-out services (Bach 1998).

The third part of the government reform strategy focused on the creation of a system of 'internal markets', intended to mimic the competitive relations found in the private sector. In the NHS, and to a lesser extent in schools, universities and the civil service, service providers have been separated from purchasing authorities. In particular, hospital managers encounter a high level of financial uncertainty, unsure about their annual contract income, which depends on the purchasing decisions of numerous health authority and GP fundholders. These uncertainties have required tight control of labour costs and increasing use of temporary contracts (Sly and Stillwell 1997).

For the personnel function, a major challenge has been to articulate a new set of values and personnel practices which capture and reinforce these new organisational realities. Personnel specialists have been expected to establish effective communication with staff and ensure that employees have the required competences to perform effectively. At the same time the establishment of separate business units, with budgetary control devolved to service managers, has encouraged line managers to take a more active role in the management of human resources (Bach 1995; Kessler and Purcell 1996; Kessler 1997).

Human resource management and the new public management

These structural reforms have fundamentally altered the context in which managers work and have challenged the traditional role of the personnel function. An emphasis on value for money, customer service and flexibility has eroded the traditional notions of fairness, standardisation and probity that characterised management in the public domain (Stewart and Ranson 1988). These alterations in management style have been termed the new public management (see Hood 1991; Ferlie *et al.* 1996). Although it has become a contested term, in its employment philosophy new public management shares much of the same pedigree as human resource management (HRM). Suggested changes in employment practices include tighter control of staff through clearer performance targets, linked with individual performance-related pay and more forceful management of issues such as absenteeism (see Ferlie *et al.* 1996: 10–15). These prescriptions resonate with HRM which comprises 'a set of policies designed to maximise organisational integration, employee commitment, flexibility and quality of work' (Guest 1987: 503). Guest's emphasis on the value of employees to organisational success, termed 'soft' HRM, has been contrasted with a more instrumental, calculative approach to personnel management termed 'hard' HRM in which the emphasis is firmly on cost minimisation (Storey 1989). How far have the policies and practices associated with HRM and the new managerialism taken root in the public services?

A unifying theme of HRM and the new public management has been the lionising of managers in establishing higher levels of performance from a more flexible and committed work force. Successive Conservative governments aimed to recruit a new cadre of managers, from outside the public sector, who favoured radical reforms of employment practices. In the civil service of the 131 agency chief executives recruited by the end of 1996, 69 per cent were recruited by open competition and 37 per cent of the posts were filled by candidates from outside the civil service (House of Lords 1998: 51). However, within the Senior Civil Service as a whole, outsiders remain a small proportion (Talbot 1997: 20) and this led the Conservative government to announce new plans to increase external recruitment (Cm 3321 1996: 34). In the NHS, the first two appointments to the chair of the NHS Management Board (chief executive) were outsiders, but subsequent NHS chief executives have been career NHS managers, mirroring the dominant trend in the NHS.

Private sector appointees have rarely fulfilled the transformational role assigned to them and concern has been expressed about the impact on civil service morale, political impartiality and management continuity of the widespread use of recruitment from outsiude the civil service (House of Lords 1998: 52). The reputation of external recruits has been tarnished by the dismissal of the chief executives of the Prison Service and the Child Support

Agency. This largely reflected unresolved problems about the division of responsibility between ministers and agency chief executives for policy matters and ambiguity about who was ultimately accountable for the performance of individual agencies. Similar problems arose for Victor Paige, the first NHS 'chief executive', who resigned in frustration (Paige 1987). This chequered history indicates that it has been difficult for top managers to steer their organisations in a strategic fashion because of unpredictable political interventions, raising doubts about the capacity of personnel specialists to pursue a strategic agenda.

Training and development have been viewed as a litmus test of HRM because an organisation that demonstrates commitment to its work force by investing in training will wish to protect that investment. There has been a concerted effort to boost management training and to extend it to professional staff. For example, in the NHS, which contains many occupational groups hostile to managerial values, it has become commonplace for professional staff to gain management qualifications, such as an MBA. In secondary education the expectation is that all head teachers appointed for the first time will hold a professional headship qualification demonstrating their leadership skills and management proficiency (Department for Education and Employment 1997: 46).

Training activity has been linked with the identification of core competences which are the key skills necessary to ensure effective performance. The development of competence frameworks is widespread throughout the civil service, enabling job requirements to be better defined, skill gaps to be identified and training provision to be linked with the aquisition of core competences (Cm 3321 1996: 23). This process is not confined to managerial posts as competence-based NVQs have been used to increase training and career opportunities for lower-level staff, such as health care assistants and others working in personal social services (LGMB and CCETSW 1997: 101–5). Public sector organisations have sought to gain the national Investors in People standard, not least because it is a stated government objective that all civil servants will be employed in organisations recognised as Investors in People by the year 2000 (Cm 3321 1996: 19). These reforms in employee resourcing are designed to ensure increased flexibility and higher performance standards (see chapters 6 and 8).

Doubts exist about these initiatives because survey evidence (Talbot 1994) reveals that management development practice has changed least out of seven areas identified to gauge the degree of public sector change. Almost a third of respondents felt that the level of management development support was inadequate and a further 20 per cent were unsure whether managers' needs were being met (Talbot 1994: 63). Commitment to management development is further called into question by the absence of increased central government funding for training and development in the civil service (Talbot 1997: 24). In short, these developments signify that more attention is being assigned to personnel matters, but can this be equated with an enhanced role for the personnel function?

The organisation and role of the personnel function

The restructuring of the public services and experimentation with HRM techniques could be expected to have had a major impact on the organisation and role of the personnel function. Kessler and Purcell (1995) argue that some of the distinctive features of public service organisation have diminished, not least owing to the establishment of multi-divisional organisational structures within the public sector, including the NHS (Bach 1995). The experience of the private sector indicates that these developments influence a range of personnel decisions (Purcell and Ahlstrand 1994; Marginson *et al.* 1995).

The implications of the devolution process are not straightforward because it can occur at a number of different levels and take different forms. First, there has been a shift in personnel responsibilities from national level to the enterprise level which has accompanied the fragmentation of each public service into a myriad of separate employers. The expectation has been that personnel specialists would play a more pivotal role as they were granted greater autonomy to shape personnel practice, but these expectations have been only partially fulfilled.

Second, particularly within the larger employers a further process of devolution has occurred as individual agencies, local authorities and trusts have been broken up into their constituent 'business units'. The logic of such an approach has been that personnel practice would be more closely related to the requirements of each business unit and a more differentiated pattern of personnel management would emerge. A third, qualitatively different, form of devolution does not focus on the level of decision making but concerns the devolution of responsibility from personnel specialists to line managers which could, in principle, occur at any level within the organisational hierarchy. Personnel specialists have suggested that this process would allow them to concentrate on more strategic activities whilst empowering line managers to take more responsibility for personnel practice. It is the interplay of these three processes which has, in large part, shaped the recent trajectory of the personnel function in the public services, as the following examination of the civil service, NHS and local government illustrates.

The civil service

In the civil service the most important development has been the establishment of executive agencies, which employ approximately 75 per cent of civil servants. Central to their development has been the delegation of personnel activities in areas such as pay and conditions from central government to individual agencies, and in 1996 service-wide pay bargaining was ended. These delegated powers have undoubtedly enhanced the operational freedom of agency managers and have spawned a variety of reforms of pay and grading structures, work organisation and employee involvement (House of

Lords 1998; IDS 1998). Nonetheless, the discretion, and by extension the authority, of agency personnel specialists remains constrained. First, it is striking that, despite the original emphasis on agency autonomy, survey evidence (Development Division 1997b: 15) suggests that it is only by a narrow margin – 53 per cent – that agency managers view themselves as the dominant influence on the overall personnel agenda. In areas such as pay policy the combined influence of the parent department and the Treasury is judged to be the dominant influence on agency policy. These findings are corroborated by Farnham and McNeil (1997: 44), who report frustration among agency senior managers about the restrictions placed on the pursuit of their personnel agenda, particularly in respect of pay awards.

It is perhaps unsurprising that the Treasury continues to intervene actively in such a sensitive political and economic issue as pay policy, but central government influence is not confined to pay. The personnel agenda has been strongly shaped by a series of central government initiatives which have been imposed on the agencies, as the obligation placed on all civil service agencies and departments to achieve Investors in People status by the year 2000 illustrates (Cm 3321 1996: 19).

In terms of devolution within agencies, there has been a tendency to separate personnel policy formulation undertaken by a corporate personnel function from the more operational personnel work which is increasingly located within the appropriate business units (Development Division 1997a, b). The main responsibilities of the corporate personnel role are to establish the overall personnel strategy, linked with the requirements of the business, to promote core organisational values and to ensure that there is a sufficient pool of senior management talent. Consequently corporate personnel specialists in agencies like the Vehicle Inspectorate suggest that the specific features of their agency have facilitated a primarily strategic and 'change-maker' role (see Clark 1997: 13) with a slimmed down central personnel function. The corollary of these reforms is that much greater emphasis has been placed on developing the personnel function within individual business units. Within many of the larger agencies, such as the Benefits Agency, the size of the personnel function has increased as most business units have established their own personnel management units (Kessler 1997: 17).

The assumption of this type of structure is that local business units should have discretion to establish their own policies geared to their local requirements and be liberated from the centre. In agencies with diverse businesses significant differences in personnel practice could be expected to develop. However, this sits uneasily with the concern of agency managers to develop strong corporate cultures (Fogden 1993; Clark 1997) and the need to ensure that accountability to central government is maintained. In resolving these tensions between local discretion and central accountability, in most cases the latter appears to be the dominant force.

The devolution of responsibilities from personnel specialists to line managers has been an integral part of the reform process, with official guidance extolling the virtues of line management empowerment (Development Division 1993; Cm 3321 1996: 41). Line managers are expected to play the primary role in the selection and development of their staff by cultivating a learning culture, providing feedback and ensuring effective communication of the business plan so that staff are aware of their contribution to the organisation (Cm 3321 1996: 42). If intentions are clear the outcomes are more ambiguous. Within agencies line managers are viewed as much less influential than personnel specialists even in relation to issues such as recruitment and selection and training and development which have been the primary focus of these initiatives. Despite line management influence being greater concerning absenteeism, appraisal and performance-related pay the authors conclude that 'Nevertheless the low level of line management influence versus central management influence (Board and HR) is surprising, given the apparent trend towards delegation to the line' (Development Division 1997b: 12).

This uneven development reflects the ambivalent attitudes of line managers and personnel specialists to devolution. Line managers are not opposed to devolution in principle but because of increased work load pressures are reluctant to take on further responsibilities. They are concerned that a 'downsized' central personnel function is attempting to offload responsibilities on to them without providing the necessary training and support, fostering cynicism and distrust (Development Division 1993: 9, 1997a: 23; Hall and Torrington 1998: 49).

The National Health Service

The establishment of NHS trusts envisaged the delegation of personnel practice from central government to local level, with employers granted considerable discretion to devise their own terms and conditions of employment. Trust managers have responded by establishing new employment roles which cut across existing occupational groupings; altered the composition of the work force by boosting the proportion of support workers; made greater use of a range of employment contracts, particularly fixed-term contracts; tightened up on the performance of staff, particularly through more rigorous management of absence; and reduced the importance of the relationship with trade unions by fostering other channels of communication (see Bryson *et al.* 1996; Corby and Higham 1996; IRS 1997a; Bach 1998). Despite these significant innovations, the personnel agenda at trust level remains heavily circumscribed by the financial circumstances and policy framework under which trusts operate (Bach and Winchester 1994; Bach 1998).

Each trust's financial position has been heavily dependent on the funding made available to its local purchasers and, with contracts agreed on an annual basis, it has usually been a few months into the financial year before each trust's financial position has become reasonably clear. Trust managers have complained that purchasers have not made adequate allowance for the pay element, with pay increases largely excluded from contract negotiations. This restrictive budgetary context, exacerbated by the requirement to achieve tough financial targets, has made it difficult to bring about systematic long term changes in employment practices. This view has been endorsed by the nurses' review body in its explanation of the slow development of local pay (Nurses' Pay Review Body 1997).

Second, the personnel agenda within trusts has in large part been shaped by responding to a series of frequently contradictory national policy initiatives and meeting a variety of national performance targets. Trust managers have been required to develop local pay machinery, to competitively tender support services, to reduce junior doctors' hours and to meet their Opportunity 2000 targets. There has been great uncertainty amongst senior managers about how much they could depart from national policy guidance on issues such as market testing (Bach 1998).

Within individual trusts the personnel function has been shaped by the division of the organisation into a number of separate clinical directorates. Three main options for the structure of the department are possible. Personnel can remain centralised but allow divisions to negotiate the range and cost of personnel services provided from the centre through service level agreements (SLAs). An alternative is that personnel specialists can remain responsible to the central personnel director but be located with the divisions, establishing closer working relations with the core businesses. Finally, a small central department can be retained which focuses on strategic issues and the divisions are responsible for their own personnel staff.

There are variations between trusts in the approach they have adopted. Evidence drawn from case studies of three acute NHS trusts suggests that the extent of devolution to clinical directorates depends on the size of the trust, the service mixture and senior management views about the benefits of devolution (Bach 1998). Survey evidence confirms these variations and indicates that there have been concerted attempts to devolve personnel tasks to clinical directorates and, within directorates, to pass responsibilities to line managers (IRS 1996). Greater control of the personnel function is exercised by line managers in the business units, who are the customers of the predominantly operational personnel service.

Line managers suggested that the contribution of personnel specialists has been enhanced when they are more focused on the requirements of individual directorates. However, too great an emphasis on the freedom of individual directorates can create tension between the need for central personnel to take a corporate view in the interests of the whole trust as opposed to the needs of the individual business units whose focus will be more short term. Conflicts of loyalty can arise for personnel specialists working at business unit level, who have to meet the different expectations of senior management in central personnel and the business units. Inconsistencies in the way that staff are managed between directorates has led to feelings of dissatisfaction and inequity amongst the work force (Bach 1995).

To avoid some of these shortcomings, and to reduce the increased expenditure associated with devolution to clinical directorates, trust managers appear to be attempting to develop more corporate management styles which play down the emphasis on clinical directorate autonomy that characterised the early years of the NHS reforms. Within a context in which trust autonomy remains heavily circumscribed, owing to the influence of national pay arrangements for most staff, emphasising clinical autonomy makes little sense. Strong centralising tendencies therefore remain, not least because of the financial difficulties which most trusts face which can be resolved only on a trust-wide basis (Bach 1998; Kessler 1997: 14).

Local authorities

In contrast to agencies and trusts, local authorities have always constituted separate employers. Historically they have had greater discretion about whether they would adhere to national agreements, and have had some freedom to interpret such agreements in the light of local priorities. In comparison with agencies and trusts, local authorities are distinctive in offering a wider range of services with their own service based personnel agenda. For example, social service departments are subject to specific legislative requirements and funding arrangements, reflected in the guidance for personnel specialists (see, for example, LGMB and CCETSW 1997).

During recent years there have been major reforms of working practices (White 1997) and further changes may arise from the adoption of a new single status agreement (IRS 1997b). These developments have occurred in a context in which the overall discretion available to local authorities to shape their personnel agenda has diminished (Winchester and Bach 1995: 327; Leach 1996: 159). This has occurred most clearly in education, with the diminution of the role of local education authorities (LEAs), but in all spheres the financial and legislative control exercised by central government has increased.

The diversity of local government services with different financial regimes, variable requirements arising from compulsory competitive tendering and differing levels of competition has fragmented local authorities and encouraged the devolution of personnel practice to individual business units in a more substantial manner than has occurred in the NHS (Audit Commission 1994; Keen and Vickerstaffe 1997; Kessler 1997). By 1994 over 50 per cent of personnel staff worked outside central departments, a much higher proportion than was the case in finance and information technology departments (Audit Commission 1994: 4). Even prior to CCT for personnel services, the personnel function was affected by the reorganisation of local authorities into client and contractor functions. Personnel as a provider of support to CCT affected services (for example, for the payroll) came under pressure from service managers because they were resistant to paying for central services which they viewed as of little value and a cost over which they had little control (Davis 1996: 14; Walsh 1996: 63). When authorities were required to tender competitively for personnel services from the late 1980s these market pressures were formalised. In the first instance authorities were required to tender for or contract out 30 per cent of their personnel activities measured by cost with the intention to raise this threshold to 40 per cent (Fowler 1997).

The direct impact of CCT an personnel services has been dissipated because, by contracting out aspects of training, recruitment and selection and occupational health services, local authorities have ensured that the whole personnel function is not subject to the full rigours of CCT (Fowler 1996). The process of local government reorganisation and the prospect of the Conservative government's electoral demise diluted further the pressure towards CCT for personnel services.

The indirect impact has been more pronounced. In response not only to service fragmentation arising from CCT but also to local government reorganisation, authorities have reintegrated by developing a corporate management model intended to replace traditional functional management. In some cases, as in Hackney, there is a division between a small core personnel function responsible for strategy and a self-financing trading personnel unit (Mullen 1998: 42). There are doubts, however, about the capacity of the personnel function to provide a policy lead to the business units in such circumstances because the usual framework is that the head of personnel reports to a director of corporate affairs. This has effectively encouraged the removal of senior personnel posts and a downgrading of personnel from the top team (Mullen 1998: 44).

In these circumstances it might be assumed that personnel specialists within individual business units would be taking advantage of their discretion to shape personnel practice without hindrance from a central personnel department. The extent to which this has occurred has been uneven, not least because of central financial controls and dwindling financial resources (Keen and Vickerstaffe 1997; Kessler 1997). In their case study of Barset County Council, Keen and Vickerstaffe suggest that service managers had been given the freedom to save money but not to spend it. These managers complained that increasingly they had to obtain permission from more senior managers about staffing decisions which undermined their belief that they had genuine scope to develop innovative personnel practices.

In the school sector substantial devolution of management responsibility to schools occurred as result of the 'local management of schools' reforms coupled with the scope for schools to become grant maintained and opt out of direct control by the local education authority. These reforms were designed to erode the power of LEAs and to increase the influence of head teachers and governing bodies within schools, especially as regards financial management. For the personnel function, located within the LEA, this opened up the spectre that its influence would be eclipsed as the influence of the LEA dwindled (Ironside and Seifert 1995).

Schools are not sufficiently large organisations to support the employment of a personnel specialist, and head teachers and their deputies have become the fulcrum of personnel activity, with considerable discretion over staffing matters. In conjunction with at least one school governor, the head with the deputy has a central role in teacher recruitment and selection, and no appointment is made without the head teacher's approval. Particularly with senior appointments, an LEA adviser may still participate in appointment panels, as used to be the case prior to LMS, but the LEA adviser would be present at the invitation of the school, and paid by the school, in the case of grant-maintained schools.

The extent to which the strengthening of the head teacher's and governors' role in personnel policy has eclipsed the personnel advisory role varies between LEAs. They have responded to the educational reforms differently, with some LEAs maintaining a more interventionist stance than others (Riley 1996). Moreover, the relationship between an individual school and the LEA is crucial. Some schools, dissatisfied with the personnel service available from their LEA, have purchased personnel services from non-LEA sources (Thatcher 1994). However, over 90 per cent of head teachers rated their LEA personnel service as 'good' or 'very good', a greater degree of satisfaction being expressed with personnel than with any of the other eleven LEA support services which they were asked to rank (Bullock and Thomas 1997: 107). Many schools therefore continue to enjoy good relations with their LEA and use LEA personnel advice, on a contract basis, particularly for complex redundancy and employment law cases. Even if this is the case, the shift to the school as the focus of personnel activity, with the LEA becoming the client of the school, represents a major change in the relationship between LEAs and schools.

In summary, across the public services there have been cross-cutting patterns of devolution, with the catalyst being the reorganisation of public services into separately constituted employer units. Not surprisingly, given the historical legacy of stultifying centralised personnel practice, most managers have been eager to embrace devolution in its various guises. Their aspirations have not always been converted into practice, reflecting unrealistic management expectations about the prospects of devolution and some trade union opposition, matched by increased managerial awareness of the shortcomings of devolution.

Discussion: the limits of a strategic approach

Underpinning the experimentation with human resource management practices and the changing organisation of the personnel function, some commentators have discerned a shift to a more strategic role for the personnel function across the public services (Barnett *et al.* 1996: 34–5; Farnham and Horton 1996: 324–5). The most important facets of such an approach include integrating personnel policies with business strategy and ensuring that personnel demonstrates its contribution to the organisation, not least by focusing on strategic rather than operational activities. These sentiments are widely endorsed by public service managers, judging by the volume of reports espousing the importance of a strategic approach to HRM (Development Division 1997a, b; NHS Executive 1997; LGMB 1994).

Discerning how far a strategic approach has emerged is by no means straightforward. The human resource management literature is replete with warnings about the difference between the rhetoric and the reality of HRM practice (Sisson 1994; Legge 1995). Consequently, policy documents which suggest that business strategy is linked with HRM strategy are, at best, a necessary but not a sufficient condition of a strategic approach. The fullest analysis of these issues has been conducted in the civil service with a detailed assessment of executive agency and departmental documents accompanied by a survey of human resource managers (Development Division 1997a). This analysis suggested that although personnel issues were often mentioned they were insufficiently integrated into corporate plans: 'For many HR issues there is a large discrepancy between how important for organisational success such issues are viewed to be by HR managers, and how much they actually surface as important in agency and departmental plans' (Development Division 1997a: 6).

Similarly in local government the Society of Chief Personnel Officers (SOCPO), the national body for personnel directors, has acknowledged that setting strategic objectives has been one of the weakest aspects of personnel practice (SOCPO 1997: 6). In the health service expectations that with the advent of trusts a more strategic approach to the management of human resources would be developed have been disappointed. By the middle of 1997, despite exhortations from the NHS Executive about the importance of a formal human resource strategy, only just over half of trusts surveyed had implemented a formal human resource strategy (IRS 1997a: 3). In an uncharacteristically blunt analysis of the state of HRM in the NHS the NHS Executive (1997: para. 3) admitted there had been major failings at trust level:

> However, not all local employers have placed HR on their strategic agenda in a way which encourages a well thought out approach. As a result, development of human resource management capacity and best practice in human resources has been patchy.

A variety of other indicators would seem to cast doubt on the degree to which a strategic approach to personnel management has emerged. The existence of staff shortages within some occupational groups, particularly teachers and nurses (Nurses' Pay Review Body 1997; Schoolteachers' Review Body 1998), relatively high levels of absenteeism, concerns about heath and safety standards and stress, particularly in the 'caring professions' (Balloch 1997; National Audit Office 1996), provide little support for a strategic approach to personnel management. What accounts for this relatively negative picture?

First, the capacity of personnel specialists to contribute strategically has been influenced by their lack of representation at top management level. In the civil service, the Conservative government acknowledged that the emphasis on generalist skills has inhibited the development of an influential personnel function (Cm 3321 1996: 25–7). This has contributed to personnel specialists remaining, by their own admission, in a predominantly administrative capacity (Development Division 1997b: 16). In the NHS personnel specialists are rarely represented at trust board level. This reflects the views of senior trust managers, particularly chief executives, that Personnel has only a limited contribution to make (Bach 1995; NHS Executive, 1997). In local government similar trends are evident, as noted above, with personnel specialists largely excluded from the top management tier (Mullen 1998).

Second, market-style reforms have created considerable managerial uncertainty which has fostered a short term agenda oriented to cost minimisation and opportunistic personnel practice (Corby 1995: 180; Bach 1998). For example, in the health service personnel practice has been shaped by restrictive financial targets, budgetary constraints and the uncertainty attached to trust income because of the conflictual and complex nature of the annual contracting cycle. Despite some greater operational freedoms which trust status has brought, managers have been largely excluded from NHS policy making, which has left them to implement a plethora of frequently contradictory policy initiatives whilst they have been increasingly judged against rigid, centrally defined performance targets. This has prevented the development of a strategic lead, as has been acknowledged by the NHS Executive (1997: para. 7):

> The lack of a clear strategic framework which locks human resource management effectively into the government's health care policies and service development objectives has been a major impediment to progress. Equally, human resource management capacity is insufficiently developed across the whole of the service to make a vital contribution.

A third difficulty, illustrated by the above quotation, is that within an increasingly fragmented public service sector the responsibility for the development of a framework for effective personnel practice has become unclear, and as a consequence this role has been neglected. The pretence of trust, school and agency autonomy has hindered the process, because central government has been able to abdicate responsibility for personnel policy, as can be illustrated by the failure of the NHS Executive to develop effective personnel capacity to make a reality of local pay determination (Deegan 1995). Even if the will existed to develop a coherent framework for personnel policy, within individual public services responsibility for personnel policy is divided between government and employers and competing trade union and professional organisations, which inhibits coherent policy.

The election of a Labour government whose manifesto gave particular prominence to improving education and health services, and included a commitment to the replacement of CCT and the introduction of a national minimum wage, potentially amounts to a considerable agenda of change for public service personnel practice. However, any such developments have to be tempered by two features of Labour policy which suggest strong elements of continuity in policy towards the public sector.

First, the Labour government endorsed the public expenditure plans which it inherited from the previous Conservative government for the first two years it was in office. Although this did not prevent additional expenditure in high priority areas such as education and health, it signalled the Labour government's intention to maintain tight control of public expenditure. Tight budgetary constraints can be expected to foster a short term personnel agenda by reinforcing managerial uncertainty and by preventing personnel specialists 'paying for change', as has invariably been required to achieve major reforms of personnel practice in other sectors. Moreover, the Labour government's commitment to reduce management costs could make personnel managers vulnerable in any future cost-cutting exercises. Second, the Labour government, whilst favouring co-operation rather than competition, has expressed support for the continuation of devolved systems of decision making within NHS trusts and other public services, sustaining the emphasis on local flexibility, albeit within a more explicit national framework (Department of Health 1997).

The Labour government has expressed more vocal commitment to the work force which reflects its understanding that high quality public services cannot be sustained alongside a demoralised public service (Department for Education and Employment 1997). In the NHS there has been recognition that higher priority should be assigned to human resource development and that this needs to be developed within a more coherent national framework (Department of Health 1997: 51). However, this support for a softer developmental agenda continues alongside a hard human resources agenda oriented to 'weeding out' poor performers and maintaining tight cost control, with important ramifications for personnel practice.

The experience of the last two decades suggests that considerable scepticism exists about the transformation of personnel practice in the public services. Personnel specialists, implicated in the gap between personnel policy and practice, face formidable difficulties in moving centre stage and breaking free of the reactive, predominantly administrative role that has characterised the development of the personnel function. Despite almost twenty years of continuous public sector reform, distinctive features of public sector personnel practice remain intact and continue to inhibit the quest for a more strategic role for the personnel function.

References

Adams, K. (1991) 'Externalisation *v.* specialisation: what is happening to personnel?' *Human Resource Management Journal* 1 (4): 40–54.

Audit Commission (1994) *Behind Closed Doors: the Revolution in Central Support Services,* London: HMSO.

Bach, S. (1989) *Too High a Price to Pay,* Warwick Papers in Industrial Relations 25, Coventry: Industrial Relations Research Unit.

Bach, S. (1995) 'Restructuring the personnel function: the case of NHS trusts', *Human Resource Management Journal* 5 (2): 99–115.

Bach, S. (1998) 'The Management of Employment Relations in the NHS: Pay, Work Organisation and the Internal Market', unpublished Ph.D. thesis, Coventry: University of Warwick.

Bach, S. and Winchester, D. (1994) 'Opting out of pay devolution? The prospects for local pay bargaining in UK public services', *British Journal of Industrial Relations* 32 (2): 263–82.

Bains, M. (1972) *The New Local Authorities: Management and Structure,* London: HMSO.

Balloch, S. (1997) 'Issues facing the social services workforce' in M. May, E. Brunsdon and G. Craig (eds) *Social Policy Review 9,* London: Social Policy Association.

Barnett, S., Buchanan, D., Patrickson, M. and Maddern, J. (1996) 'Negotiating the evolution of the HR function: practical advice from the health care sector', *Human Resource Management Journal* 6 (4): 18–37.

Bryson, C., Jackson, M. and Leopold, J. (1996) 'Human resource management in NHS trusts', *Health Services Management Research* 9 (2): 98–106.

Bullock, A. and Thomas, H. (1997) *Schools at the Centre? A Study of Decentralisation,* London: Routledge.

Clark, M. (1997) 'Testing times at the vehicle inspectorate', *Work and Employment* 4: 11–14.

Colling, T. (1997) 'Managing human resources in the public sector' in I. Beardwell and L. Holden (eds) *Human Resource Management: a Contemporary Perspective,* London: Pitman.

Colling, T. and Ferner, A. (1995) 'Privatization and marketization' in P. Edwards (ed.) *Industrial Relations: Theory and Practice in Britain,* Oxford: Blackwell.

Corby, S. (1995) 'Opportunity 2000 in the NHS: a missed opportunity for women', *Employee Relations* 17 (2): 23–37.

Corby, S. (1996) 'The National Health Service' in D. Farnham and S. Horton (eds) *Managing People in the Public Services,* London: Macmillan.

Corby, S. and Higham, D. (1996) 'Decentralisation in the NHS: diagnosis and prognosis', *Human Resource Management Journal* 6 (1): 49–63.

Cm 3321 (1996) *Development and Training for Civil Servants: A Framework for Action,* London: HMSO.

Davis, H. (1996) 'The fragmentation of community government' in S. Leach and H. Davis (eds) *Enabling or Disabling Local Government,* Buckingham: Open University Press.

Deegan, M. (1995) 'Making it pay the local way', *Health Service Journal* 105 (5477): 19.

Department for Education and Employment (1997) *Excellence in Schools,* Cm 3681, London: Stationery Office.

Department of Health (1997) *The New NHS,* Cmd 3807, London: Stationery Office.

Development Division (1993) *Encouraging and Supporting the Delegation of Human Resource Development Responsibilities to Line Managers*, London: Cabinet Office.

Development Division (1997a) *The Changing Role of the Human Resource Function: Main Report*, London: Cabinet Office.

Development Division (1997b) *The Changing Role of the Human Resource Function: Research Findings and Individual Project Work*, London: Cabinet Office.

Farnham, D. and Horton, S. (1996). 'Traditional people management' in D. Farnham and S. Horton (eds) *Managing People in the Public Services*, London: Macmillan.

Farnham, D. and McNeill, J. (1997) 'Pay delegation in Next Steps agencies: some initial research findings', *Public Policy and Administration* 12 (4): 35–46.

Ferlie, E., Ashburner, L., Fitzgerald, L. and Pettigrew, A. (1996) *The New Public Management in Action*, Oxford: Oxford University Press.

Fogden, M. (1993) 'Managing change in the employment service', *Public Money and Management* 13 (2): 9–16.

Fowler, A. (1996) 'Winds of change lash council staff', *People Management*, 18 April, pp. 22–7.

Fowler, A. (1997) 'How to outsource personnel', *People Management*, 20 February, pp. 40–2.

Fulton (1968) *The Report of the Committee on the Civil Service* (the Fulton report), Cmnd 3638, London: HMSO.

Guest, D. (1987) 'Human resource management and industrial relations,' *Journal of Management Studies* 24 (5): 503–21.

Hall, L. and Torrington, D. (1998) 'Letting go or holding on: the devolution of operational personnel activities', *Human Resource Management Journal* 8 (1): 1–55.

Hood, C. (1991) 'A public management for all seasons?' *Public Administration* 69 (2): 3–19.

House of Lords (1998) *Report*, Select Committee on the Public Service, session 1997–98, paper 55, London: Stationery Office.

Incomes Data Services (1998) *Civil Service Pay Bargaining in 1997*, IDS Report 753, pp. 25–31.

Industrial Relations Services (1996) 'The changing world of personnel', *Employment Trends* 604: 4–11.

Industrial Relations Services (1997a) 'Annual review of pay and employment practices' I, 'A survey of 137 NHS trusts', *Health Service Report*, Autumn, pp. 2–11.

Industrial Relations Services (1997b) 'Historic single-status deal in local government', *Employment Trends* 639: 5–10.

Ironside, M. and Seifert, R. (1995) *Industrial Relations in Schools*, London: Routledge.

Keen, L. and Vickerstaffe, S. (1997) '"We're all human resource managers now": local government middle managers', *Public Money and Management* 17 (3): 41–6.

Kessler, I. (1997) 'Business, New Organisational Forms and Employment Relations in the Public Service Sector', paper presented at the fifth IIRA Regional Industrial Relations Conference, Dublin, August.

Kessler, I. and Purcell, J. (1996) 'Strategic choice and new forms of employment relations in the public service sector', *International Journal of Human Resource Management* 7 (1): 206–29.

Leach, S. (1996) 'Conclusion: scenarios for change' in S. Leach and H. Davis (eds) *Enabling or Disabling Local Government*, Buckingham: Open University Press.

Legge, K. (1995) *Human Resource Management: Rhetorics and Realities*, London: Macmillan.

Local Government Management Board (1994) *The Changing Role of the Human Resource Function*, Luton: LGMB.

Local Government Management Board and Central Council for Education and Training in Social Work (1997) *Human Resources for Personal Social Services*, London: LGMB.

Marginson, P., Edwards, P., Armstrong, P. and Purcell, J. (1995) 'Strategy, structure and control in the changing corporation: a survey-based investigation', *Human Resource Management Journal* 5 (2): 3–27.

McCarthy, M. (1983) 'Personnel management in the health service', *Personnel Management* September, pp. 31–3.

Mullen, J. (1998) 'Local and aesthetic?' *People Management*, 5 February, pp. 42–4.

National Audit Office (1996) *Health and Safety in NHS Acute Hospital Trusts in England*, London: HMSO.

NHS Executive (1997) *Managing Human Resources in the NHS – a Service-wide Approach*, Leeds: NHSE.

Nurses' Pay Review Body (1997) *Fourteenth Report*, Cm 3538: London: Stationery Office.

Paige, V. (1987) 'The development of general management in the NHS, with particular reference to the implementation of the NHS management board', *Health Summary*, June, pp. 6 8.

Pratchett, L. and Wingfield, M. (1996) 'The demise of the public service ethos' in L. Pratchett and D. Wilson (eds) *Local Democracy and Local Government*, London: Macmillan.

Purcell, J. (1995) 'Corporate strategy and its link with human resource management strategy' in J. Storey (ed.) *Human Resource Management Strategy: a Critical Text*, London: Routledge.

Purcell, J. and Ahlstrand, B. (1994) *Human Resource Management in the Multi-divisional Company*, Aldershot: Dartmouth.

Riley, K. (1996) 'The changing framework and purposes of LEAs' in S. Leach and H. Davis (eds) *Enabling or Disabling Local Government*, Buckingham: Open University Press.

School Teachers' Review Body (1998) *Seventh Report*, Cm 3836, London: Stationery Office.

Sisson, K. (1994) 'Personnel management in Britain: paradigms, practice and prospects' in K. Sisson (ed.) *Personnel Management: a Comprehensive Guide to Theory and Practice in Britain*, Oxford: Blackwell.

Sly, F. and Stillwell, D. (1997) 'Temporary workers in Britain', *Labour Market Trends*, September, pp. 347–54.

Society of Chief Personnel Officers (1997) *Personnel: Adding Value in the Competitive Environment* II, London: SOCPO.

Stewart, J. and Ranson, S. (1988) 'Management in the public domain', *Public Money and Management* 8 (1): 13–19.

Storey, J. (1989) *New Perspectives on Human Resource Management*, London: Routledge.

Storey, J. (1992) *Developments in the Management of Human Resources*, Oxford: Blackwell.

Talbot, C. (1994) *Reinventing Public Management: a Survey of Public Sector Managers' Reactions to Change*, Corby: Institute of Management.

Talbot, C. (1997) 'UK civil service personnel reform: devolution, decentralisation and delusion', *Public Policy and Administration* 12 (4): 14–34.

Thatcher, M. (1994) 'Learning a lesson from the private sector', *Personnel Management*, April, pp. 34–7.

Torrington, D. (1989) 'Human resource management and the personnel function' in J. Storey (ed.) *New Perspectives on Human Resource Management*, London: Routledge.

Walsh, K. (1996) 'The role of the market and the growth of competition' in S. Leach and H. Davis (eds) *Enabling or Disabling Local Government*, Buckingham: Open University Press.

White, G. and Hutchinson, B. (1996) 'Local government' in D. Farnham and S. Horton (eds) *Managing People in the Public Services*, London: Macmillan.

White, G. (1997) 'Employment flexibilities in local government', *Public Policy and Administration* 12 (4): 47–59.

Winchester, D. (1983) 'Industrial relations in the public sector' in G. Bain (ed.) *Industrial Relations in Britain*, Oxford: Blackwell.

Winchester, D. and Bach, S. (1995) 'The state: the public sector' in P. Edwards (ed.) *Industrial Relations: Theory and Practice in Britain*, Oxford: Blackwell.

10 Trade unions

The challenge of individualism?

Hamish Mathieson and Susan Corby

> Trade union organisation has always been influenced by the character
> of the employment relationship, the structure of industry and labour
> markets and the composition of the labour force.
>
> (Winchester 1988: 493)

No consideration of public service trade unions can be isolated from the
political, legal and economic context in which they operate. Nor can trade
unions be divorced from their main function of negotiating pay. However,
readers are referred to other chapters in this book, as the context is not
rehearsed here. Instead, this chapter focuses on the public service unions
themselves, essentially since 1979. After briefly looking at the background,
it examines trends in union membership and density, then goes on to consider
union behaviour in terms of structure, organisation and industrial action.
The main points are that:

- Union membership in the public services is becoming an increasing
  proportion of all union membership.
- Public service union density has declined, albeit to a lesser extent than
  in the private sector.
- On the whole, single occupation unions have grown more than their
  multi-occupation counterparts.
- There has been a spate of union merger activity.
- Public service unions have become more political and more militant.
- There has been a noticeable move to managerial unionism, with a shift
  from an activist focus to a member focus.

Background

From the end of the First World War to 1979 public service unions essentially operated in an environment which assisted their growth and development. The government, as either direct or indirect employer, encouraged
collective bargaining and joint consultation, for instance through so-called
Whitley Committees. It also encouraged union membership. From 1979,

however, this changed. The Conservative government was of the view that the public services were 'the home of powerful trade unions which were unconstrained by market forces' (Kessler and Bayliss 1995: 149). Accordingly, public service employers withdrew union recognition in some organisations. The most high profile case was the withdrawal of union membership rights at Government Communication Headquarters (GCHQ) in 1984, but other examples include the withdrawal of union recognition at the National Maritime Museum and in some NHS trusts, such as Northumbria Ambulance and Mulberry. The government, as employer, also withdrew collective bargaining rights, for instance from schoolteachers and certain senior civil servants.

Allied with this was a shift in emphasis from a collectivist to a more individualistic approach, for instance the use of performance pay in the civil service, communications by managers to employees individually, rather than through workplace representatives, and a range of quality initiatives (see chapter 8). Also, essentially through contracting out, privatisation and increased control over labour costs, there has been a reduction in the number of those directly employed in the public services, thus cutting the pool of potential and actual union members. In addition, there was a legislative programme imposing increasing legal restraints on all trade unions in respect of industrial action and making industrial action by prison officers unlawful.

In sum, the environment became more hostile for public service unions from 1979 to 1997 as employers departed from consensus-based formal jointism to display, to a greater or lesser extent, the characteristics of union marginalisation. This is illustrated by the handbook for civil servants. Up to the late 1980s the *Handbook for the New Civil Servant* encouraged civil servants to join the union appropriate to their grade and play an active part. Then it was changed to say that civil servants were encouraged to play an active part in their union, if they decided to join. By 1997 at least one large executive agency in its handbook for new recruits was silent about union membership (Corby 1998).

With the change of government in 1997 came signs of a more friendly environment for public service unions. For instance, union rights were restored to those at GCHQ, albeit on a no-strike basis. Nevertheless, there has been no marked break with the past in terms of public expenditure (see chapter 2) or pay (see chapter 4).

Having briefly considered the background, this chapter now looks at trends in union membership and density.

Union membership and density

Union membership

Union membership in the public services grew during the twentieth century until 1979 (Fryer 1989). The most remarkable growth was in the post-war

Table 10.1 Membership of public service trade unions, TUC-affiliated and non-TUC-affiliated, and police federations, at the end of 1979, 1985, 1991 and 1996

Organisation	1979	1985	1991	1996
TUC-affiliated unions	2,899,094	2,729,054	2,561,442	2,578,245
Non-affiliated unions	527,742	695,823	790,809	791,099
Total	3,426,836	3,424,877	3,352,251	3,369,344
Police federations	113,050	120,462	126,885	124,710
Total for public services	3,539,886	3,545,339	3,479,136	3,494,054

Sources: Certification Office data; Police Federation data.

period. According to Bain and Price (1983), public service union membership grew by 160 per cent between 1948 and 1979. However, in 1979–96 aggregate membership growth has been reversed: total membership, including the police federations, fell by 1.3 per cent, or 1.7 per cent if the latter are excluded. (The police federations have a representational role but they are not trade unions in law.)

The decline in the membership of unions organising predominantly or exclusively in the public services (a 2 per cent decline) is far less severe than for the whole economy, where membership fell by 40 per cent over the period 1979–96. As a result, union members in the public services are becoming an increasing proportion of total union membership. The proportion was 26 per cent in 1979 but by 1996 it had risen to 42 per cent. In addition, some of the large private sector TUC-affiliated unions such as GMB (formerly GMBATU, the General Municipal Boilermakers' and Allied Trades' Union), the Transport and General Workers' Union (TGWU) and the Manufacturing Science and Finance Union (MSF) have significant numbers of members in the public services. In 1996 about one in three GMB members was employed in the public services. The figures for MSF and the TGWU were one in seven and one in nine respectively. Taking into account the contribution of the general unions, almost half of total union membership was located in the public services in 1996. Moreover, eight out of the seventeen unions with over 100,000 members were public service based (Certification Office 1997).

As table 10.1 shows, TUC and non-TUC unions fared differently. TUC-affiliated public service unions lost 11 per cent of their membership between 1979 and 1996, whereas non-affiliated union membership increased by 50 per cent. The bulk of the increase in the membership of non-affiliated public service unions occurred in the first half of the 1980s. Farnham and Giles (1995) attribute the increase to a favourable combination of expansion in employment for public service professionals, the shock of restructuring and concern among moderate staff about taking the sort of industrial action favoured by TUC-affiliated unions.

Tables 10.2 and 10.3 look at unions individually. Kelly categorises unions as militant or moderate. Militant unions are defined as willing to take industrial action, having an ideology of conflicting interests and relying strongly on the mobilisation of members. Moderate unions are defined as taking industrial action infrequently or not at all, having an ideology of partnership and strongly relying on employers. (For a full discussion of militant and moderate trade unions see Kelly 1996.) In fact, the militancy/moderation thesis does not explain the membership gains and losses among public service unions. For instance, the moderate Association of Professional Ambulance Personnel (APAP) experienced a severe decline (43 per cent from 1985 to 1996), but the moderate Association of Teachers and Lecturers (ATL) grew by 91 per cent over the period 1979–96. Over the same period the militant Prison Officers' Association (POA) significantly increased its membership (by 33 per cent), but the most militant of the teachers' unions, the National Union of Teachers (NUT), declined by 7 per cent.

Another inadequate explanation is TUC affiliation. Some unions which have seen sizeable increases are TUC-affiliated, such as the Association of First Division Civil Servants (FDA), which caters for senior civil servants and has seen its membership increase by 63 per cent between 1979 and 1996. But some are not, such as the doctors' union, the British Medical Association (BMA), which has seen a 54 per cent increase over the period 1979–96.

Size is also an unconvincing explanation. Looking at the period 1979–96, the 300,000 strong nurses' union, the Royal College of Nursing (RCN), grew by 90 per cent and the 200,000 strong teaching union, the National Association of Schoolmasters and Union of Women Teachers (NAS/UWT), by 54 per cent. Yet the Royal College of Midwives (RCM), with 35,000 members in 1996, grew by 75 per cent from 1979 to 1996 and the British Association of Occupational Therapists (BAOT), with 15,000 members, grew by 139 per cent. A more robust explanation may be related to occupational coverage. The more general unions have declined while most, though not all, single occupation unions have grown.

A further important trend is the continued feminisation of public service trade union membership. According to the Certification Officer the number of female members rose by 333,935 or 18 per cent between 1979 and 1996. At the same time the number of male union members declined by 391,427, or 25 per cent. As a result the proportion of female membership of public service trade unions was 66 per cent in 1996. This is slightly higher than women's share of the public sector labour force.

Union density

The strength of unionisation may also be measured by the proportion of actual members expressed as a percentage of potential members, i.e. those in employment in the relevant occupation/sector. This provides a more

Table 10.2 Membership of TUC-affiliated public service unions, at the end of years 1979, 1985, 1991 and 1996.

Union	1979	1985	1991	1996	% change 1979–96
General public services					
National and Local Government Officers Association[a]	753,226	752,151	759,735	–	+0.8
National Union of Public Employees[a]	691,770	663,776	551,165	–	–20.3
Unison[b]	–	–	–	1,374,583	–
Total	1,444,996	1,415,927	1,310,900	1,374,583	–4.9
Central government					
Association of First Division Civil Servants[c]	5,820	5,509	9,994	9,473	+62.8
Civil and Public Services Association[d]	223,884	146,537	124,566	116,681	–17.9
Civil Service Union	45,464	31,212	–	–	–
Inland Revenue Staff Federation[e]	65,257	55,118	57,011	–	–12.6
Institution of Professionals Managers and Specialists	102,142	89,238	90,434	77,818	–23.8
National Union of Civil and Public Servants[f]	107,957	84,275	112,761	–	+4.4
Prison Officers' Association	20,469	23,777	27,224	27,322	+33.4
Public Services Tax and Commerce Union[g]	–	–	–	149,262	–
Scottish Prison Officers' Association	2,567	3,021	4,099	3,218	+25.4
Total	573,560	438,687	426,089	383,774	–33.1
Education					
Association of University Teachers	30,881	31,232	32,960	37,054	+20.0
Educational Institute of Scotland	48,550	43,324	47,169	50,185	+3.4
National Association of School Masters/Union of Women Teachers[h]	152,222	169,839	179,937	238,472	+56.7
National Association of Teachers in Further and Higher Education	70,652	77,386	73,907	70,157	–0.7
National Union of Teachers[h]	290,740	253,672	214,675	271,299	–6.7
Undeb Cenedlaethol Athrawon Cymru[i]	–	–	–	3,613	–
Total	593,045	575,453	548,648	670,780	+13.1
Local government and related					
Association of Magisterial Officers[j]	–	–	–	5,280	–

Table 10.2 (Continued).

Union	1979	1985	1991	1996	% change 1979–96
Community and Youth Workers Union[k]	–	–	–	2,393	–
Federated Union of Managerial and Professional Officers[l]	–	–	–	10,897	–
Fire Brigades Union	41,533	45,895	51,881	55,341	+33.2
Greater London Staff Association[m]	17,089	15,449	–	–	(–9.6)
National Association of Probation Officers[n]	–	6,225	6,765	6,779	+8.8
Total	58,622	67,569	58,646	80,690	+37.6
Health					
British Orthoptic Society[o]	–	–	–	1,032	–
Chartered Society of Physiotherapy[p]	–	–	–	47,903	–
Community and District Nursing Association[q]	–	–	–	4,133	–
Confederation of Health Service Employees[r]	212,930	212,980	201,993	–	–5.1
Health Visitors' Association[s]	12,185	15,952	–	–	+31.0
Hospital Consultants' and Specialists' Association	3,756	2,486	2,351	2,264	–39.7
Society of Radiographers[t]	–	–	12,815	13,086	+2.1
Total	228,871	231,418	217,159	68,418	–70.1
Total for public services	2,899,094	2,729,054	2,561,442	2,578,245	–11.1

Source: Certification Office data.

Notes
a Percentage change in membership refers to the period 1979–91. Includes members in the public utilities.
b UNISON was formed by the amalgamation of COHSE, NALGO and NUPE in 1993. Includes members in the public utilities.
c Figures for the Association of First Division Civil Servants from 1991 include those for the Association of HM Inspectors of Taxes, which transferred engagements in 1989.
d The CPSA and Public Services Tax and Commerce Union (PTC) amalgamated in 1998 to form the Public and Commercial Services Union (PCS).
e IRSF amalgamated with NUCPS in 1996 to form PTC. Percentage change in IRSF membership relates to 1979–91.
f The NUCPS was formed as a result of the merger of the Society of Civil and Public Servants and the Civil Service Union in 1988. NUCPS amalgamated with the Inland Revenue Staff Federation to form the Public Services Tax and Commerce Union in 1996.
g PTC was created on 1 January 1996 out of the merger of IRSF and NUCPS.
h Membership figures include non-serving teachers, retired and student members.
i UCAC (National Association of Teachers in Wales) affiliated to the TUC in 1995. Membership increased by 40.8% over the whole 1979–96 period. For 1979–91 figures see table 10.4.
j Affiliated to the TUC in 1995. Membership increased by 13.1% over the whole 1979–96 period. For 1979–91 membership figures see table 10.4.

k Affiliated to the TUC in 1995. Membership increased by 51.2% over the whole 1979–96 period. For 1979–91 membership figures see table 10.4.
l MPO affiliated to the TUC in 1996. Membership increased by 75% over the whole 1979–96 period. For 1979–91 membership figures see table 10.4.
m The GLSA transferred engagements to the GMB in 1988.
n Affiliated to the TUC in 1983. Figures relate to 1985–96.
o BOS affiliated to the TUC in 1996. Membership declined by 15.1% over the period 1985–96. For 1985–91 membership figures see table 10.4.
p Affiliated to the TUC in 1992. Membership increased by 32.9% over the whole 1979–96 period. For 1979–91 membership figures see table 10.4.
q CDNA affiliated to the TUC in 1996. It received a certificate of independence from the Certification Office in 1995.
r COHSE amalgamated with NALGO and NUPE in 1993 to form Unison.
s The HVA merged with MSF in 1990.
t Affiliated to the TUC in 1990. Membership increased by 59.4% over the whole 1979–96 period. For 1979–85 membership figures see table 10.4.

Table 10.3 Membership of non-TUC-affiliated unions in the public services with over 1,000 members, and Police Federation, at end of years 1979, 1985, 1991 and 1996

Union	1979	1985	1991	1996	% change 1979–96
Central government					
Association of Government Supervisors and Radio Officers[a]	12,026	–	–	–	–
Association of HM Inspectors of Taxes[b]	2,518	2,426	–	–	(–3.6)
Immigration Service Union[c]	–	1,192	1,724	2,183	(+83.1)
Prison Governors Association[d]	–	–	1,155	1,032	(–10.6)
Prison Service Union[e]	–	–	–	2,316	
Total	14,544	3,618	2,879	5,531	–62.0
Education					
Association of Cambridge University Assistants[e]	1,166	1,096	1,159	1,085	–6.9
Association for College Management[f]	–	–	1,466	3,277	(+123.5)
Association of Educational Psychologists[c, j]	–	1,163	1,728	2,096	(+80.2)
Association of Head Teachers in Scotland[f]	–	–	1,240	1,466	(+18.2)
Association of Teachers and Lecturers[g]	87,407	113,453	141,504	166,793	+90.8
Association of University and College Lecturers[h]	3,006	3,021	3,019	3,029	+0.7
National Association of Educational Inspectors, Advisers and Consultants	1,095	1,394	2,341	2,452	+123.9
National Association of Head Teachers	23,329	29,762	38,140	43,617	+87.0

Table 10.3 (Continued).

Union	1979	1985	1991	1996	% change 1979–96
National Association of Teachers in Wales (Undeb Cenelaethol Athrawan Cymru)[i]	2,566	3,064	3,311	–	(+29.0)
National Society for Education in Art and Design[j]	2,495	2,223	2,505	2,365	–5.2
Professional Association of Teachers	19,294	39,333	41,174	40,178	+108.2
Scottish Further and Higher Education Association	1,748	1,679	1,780	1,253	–28.3
Scottish Secondary Teachers' Association	8,720	7,598	7,246	7,116	–18.4
Secondary Heads' Association	4,451	6,704	7,776	8,696	+95.4
Total	155,277	210,490	254,389	283,423	+82.5
Local Government and related					
Association of Magisterial Officers[k]	4,668	3,928	4,170	–	(–10.7)
Association of Public Service Finance Officers[l]	3,220	2,877	–	–	(–10.6)
Association of Public Service Professional Engineers[l]	1,938	1,841	–	–	(–5.0)
British Union of Social Work Employees[m]	–	1,235	2,480	3,818	(+209.1)
Community and Youth Workers' Union[k]	1,583	2,001	2,246	–	(+41.8)
Federated Union of Managerial and Professional Officers[n]	6,225	8,770	11,956	–	(+92.1)
National Association of Fire Officers[o]	3,933	3,999	–	–	(+1.7)
Retained Firefighters' Union	8,741	5,340	4,198	4,061	–53.5
Total	30,308	29,991	25,050	7,879	–74.0
Police federation					
Total[p]	113,050	120,462	126,885	124,710	+10.3
Health					
Association of Clinical Biochemists	1,870	2,260	2,561	2,244	+20.0
Association of NHS Officers[q]	5,179	4,477	4,318	–	(–16.6)
Association of Optometrists[r]	–	4,541	4,956	–	(+9.1)
Association of Professional Ambulance Personnel	–	4,584	2,978	2,626	(–42.7)
British Association of Dental Nurses[s]	2,574	2,631	2,642	2,406	–6.5
British Association of Occupational Therapists[t]	6,417	7,682	11,503	15,367	+139.5

Table 10.3 (Continued).

Union	1979	1985	1991	1996	% change 1979–96
British Dental Association	12,424	15,516	15,206	15,435	+24.2
British Dietetic Association[u]	–	2,375	2,936	4,128	(+73.8)
British Medical Association	65,624	78,147	86,043	101,334	+54.4
British Orthoptic Society[v]	–	1,216	1,185	–	(–2.5)
Chartered Society of Physiotherapy[w]	36,052	31,528	36,521	–	(+1.3)
General Dental Practitioners Association[j]	2,074	2,428	3,656	1,980	–4.5
Hospital Physicists' Association[x]	1,264	1,423	1,481	–	(+17.2)
Royal College of Midwives	20,631	26,518	34,710	35,194	+70.6
Royal College of Nursing	161,962	251,127	293,193	307,094	+89.6
Society of Chiropodists and Podiatrists[y]	4,497	5,145	5,761	6,458	+43.6
Society of Radiographers[z]	8,211	11,222	–	–	(+36.7)
Total	328,779	452,820	509,650	494,266	+50.3
Total for public services	641,958	817,381	918,853	915,809	+42.6

Sources: Certification Office data; Police Federation data.

Notes
a   Merged with IPCS in 1984.
b   Percentage change relates to 1979–85. Transferred engagements to FDA in 1989.
c   Percentage change relates to 1985–96.
d   Percentage change relates to 1991–95.
e   Figure relates to end-1997. PSU received a certificate of independence in 1995.
f   Percentage change relates to 1991–96.
g   This organisation was named Assistant Masters' and Mistresses' Association until 1992.
h   Last figure relates to August 1997. This organisation was named the Association of Polytechnic Teachers until 1990 and the Association of Polytechnic and College Teachers until 1992. AUCL merged with the Association of University Teachers in September 1997.
i   Percentage change relates to 1979–91. UCAC affiliated to the TUC in 1995.
j   Received a certificate of independence between 1985 and 1991.
k   Percentage change relates to 1979–91. Affiliated to TUC in 1995.
l   Transferred engagements to FUMPO in 1986.
m   Percentage change relates to 1985–97.
n   Received a certificate of independence in 1985. Affiliated to the TUC in 1996. For 1996 membership see table 10.2.
o   Percentage change figures relate to 1979–85. Transferred engagements to EETPU in 1990.
p   Figures relate to England and Wales.
q   Percentage change relates to 1979–91. Transferred engagements to NALGO in 1992.
r   Percentage change figures relate to 1985–91. This organisation's certificate of independence as a union was withdrawn by the Certification Officer in 1994.
s   This organisation was named the Association of British Dental Surgery Assistants until 1994. Received a certificate of independence between 1979 and 1985.
t   Last figure relates to 30 September 1997.
u   Last figure relates to end February 1997. Affiliated to the TUC in 1997.
v   Percentage change figures relate to 1985–91. Affiliated to the TUC in 1996. For 1996 membership see table 10.2.
w   Figures relate to 1979–91. Affiliated to the TUC in 1992. For 1996 membership see table 10.2.
x   Transferred engagements to MSF in 1993.
y   Affiliated to the TUC in 1997.
z   Figures relate to 1979–85. Affiliated to the TUC in 1990. For membership figures 1991–96 see table 10.2.

accurate estimate of union penetration, as it reduces the risk of inflating figures by the inclusion of retired and unemployed members.

Union density in the public services, like union membership, was highest in 1979, when it was estimated at 96 per cent in central government, 78 per cent in local government and education and 76 per cent in health services (Waddington and Whitston 1995). Across the public services as a whole density was 80 per cent. By 1987 density in central government had declined sharply, to 76 per cent, and in health services marginally, to 73 per cent, while in local government and education it had risen by almost five percentage points. Accordingly, in 1987 across the public services as a whole, union density remained virtually unchanged (79 per cent, compared with 80 per cent in 1979). This presented a sharp contrast with the marked decline in union density in manufacturing, from 73 per cent to 60 per cent over the period 1979 to 1987 (Waddington and Whitston 1995).

Labour Force Survey findings (see Bird and Corcoran 1994; Cully and Woodland 1997) permit detailed analysis of density trends since 1989. The findings make sobering reading for public service unions and put membership trends in perspective. Union density has declined across the public services from 80 per cent in 1979 to around 55 per cent in 1996. The largest drop has occurred in central government (from 96 per cent to 61 per cent) but a substantial decline has also taken place in health services. For example, density in hospitals fell by thirteen percentage points between 1989 and 1996 to 54 per cent. In contrast, union density in schools was more stable – 63 per cent in 1989 and 59 per cent in 1996 – and density levels among particular segments of the public sector workforce, such as teachers, nurses, firefighters and professions allied to medicine, remained high, over 75 per cent in 1996. Moreover, public service unions' density levels are still significantly higher than that of all unions.

The decline in union membership and density has been explained by the reluctance of individuals to join a union born out of anti-collectivist ideology and failures in union organising capacity (Bailey 1994; Kelly 1990). Waddington and Whitston (1997), however, qualify this. In a large scale survey of over 5,000 respondents across the public services they reported that collective reasons, such as the need for mutual support and improved pay and conditions, were central to the decision to join a union. Over 70 per cent said that they had joined to obtain 'support if I had a problem at work'. But in health services members were also concerned that the union served perceived 'professional' needs at work, such as legal advice and training. Waddington and Whitston concluded that their evidence 'provides little support to those arguing that individualisation has dissolved labour movements since 1979' (1997: 537). Such conclusions echo those of Kerr, whose study of local government and health workers found that 'there appear to be no fundamental attitudinal reasons why non-unionists in these industries would not join a union' (1992: 52).

Waddington and Whitston also examined the role of union organisation in the recruitment of new members. Respondents were asked whether their recruitment into the union had been the result of an initiative taken by the union, or of themselves, or on the recommendation of management. Findings relating to the public services indicate that a higher proportion of members had joined as a result of their own initiative in contacting the union (a third) than had been recruited by a workplace union representative (a quarter). Only 5 per cent had been encouraged to join by management. The relative weakness of workplace recruitment is highlighted by comparison with engineering and other manufacturing, where shop stewards accounted for half of recruitment. These findings suggest that deficiencies in local union organisation in the public services are hindering recruitment efforts.

Union structure

Open/closed unions

The analytical distinction drawn by Turner (1962) between 'open' and 'closed' unions is useful in seeking to classify unions in the public services by their recruitment strategies. An open union is one which is 'actively recruiting, or seeking mergers with other unions in new occupational or industrial areas', while a closed union 'concentrates on its existing territory, aiming to make that a strong point of organisation and bargaining strength' (Coates and Topham 1980: 35).

Many public sector unions are closed, for instance, the teachers' unions such as the NUT and the NAS/UWT, the National Association of Probation Officers (NAPO), the Fire Brigades' Union (FBU) and APAP. Seifert, referring to the unions catering for the professions allied to medicine, considers that they seek 'to control the qualifications of their professions and to act to enhance and protect the labour supply side of their activities' (1992: 96). As noted above, there are also a few open unions operating in the public services, such as MSF, GMB and the TGWU. They are predominantly private sector, multi-occupational unions eager to increase recruitment in the public services to make up for losses in their traditional heartlands.

Moreover, there are degrees of openness and closedness. A union can, for example, be closed vertically, in that it has no ambition to recruit a range of grades and occupations, while being open horizontally, recruiting a grade across industrial boundaries. For instance, the RCN is open only to qualified nurses but recruits both those employed in the National Health Service (NHS) and in private health care organisations. The position is not static. For instance, the civil service union, the Institution of Professionals Managers and Specialists (IPMS), has followed its members when their organisations have been privatised, as has Unison.

Number of unions

The total number of independent unions in the public services rose from fifty-eight in 1979 to sixty-four in 1985 and then fell to fifty-three at the beginning of 1998, the quickened pace of amalgamations reducing the number. Nevertheless, despite amalgamations, there is still much multi-unionism, though its form varies. For instance, in central government, where there are eight unions with over 1,000 members, there are relatively clear jurisdictional lines. In local government and in health care, where there are twenty-two unions with over 1,000 members, there are overlapping organising territories. For instance, five unions seek to represent nurses.

Looking solely at the TUC camp, the number of unions remained relatively constant throughout the 1980s but actually rose in the 1990s. This reflects a spate of affiliations of relatively small unions, such as the Society of Radiographers and the Chartered Society of Physiotherapists. By 1997 53 per cent of all public service unions were TUC-affiliated, while the proportion of total TUC-affiliated unions accounted for by unions in the public services rose from 23 per cent in 1979 to 37 per cent in 1997.

Mergers

Change in union structure encompasses both merger activity and arrangements which fall short of merger but aim to improve co-operation between unions (Willman and Cave 1994). Although merger activity in public service unionism was muted in the 1980s, more radical developments followed in the 1990s in all areas except education. Mergers take two principal forms in law: a transfer of engagements, which involves the absorption of the transferring organisation into a larger body whose legal identity remains unchanged, or amalgamation, where a new union replaces the amalgamating organisations. Undy *et al.* further distinguish between the two forms of merger by noting that in amalgamations 'the two parties are likely to see themselves as having similar status or as equals'. In transfers of engagements 'the minor union . . . is normally involved in surrendering autonomy in exchange for some gain such as security' while the larger union 'will probably not change significantly their present system of organisation and power structure in order to accommodate the incoming union' (1996: 48).

In the civil service, for example, the union for executives, the Society of Civil and Public Servants (SCPS), amalgamated with the union for support grades, the Civil Service Union (CSU) in 1988, then the amalgamated union, the National Union of Civil and Public Servants (NUCPS), joined up with the Inland Revenue Staff Federation (IRSF) in 1996, then that amalgamated union, the Public Services Tax and Commerce Union (PTC), joined up with the union for clerical workers, the Civil and Public Services Association (CPSA) to form the Public and Commercial Services Union (PCS) in 1998. Underlying such structural change has been a decline in civil service employment (see chapter 1) combined with the devolution of bargaining over terms and conditions to departments and executive agencies, which has put a strain on unions' resources and caused intensification of effort in servicing members. As the PTC leadership said: 'large savings will be possible inside a single union. Plain logic and common sense say that you need a single union to represent all the grades and types of work in which you are now involved' (PTC 1997: 2).

Changes in the external environment are also important in explaining the amalgamation between three unions: the Confederation of Health Service Employees (COHSE), the National Union of Public Employees (NUPE), which mainly organised manual workers in local government, water and the universities and unqualified health workers, and the National and Local Government Officers' Association (NALGO), which mainly organised administrative and clerical workers in local government, health, education and the utilities. Together these three unions formed Unison in 1993. The areas where these unions organise have been subject to privatisation, contracting out and restructuring into semi-autonomous provider units. Like the civil service, this has resulted in a decline in the number of employees and, in the health services at least, some proliferation of bargaining units.

The merger to form Unison sought to fulfil a number of objectives. First, it aimed to eliminate the potential for inter-union competition for members, of which there was a history in the 1980s, particularly between NALGO and NUPE (Undy *et al.* 1996) as, unlike the civil service, there are no discrete organisational lines in health and local government (see above). Secondly, the merger sought to enhance the eligibility of the new union to represent all sections of the workforce, a potential attraction for employers in terms of recognition for local bargaining (Waddington and Whitston 1995). Thirdly, the merged union sought to deploy the attributes of size and resources as part of its recruitment appeal, particularly among the professions allied to medicine in the NHS, which are often without direct representation at single bargaining tables in NHS trusts (Corby 1992).

However, as Terry notes, the formation of Unison is likely to do little to reduce its underlying recruitment rivalries with the traditional general unions. The latter, such as the GMB, which formed a public services section in 1992, and the TGWU, are 'constantly looking to expand their membership base into new sectors and occupations' (Terry 1991: 100). Similarly, the formation of Unison does nothing to prevent the continued competition for nurses between Unison and the RCN.

A number of mergers were effected through transfers of engagements. They took three forms. First, small TUC-affiliated unions became absorbed into larger TUC-affiliated unions. Examples include the 16,000 strong Greater London Staff Association taking shelter in the GMB in 1988 and the 16,000 strong Health Visitors' Association joining MSF in 1990. Second, small non-TUC-affiliated organisations joined large TUC unions. Examples include the 840 strong Scottish Health Visitors' Association merging with Unison in 1996 and the Association of University and College Lecturers (AUCL), with 3000 members, joining the Association of University Teachers (AUT) in 1997, providing the latter with a toehold in the 'new' universities and giving rise to competition with the National Association of Teachers in Further and Higher Education (NATFHE), the erstwhile polytechnic lecturers' union.

Third, smaller non-TUC-affiliated organisations moved into larger non-TUC-affiliated organisations. For example, in 1986 no fewer than nineteen organisations of local authority officers, most with membership levels in tens and hundreds, voted to merge with FUMPO, a specialist and senior managerial public service union.

In short, although merger activity has led to some simplification of union structure in the public services, there are still a plethora of unions and many areas of inter-union competition.

Inter-union co-operation

An exclusive focus on merger activity ignores the growth in other forms of inter-union collaboration. Firstly, federal arrangements have been attempted as an alternative to a full merger. Thus IPMS, faced with declining membership and the need to service members covered by an increasing variety of bargaining units, became part of a federation with the Post Office's Communication Managers Association (CMA) and British Telecom's Society of Telecom Executives (STE) in 1992. These three unions sought savings by pooling common non-bargaining services, such as research, education, legal services, press and publicity, while maintaining their separate identities and industrial autonomy (Willman and Cave 1994). However, the federation fell apart in 1995. According to the IPMS annual report of 1995, this was because of a 'clash of cultures and the independence required by all partner unions'.

Another unsuccessful attempt at federal arrangements occurred in higher education. With the ending of the so-called binary divide between universities and polytechnics, the two unions for academics, NATFHE, which organised in the polytechnics, and the AUT, which organised in the universities, set up a confederation in 1993 aimed at developing common policies and sharing staffing and other resources (IRS 1993b). However, this was discontinued in 1996, largely because of policy differences, and in fact, as a result of AUCL's merger with the AUT (see above), there is inter-union competition where previously there was none.

More successful than these short lived federations have been the service agreements between MSF and the midwives' union, RCM, and between Unison and the occupational therapists' union, BAOT. Under these agreements the two large TUC-affiliated unions, MSF and Unison, provide industrial relations services such as negotiation and shop steward training for their smaller, non-TUC associates (Bryson *et al.* 1995; Labour Research 1995).

Formal mechanisms apart, there is evidence, from NHS trusts and schools, that there has been more workplace level collaboration in the 1990s than hitherto, notably across the TUC/non-TUC divide (Bryson *et al.* 1995; Ironside *et al.* 1997; Lloyd 1997).

Political funds

The public service unions are becoming increasingly politicised: thirteen such unions, all of them TUC-affiliated, established political funds following membership ballots under the 1984 legislation. Only one union, the small Retained Firefighters' Union, which is not affiliated to the TUC, closed its fund. The only large TUC public service union not to have a political fund is the 250,000 strong teachers' union, the NUT. In 1995, 70 per cent of members of public service unions contributed to political funds. Moreover, public service contributors accounted for 36 per cent of all union members paying into such funds.

However, having a political fund is one thing. Affiliation to the Labour Party is another. None of the unions which have set up political funds in the last decade has affiliated to the party. Moreover, none of the civil service unions is affiliated to the party, mindful that civil servants are politically neutral. As to Unison, members have a choice of two political funds: a general fund which is politically neutral or a fund affiliated to the Labour Party.

Union organisation and representation

This section looks at the impact of public service restructuring on internal union organisation and membership relations. A significant feature is the growing importance of the lay workplace representative. Such representatives go under a variety of names, for instance 'steward' in many unions operating in the NHS and 'branch secretary' in many unions operating in the civil service.

Workplace vitality?

Workplace union organisation in the public services was largely absent until the1970s. Its development has been attributed in part to employer initiative: managerial sponsorship of shop steward organisation flowed from 'the traditional "good employer" model of widespread union recognition and union-based consultation and negotiation ... being extended to the workplace' (Terry 1995: 206–7). At the same time the dominance of a decentralised, lay member based concept of union government, which Heery and Kelly (1994) call 'participative unionism', ensured official union support for the increased role of stewards, at least in certain unions, e.g. NALGO, NUPE, COHSE.

Yet until the 1990s union structures tended to be highly centralised, with national officers concluding national agreements, which applied with little variation. Accordingly, workplace representatives were largely concerned with recruitment, information giving and individual case work. In the 1990s, however, when national bargaining arrangements either ended, as in the civil service and a few NHS trusts, or became looser, as in local government, workplace representatives expanded their role to cover negotiating terms and conditions, receiving support from union headquarters, for instance new training courses and information bulletins (IRS 1993a; Labour Research 1996b). Moreover, Unison developed a software package, Local Negotiator, which draws on electronic databases to allow negotiators to calculate the effect of a pay claim on members' earnings or the employer's pay bill (Labour Research 1996a). Research by Corby and Blundell (1997) into three NHS trusts suggested that stewards were coping remarkably well with their enhanced roles.

Fairbrother (1996), looking at some civil service local offices in the Benefits Agency and two social services departments in local authorities, argues that the moves towards decentralised forms of management and the consequent growing importance of workplace unionism offer the prospect of union renewal. There is an opportunity, claims Fairbrother, for egalitarian forms of union organisation rather than hierarchy, and for involvement rather than remoteness, although he admits that this is not a straightforward or inevitable process. As yet, there is little evidence to support or refute Fairbrother's contention, but Colling (1995), looking at competitive tendering in local authorities, found that in the main there had not been union renewal.

Steward/FTO relationships

Many public service unions, in an attempt to match the increasingly devolved industrial relations arrangements of employers, have decentralised their structures. For instance, Unison has 'service groups' with their own policy-making conferences for the different industrial sectors in which it organises, and the civil service union, the PCS, has 'occupational associations', which have limited autonomy: the national executive committee has 'final direction' where it considers matters 'affect the union's general interest' (PTC 1997: 11).

The public service unions have also set up regional offices. For example, the RCM in 1992 established an office for the north of England, based in Leeds, in addition to its headquarters in London. The civil service union, IPMS, had five regional offices in 1997, whereas a decade ago it had none. Such developments have brought full-time officers (FTOs) physically closer to their workplace representatives.

Kelly and Heery (1994), looking at unions operating in both the public and the private sectors, found that relations between workplace representatives and full time officers were on the whole harmonious. There was a large measure of consensus and a high degree of interdependence. Other research in the NHS and schools came to a similar conclusion (Lloyd 1997; Corby and Blundell 1997; Ironside *et al.* 1997), while in another study 59 per cent of those with experience of decentralisation said that relations had improved, compared with 10 per cent who said they had worsened (IRS 1992).

Managerial unionism

Many public service unions have exhibited features of managerial unionism, as outlined by Heery and Kelly. They define managerial unionism as responding to members' instrumental needs, often identified by surveys of members. Managerial unionism arose in the 1980s, partly in response to the decline in membership and partly out of a critical analysis of the perceived weaknesses of the activist based, often politically driven, so-called participative trade union model of the 1970s. It was allied to concern about the unions' representativeness of the particularities of membership interests and composition (Terry 1996) and resulted in the union leadership 'designing and promoting union services to match [members' needs] and planning the organisation, training and deployment of its own human resources to support service delivery' (Heery and Kelly 1994: 7).

Heery and Kelly maintained that managerial unionism is widespread throughout the public and private sector. Undoubtedly, numerous examples from the public services support their contention. Thus the teachers' unions such as the ATL, AUT and NUT have emphasised their role in defending the professional interests of members, while other unions such as those for professional ambulance staff (APAP), the Federated Union of Managerial and Professional Officers (FUMPO) and the Professional Association of Teachers (PAT) 'have deliberately stressed their lack of militancy in an attempt to diminish both the psychological and potential economic costs to employees of taking out membership' (Heery 1996: 184). The RCN, after research among its members, established a twenty-four-hour telephone hot line to give advice to members on employment, professional and legal issues (Brindle 1998).

Constitutional reforms which have accompanied the amalgamations creating Unison and PCS also reflect the tide of managerial unionism. For example, in the new 'member centred' PCS 'greater emphasis is placed on the votes and opinions of all members, including those who may not be able to attend regularly at local branch meetings' (PTC 1997: 3). So at the heart of the new constitution is the 'overriding authority' of individual member ballots. All branch officers and senior lay representatives are elected by individual secret ballot, replacing branch bloc voting. Moreover, decisions taken at delegate conference (now held every two years, instead of every year, as in the partner unions) can be overridden by a membership ballot called by the national executive committee. While the PTC joint general secretary claimed that the new union would 'give power to ordinary members, [who] will take all the important decisions' (Labour Research 1997) others will interpret the rule changes as enhancing the position of the national leadership and diminishing the influence of traditional activist and conference based systems of decision making.

A number of public service unions have taken initiatives designed to serve and articulate the interests of particular groups of members. The most innovative are those taken by Unison. It has adopted the principle of proportionality, i.e. set targets to ensure that women are represented in its decision making processes in proportion to their numbers by the end of the century. Thus it has reserved seats on its national executive committee for women and low paid women. It has also established so-called self-organised groups for gays and lesbians, black members and disabled members. In 1994 42 per cent of its national executive were women. The figure for 1997–98 was 65 per cent against a female membership of 78 per cent in 1996 (Labour Research 1998). A number of other public service unions also reserve seats on their national executive committees for women, but progress in increasing the number of female full time officers has been less marked. For instance, in Unison women account for 38 per cent of national officers. Only four very small TUC affiliates have female general secretaries at the time of writing. The largest is the 7,000 strong probation officers' union, NAPO. The position is slightly better among non-TUC affiliates, where both the RCM and RCN have female general secretaries.

Public service unions have also shown interest in the application of managerial techniques to organisation questions. In the cases of Unison and PTC the impetus to seek outside advice on union management (from Cranfield Management School and a freelance personnel consultant) arose from their requirement to manage the post-merger situation. Senior officials and national executive committee members of other public service unions, such as the FDA and NATFHE, have also attended Cranfield courses on strategy development and strategic management skills together with appropriate human resource issues.

Industrial action

In the 1950s and 1960s industrial disputes were rare in the public services. In the 1970s, however, this changed, primarily in response to a series of incomes policies and public expenditure reductions (see chapter 2), culminating in the so-called winter of discontent in 1979. In the process, the public sector unions 'banished their traditionally moderate image' (Winchester and Bach 1995: 309). Indeed, for many trade unions the strikes of the 1970s were their first experience of official industrial action. For instance, the senior civil servants' union, the FDA, took industrial action for the first time in 1979, taking part in a one day protest strike by all the civil service unions. As O'Toole (1989: 174) said:

> It is not clear how many FDA civil servants took part in industrial action, but it is known that a considerable number did, including people in the rank of under secretary and also including a number of private secretaries to ministers. Both these groups have sensitive responsibilities and it is, to say the least, surprising that such members should have participated in industrial action.

Industrial action in the public services remained a conspicuous feature of the 1980s and 1990s, when an emphasis on managerial efficiency came to the fore (see chapter 1) and public expenditure was constrained (see chapter 2). Table 10.4 shows a comparison of working days lost per thousand employees for all industries and for the public services from 1980 to 1996. While health services were generally well below below the incidence rate for the economy as a whole, the rest of the public services were well above the overall incidence rate from 1986 to 1996.

This rise in militancy occurred at the same time as there was a reduction in the use of arbitration, either because the arbitration option was not available, as in the twenty-week civil service dispute of 1981, or because the arbitration option was eschewed, as in local government in 1989. It also occurred at a time when the legal constraints on industrial action were progressively tightened as a result of government legislation. Although these constraints applied to all unions, public service unions were particularly affected by the requirement that a dispute must be between workers and *their* employer if there was to be immunity and by the outlawing of secondary

Table 10.4 Working days lost per 1,000 employees in the public services 1980–96 (000)

Year	1	2	3	4	5
1980	531	49	–	48	–
1981	201	682	–	24	–
1982	249	109	–	618	–
1983	180	32	–	4	–
1984	1283	214	–	17	–
1985	298	257	–	25	–
1986	89	120	–	9	–
1987	163	244	–	5	–
1988	166	65	–	25	–
1989	182	587	–	103	–
1990	83	46	–	232	–
1991	34	96	–	1	–
1992	24	132	–	1	–
1993	30	168	12	2	–
1994	13	11	36	1	–
1995	19	69	36	6	23
1996	59	114	70	3	3

Sources: Annual review articles, *Employment Gazette* 1981–95; *Labour Market Trends* 1996–97.

Notes
1 All industries and services.
2 Public administration and defence 1980–82; public administration, sanitary services and education 1983–92; public administration and sanitary services 1993–94; public administration, defence and social security 1995–96.
3 Education, research and development 1993–94; education 1995–96.
4 Professional and scientific services 1980–82; medical and health services 1983–94; health and social work 1995–96.
5 Other community, social and personal service activities 1995–96.

action. Thus disputes across a service, especially when bargaining was decentralised, notably in the civil service, would normally result in service-wide industrial action being unlawful. Moreover, prison officers' right to take industrial action in any circumstance was removed in 1994 (see chapter 3) and union membership was withdrawn from workers at GCHQ in 1984, as mentioned above.

Analysis of data in table 10.5 shows that the proportion of strikes accounted for by the public services grew steadily from 6.7 per cent in 1980 to 43.6 per cent in 1993, falling back to 32 per cent in 1996. Moreover, the proportion of working days lost in the public services also grew. In the period 1980–89 the number of working days lost in the public services as a proportion of working days lost in the economy as a whole was 19 per cent, but the figure was 42 per cent in the period 1990–96.

There have been notable changes in the form of strike action. Large prolonged national strikes, such as those involving civil servants, health workers and teachers in the 1980s, gave way to localised action. An analysis of official data relating to all strikes leading to the loss of over 5,000 working days in 1990–96 reveals that a substantial majority of days lost were lost because of strikes confined to specific geographical areas. Staff groups involved were civil

Table 10.5 Strikes in the public services 1980–96

Year	No. of strikes	% of total	Working days lost (000)	% of total
1980	89	6.7	258	2.1
1981	84	6.3	1165	27.3
1982	124	8.1	1201	22.6
1983	115	8.5	121	3.2
1984	162	13.4	786	2.8
1985	135	15.0	990	15.4
1986	167	15.5	460	23.9
1987	123	12.1	945	26.6
1988	125	16.0	290	7.8
1989	172	24.5	2388	57.8
1990	177	28.0	520	27.3
1991	130	35.0	363	47.7
1992	110	43.4	329	62.3
1993	92	43.6	341	52.5
1994	57	27.8	92	33.1
1995	89	37.8	201	48.4
1996	78	32.0	297	22.8

Sources: Annual review articles, *Employment Gazette* 1981–95; *Labour Market Trends* 1996–97.

Notes:
Figures relate to the following categories used in the official statistics: 1980–82, 'Public administration and defence' and 'Professional and scientific services'; 1983–92, 'Public administration, sanitary services and education' and 'Medical and health services'; 1993–94, 'Public administration and sanitary services', 'Education, research and development' and 'Medical and health services'; 1995–96, 'Public administration, defence and compulsory social security', 'Education' and 'Health and social work' and 'Other community, social and personal services'.

servants, council workers, firefighters, social workers, librarians, residential care workers, community workers and further education lecturers (*Employment Gazette* 1991–95; *Labour Market Trends* 1996–97).

Accompanying the localisation trend has been a tendency for unions to employ rolling strikes, selective strikes and strikes of short duration. In 1995–96, for example, Merseyside firefighters held eight nine-hour strikes and twenty-one one-day strikes (Darlington 1998) and some civil servants carried out a programme of strikes in selected offices and Job Centres in the Employment Service which resulted in a total loss of 73,600 days. Such action ensures that the individual member's loss of pay through withdrawal of labour is limited and/or the call on the finances of the unions is limited, especially as some non-manual unions in the public services, such as NALGO (now part of Unison) and IPMS have given strike pay equivalent to take-home pay to those striking continuously. There is also evidence of the increasing incidence of unofficial strike action in the public services, particularly among non-manual workers in local government services (Gall and Mackay 1997).

Assessing the cost/benefit of strikes is well nigh impossible, as there are so many factors which are difficult to measure. For instance, in future years an employer may settle higher than would have been the case because the strike threat comes to be seen as credible. Undoubtedly, however, some unions have scored qualified successes: for instance, the health unions achieved the retention of national pay bargaining, albeit having to make some concessions to local top-up pay bargaining, after their dispute in 1995.

Not only has the form of strikes changed, but so have the reasons for strikes. Disputes over pay issues accounted for the lion's share of working days lost through the 1980s, but in the 1990s non-pay issues came to the fore, notably working time. This may be contrasted with patterns across the private sector. In the 1980s there was a roughly equal balance between pay and non-pay reasons for strikes, while in the 1990s pay reasons have predominated (*Employment Gazette* 1980–95; *Labour Market Trends* 1996–97).

Another noteworthy aspect of public service industrial action has been the extent to which it has been a reaction to strategic public policy objectives. For example, 265,000 working days were lost in the period 1988–96 as civil servants, council workers and NHS ancillary workers struck against plans for contracting-out, market testing and the privatisation of services.

Finally, however, a note of caution should be injected. Although we have highlighted a trend towards greater militancy by public service unions, it must be remembered that some public service unions either enshrine a policy of no industrial action in their rules, for instance the PAT, or in practice do not take industrial action, for instance the Immigration Service Union. Moreover, although in 1995 both the RCM and the RCN abandoned their rules prohibiting industrial action, they have not yet altered their practice.

Conclusions

This chapter has shown that public service unionism is relatively healthy, compared with its private sector counterpart, in terms of both union membership and density. Moreover, a disproportionately large number of unions operate in the public services: fifty-five out of 181 independent trade unions. To put it another way, 19 per cent of the workforce are employed in the public services, but 30 per cent of all unions are predominantly public service unions. Although there has been some rationalisation of union structure through mergers, there is still inter-union competition for members in many parts of the public services, and in the universities a merger has actually increased inter-union competition.

A key conclusion of this chapter is that the boundary between public sector and private sector unions is becoming blurred. For instance, public service unions have followed their members into the private sector when the organisations in which they worked were privatised, while some public service unions have merged with predominantly private sector unions. Furthermore, public service unions are coming into the mainstream of the wider union movement. They are increasingly willing to take industrial action. There have been a string of affiliations of professional associations to the TUC, particularly since 1990. Public service unions are substantially represented on the TUC general council and a dozen public service unions have set up political funds in the last decade. Workplace representatives in the public services are no longer largely confined to individual case work and information giving but, like their private sector counterparts, are increasingly involved in negotiating terms and conditions. Finally, public sectors unions, like their private sector counterparts, are engaged in so-called managerial unionism.

Clearly all unions, whether in the public services or not, have not found the period 1979–97 an easy one. Will they find life under a Labour government easier? Their future strength will depend primarily on external factors, including 'the general economic climate, labour markets, government pay policies and the funding and organisation of the public sector' (Lloyd 1997: 444). On these criteria, the Labour government seems to exhibit little difference from its predecessor. It has continued with some privatisations, for instance the Benefits Agency medical service and the renewal of a contract for a privately run prison (Blakenhurst), and market testing.

However, these criteria ignore the political environment. The new Labour government is showing greater willingness than its predecessor to consult the public service unions. It is also adopting a more pragmatic stance. For instance, the 'Twelve Guiding Principles' of market testing formulated by the Cabinet Office (1997) for the civil service after the general election says, twice: 'Our approach to this is pragmatic not dogmatic.' There are also signs of a partnership approach. The Cabinet Office and the civil service unions nationally have co-operated in drawing up guidance to departments and agencies in certain areas, such as racial equality. In the NHS, the government will require NHS trusts to involve staff and will establish a task force at national level to improve the involvement of front line staff in shaping new patterns of health care, and this will include NHS unions and employers (Department of Health 1998). At this juncture it is not known whether this friendlier environment, albeit with the employer strategies substantially unchanged, will lead to a growth in public service unionism or merely reduce the extent of the decline.

References

Bailey, R. (1994) 'Annual review article 1993: British public sector industrial relations', *British Journal of Industrial Relations* 32 (1): 113–36.

Bain, G. and Price, R. (1983) 'Union growth in Britain: retrospect and prospect', *British Journal of Industrial Relations* 21 (1): 46–68.

Bird, D. and Corcoran, L. (1994) 'Trade union membership and density 1992–93', *Employment Gazette*, June, pp. 189–97.

Brindle, D. (1998) 'Nurses get 24 hour hotline to union advice', *Guardian*, 25 February, p. 8.

Bryson, C., Jackson, M. and Leopold, J. (1995) 'The impact of self-governing trusts on trades unions and staff associations in the NHS', *Industrial Relations Journal* 26 (2): 120–33.

Cabinet Office (1997) 'Twelve Guiding Principles', unpublished paper, London.

Certification Office (1980–97) Annual Report of the Certification Officer, London: Certification Office for Trade Unions and Employers' Associations.

Coates, K. and Topham, T. (1980) *Trade Unions in Britain*, Nottingham: Spokesman.

Colling, T. (1995) 'Renewal or rigor mortis: union responses to contracting in local government', *Industrial Relations Journal* 26 (2): 134–45.

Corby, S. (1992) 'Industrial relations developments in NHS trusts', *Employee Relations* 14 (6): 33–44.

Corby, S. (1998) 'Industrial relations in civil service agencies: transition or transformation?' *Industrial Relations Journal* 29 (3): 194–206.

Corby, S. and Blundell, B. (1997) 'Trade unions and local bargaining in the NHS', *Health Manpower Management* 23 (2): 49–55.

Cully, M. and Woodland, S. (1996) 'Trade union membership and recognition: an analysis of data from the 1995 Labour Force Survey', *Labour Market Trends*, May, pp. 215–25.

Cully, M. and Woodland, S. (1997) 'Trade union membership and recognition', *Labour Market Trends*, June: 231–9.

Darlington, R. (1998) 'Workplace union resilience in the Merseyside Fire Brigade', *Industrial Relations Journal* 29 (1): 58–73.

Department of Health (1997) *The New NHS*, Cm 3807, London: Stationery Office.

Fairbrother, P. (1996) 'Workplace trade unionism in the state sector' in P. Ackers, C. Smith and P. Smith (eds) *The New Workplace and Trade Unionism*, London: Routledge.

Farnham, D. and Giles, L. (1995) 'Trade unions in the UK: trends and countertrends since 1979', *Employee Relations* 17 (2): 5–22.

Fryer, R. (1989) 'Public service trade unionism in the twentieth century' in R. Mailly, S. Dimmock and A. Sethi (eds) *Industrial Relations in the Public Services*, London: Routledge.

Gall, G. and McKay, S. (1997) 'Unofficial strikes in Britain', paper given at BUIRA annual conference, July.

Heery, E. (1996) 'The new, new unionism' in I. Beardwell (ed.) *Contemporary Industrial Relations: A Critical Analysis*, Oxford: Oxford University Press.

Heery, E. and Kelly, J. (1994) 'Professional, participative and managerial unionism: an interpretation of change in trade unions', *Work, Employment and Society* 8 (1): 1–22.

Industrial Relations Services (1992) 'The changing role of trade union officers' 1, 'The devolution of pay bargaining', *IRS Employment Trends* 526: 5–12.

Industrial Relations Services (1993a) 'Civil service unions and market testing', *Employment Trends* 532: 9–15.

Industrial Relations Services (1993b) 'Changing industrial relations in higher education', *Employment Trends* 536: 7–12.

Ironside, M., Seifert, R. and Sinclair, J. (1997) 'Teacher union responses to education reforms: job regulation and the enforced growth of informality', *Industrial Relations Journal* 28 (2): 120–35.

Kelly, J. (1990) 'British trade unionism 1979–89: change, continuity and contradictions', *Work, Employment and Society*, special issue, May: 29–66.

Kelly, J. (1996) 'Union militancy and social partnership' in P. Ackers, C. Smith and P. Smith (eds) *The New Workplace and Trade Unionism*, London: Routledge.

Kelly, J. and Heery, E. (1994) *Working for the Union: British Trade Union Officers*, Cambridge: Cambridge University Press.

Kerr, A. (1992) 'Why public sector workers join unions: an attitude survey of workers in the health service and local government', *Employee Relations* 14 (2): 39–54.

Kessler, S. and Bayliss, F. (1995) *Contemporary British Industrial Relations*, second edition, Basingstoke: Macmillan.

Labour Research Department (1993) 'Public service workers unite', *Labour Research*, January: 11–12.

Labour Research Department (1995) 'Union links', *Labour Research*, August: 6.

Labour Research Department (1996a) 'High-tech bargaining for Unison branches', *Labour Research*, February: 5.

Labour Research Department (1996b) 'Union activity goes local', *Labour Research*, November: 21–2.

Labour Research Department (1997) 'Civil service unions to merge despite fears', *Labour Research*, November: 3.

Labour Research Department (1998) 'Are women out of proportion?' *Labour Research*, March: 12–14.

Lloyd, C. (1997) 'Decentralization in the NHS: the prospects for workplace unionism', *British Journal of Industrial Relations* 35 (3): 427–46.

O'Toole, B. J. (1989) *Private Gain and Public Service: the Association of First Division Civil Servants*, London: Routledge.

Public Services Tax and Commerce Union (1997) *PCS: the Final Rules for a New Union*, London: PTC.

Seifert, R. (1992) *Industrial Relations in the NHS*, London: Chapman & Hall.

Terry, M. (1991) 'Annual review article 1990', *British Journal of Industrial Relations* 29 (1): 97–112.

Terry, M. (1995) 'Trade unions: shop stewards and the workplace' in P. Edwards (ed.) *Industrial Relations: Theory and Practice in Britain*, Oxford: Blackwell.

Terry, M. (1996) 'Negotiating the government of Unison: union government in theory and practice', *British Journal of Industrial Relations* 34 (1): 87–110.

Turner, H. A. (1962) *Trade Union Growth, Structure and Policy*, London: Allen & Unwin.

Undy, R., Fosh, P., Morris, H., Smith, P. and Martin, R. (1996) *Managing the Unions*, Oxford: Clarendon Press.

Waddington, J. and Whitston, C. (1995) 'Trade unions: growth, structure and policy' in P. Edwards (ed.) *Industrial Relations: Theory and Practice in Britain*, Oxford: Blackwell.

Waddington, J. and Whitston, C. (1997) 'Why do people join unions in a period of membership decline?', *British Journal of Industrial Relations* 35 (4): 515–46.

Willman, P. and Cave, A. (1994) 'The union of the future: super-unions or joint ventures?' *British Journal of Industrial Relations* 32 (2): 395–412.

Winchester, D. (1988) 'Sectoral change and trade union organisation' in D. Gallie (ed.) *Employment in Britain*, Oxford: Blackwell.

Winchester, D. and Bach, S. (1995) 'The state: the public sector' in P. Edwards (ed.) *Industrial Relations: Theory and Practice in Britain*, Oxford: Blackwell.

Index